Creating a Musical Sc

Oxford Music Education Series

The *Oxford Music Education Series* was established with Janet Mills (1954–2007) as series editor to present concise, readable, and thought-provoking handbooks for all those involved in music education, including teachers, community musicians, researchers, policy-makers, and parents/carers. The series encompasses a wide range of topics and musical styles, and aims to provide 'food for thought' for all those looking to broaden their understanding and further develop their work. Written by acknowledged leaders of education who are passionate about their subject, the books present cutting-edge ideas and aim to stimulate good practice by showing the practical implications of research.

Recent titles in the Oxford Music Education Series

Janet Mills: *Music in the School* (2005)

Janet Mills: *Instrumental Teaching* (2007)

Adam Ockelford: *Music for Children and Young People with Complex Needs* (2008)

Janet Mills and John Paynter (eds): *Thinking and Making: Selections from the writings of John Paynter on music in education* (2008)

Janet Mills: *Music in the Primary School*, 3rd edition (2009)

Creating a Musical School

David Bray

MUSIC DEPARTMENT

OXFORD
UNIVERSITY PRESS

OXFORD

UNIVERSITY PRESS

Great Clarendon Street, Oxford OX2 6DP, England
198 Madison Avenue, New York, NY 10016, USA

Oxford University Press is a department of the University of Oxford.
It furthers the University's aim of excellence in research, scholarship,
and education by publishing worldwide in

Oxford New York
Auckland Cape Town Hong Kong Karachi
Kuala Lumpur Madrid Melbourne Mexico City
Nairobi New Delhi Shanghai Taipei Toronto

With offices in

Argentina Austria Brazil Chile Czech Republic France Greece
Guatemala Hungary Italy Japan Poland Portugal Singapore
South Korea Switzerland Thailand Turkey Ukraine Vietnam

Oxford is a registered trade mark of Oxford University
Press in the UK and in certain other countries

Chapters 1–4 and 7–9 © David Bray 2009
Chapter 5 © Sharon Green 2009
Chapter 6 © Diana Pearman 2009
Foreword © Howard Goodall 2009

David Bray, Sharon Green, Diana Pearman, and Howard Goodall have
asserted their right under the Copyright, Designs and Patents Act, 1988,
to be identified as Authors of this Work

Database right Oxford University Press (maker)

First published 2009

British Library Cataloguing-in-Publication Data

Data available

Library of Congress Cataloging-in-Publication Data

Bray, David, 1957–
    Creating a musical school / David Bray.
        p. cm. — (Oxford music education series)
    ISBN 978-0-19-335588-0
    1. Music—Instruction and study—Great Britain. 2. Northampton
School for Girls (Northampton, England) Specialist Music College. I. Titl
    MT3.G7B73 2009
    780.71'242557—dc22
                                            2009006265

10 9 8 7 6 5 4 3 2 1

Typeset by RefineCatch Limited, Bungay, Suffolk
Printed in Great Britain by Ashford Colour Press Ltd.

Every effort has been made to seek permission for the use of all copyright
items in this book. In the event that any item has been overlooked, the
publishers will be glad to rectify this on reprint.

Foreword

In the field of musical education, articles and books tend to either be dryly scholarly, packed with indigestible data and consequently never read by busy teachers, or make sweeping generalizations informed by dinner-party banter and the anecdotal experience of one or other of the author's own children. Neither category helps move the musical schooling of young people on. David Bray's bold foray, though, breaks this mould by steering clear of either dry data or chattering class assumptions. His views will stimulate, inspire, and, I suspect, occasionally provoke his readers, who I very much hope will, among many others, be real teachers in real schools.

He lays down a challenge for us all to rethink the definition of a 'musical school'. This challenge is extremely timely, since the number of high schools and academies with music as a first or second specialism is growing rapidly, an abundance that contrasts sharply with the author's experience of being part of a team setting up the UK's first specialist music college in a comprehensive school just a few years ago. This growth is a tribute to the inspiring start NSG (Northampton School for Girls) made but also a cause for concern—the learning curve, which for many of these new specialized schools will be exciting but steep, is one that needs as much guidance and support as it can get. Nor is this book directed exclusively at existing or potential specialist schools. Because it is written with generous lashings of practical advice from the chalkface, it will be an invaluable tool in all learning contexts. Like everyone else who has encountered the music-making of the students of NSG, I find the school's achievements in such a short time as impressive as they are moving, but there is not a whiff of complacency in the descriptions of how NSG found its feet as a specialist music school. What's more, the insights and tough questions posed herein are as much a challenge to well-endowed independent schools, whose orchestras, choirs, and ensembles are impressive to the neutral observer and heart-warming to the prospective parent (or should one say customer?), as they are to state secondary schools with no orchestra, choir, or ensemble to speak of.

Not everything in David Bray's vision will be comfortable reading for teachers, parents, or school governors. But I cannot think of a book I'd rather have them all urgently read, since as a major provider of music to the world, Britain is a leading player in music and our young people are going to be the engine of that success for many years to come. This book addresses something that is rightly both a concern and a most exhilarating possibility—how to unleash the creative and musical potential of a whole generation, already passionately engaged with music on a personal level, not just a small percentage of children, albeit a talented and motivated percentage punching well above its weight in global terms and who represent the very best of what we as a nation can be. Halfway through these pages I was tempted to imagine what might happen if the other much larger percentage were engaged formally through their musical experiences at school—I trust my reaction was what this book was designed to invoke.

Howard Goodall
Composer and Broadcaster, National Ambassador for Singing,
www.howardgoodall.co.uk

Acknowledgements

I would like to thank the following people for their support: Mike Lovett for ensuring that I was able to work at NSG; Julie Shaw, Rob Reid, and Raydene Vaughan for putting up with my constant desire to change things; Margo Lyons and Greg Myles for their incredible support, hard work, and ability to respond to a constant barrage of new ideas and innovation; Sharon Green for her exceptional skills as a teacher and trainer; and the students and other staff at NSG for teaching me a lot. Mostly I would like to thank Penny Westwood for her exceptional leadership skills and Diana Pearman for her energy, resilience, and ability to ensure that things happen.

I would also like to record my sadness over the deaths of two important people. Janet Mills was a consistent source of support, wisdom, and practical advice during the time this book was written. Prior to this I learned an enormous amount from her sharp thinking, wisdom, and sense of humour. Revisiting some of her publications has been a humbling experience for me. Janet was a fantastic human being. She had an incredible mind but was able to talk in a commonsense way with just about anyone. She was hard to disagree with and this made her very effective when dealing with people from a very wide range of backgrounds and standpoints. I miss her greatly almost every day and treasure the conversations that we had. On one occasion when things went wrong in my life she provided a great source of support in her practical no nonsense way. Most of all I miss greatly her friendship.

Then there is Maggie Holloway. She touched the lives of hundreds of people in Northamptonshire. She did this as a teacher, organizer of music festivals, conductor, performer, singer, music centre tutor. Most of all she was a happy, bubbly, and warm person greatly loved by all her family and numerous friends. Maggie had the largest of hearts and a seemingly inexhaustible supply of energy and enthusiasm. The kind word, twinkle in her eye and her acute sense of humour complemented her immense warmth. She had the knack of being able to tune into the interests of all whom she met regardless of their age or background. She was constantly on the lookout for young people who needed a little of her extra nurturing in order to reach fulfilment. A young man, training to be a teacher and a bit of a rolling stone, confessed to me recently that she 'did right by me'. Her incredible energy and enthusiasm led to Kingshorpe Middle School being amongst the most musical schools I have had the privilege to know.

This book is dedicated to my son Joseph who loves music and playing the piano even though his teacher felt he might be too young to start and that his hands might not be big enough.

About the author

David Bray has worked as a teacher, adviser, and consultant in hundreds of primary and secondary schools. He began his career as a teacher of music and humanities in a London secondary modern school for boys, and went on to work in several secondary and primary schools before becoming an Advisory Teacher and later County Music Adviser for Northamptonshire Local Authority. He worked for several years as an OFSTED-trained inspector and for national government as an adviser on ICT projects and the development of music services. In 2004 he took up a part-time secondment leading the development of the UK's first Specialist Music College: the Northampton School for Girls.

David is a published composer and an accomplished trumpet player, singer, and conductor. In 1990 he founded the Northamptonshire County Youth Choir, which twice reached the televised national adult finals of the Choir of the Year competition. The choir was awarded prizes at the Montreux and Riva del Garda International Festivals, and achieved seven 'highly commended' and 'outstanding' performance awards at the National Festival of Music for Youth.

David's first book, *Teaching Music in the Secondary School*, was published by Heinemann in 2000.

Contents

Figures and tables

Figures

Tables

Abbreviations

CPD	Continuing Professional Development
CRB	Criminal Records Bureau
DCSF	Department for Children, Schools and Families
DfEE	Department for Education and Employment
DfES	Department for Education and Skills
GM	General Midi
ICT	Information and Communication technology
KS	Key Stage
LA	Local Authority
NFER	National Foundation for Educational Research
NQT	Newly Qualified Teacher
NSG	Northampton School for Girls
OCR	Oxford, Cambridge and RSA Examinations
OFSTED	Office for Standards in Education
PFI	Private Finance Initiative
PLTS	Personal, Learning and Thinking Skills
QCA	Qualification and Curriculum Authority
RSA	Royal Society for the Encouragement of Arts, Manufactures and Commerce
RSS	Rich Site Summary
SEF	Self-evaluation form
VLE	Virtual Learning Environment
VST	Virtual Studio Technology

Introduction

This book is a personal view of what makes schools 'musical'. It is based on considerable experience in many educational settings and more informal interactions with music and young people. My background as a teacher, adviser, examiner, and inspector means that I have had the privilege to work in, or with, hundreds of primary, secondary, and special schools over a reasonably long period of time. This has given me the opportunity to encounter musical and unmusical activities that have shaped and changed my views considerably.

I have made very few references to research, although I have for many years read and been interested in what it tells us. I would advise anyone requiring specific references to consult a publication such as *Music in the School*.[1] Those who require more detailed references will probably already know where to locate them. It is possible that a few people will seize upon this as an excuse not to accept the weight of my arguments. I am comfortable with this and also aware that some practitioners may want to reject some of what I set out because it is challenging. However my views are received (and I accept fully that they are sometimes tough and uncompromising) I hope they offer the opportunity to reflect on and question current practice. In doing so I have had one key aim in mind: to discover how we can improve the experiences all young people have of music education, so that the majority feel positive and engaged by it.

In November 2003 I attended the Northamptonshire Secondary Head Teachers' conference and started a conversation with the Head Teacher and Deputy Head Teacher at Northampton School for Girls (NSG). We talked about the possibility of the school applying to become a Specialist Music College. This new specialism for secondary schools had just been announced by the British government. At the time there was little clarity about what such a school might look like and how it could develop. My enthusiasm for the project led us to discuss the possibility of me being seconded to the school to work on a part-time basis to help get things up and running. In September 2004 NSG became the first Specialist Music College in England. The school

---

[1] J. Mills, *Music in the School* (Oxford: Oxford University Press, 2005).

also inducted on the first day of term 700 new students and 50 new teachers. The reason for this was that Northampton moved from a three-tier system of education (lower, middle, and upper schools) to a two-tier system (primary and secondary) and NSG took in three year groups at once.

This book looks at the features of a 'musical school' from a theoretical standpoint and sometimes makes specific reference to NSG, especially the two-year period from 2004 to 2006 when I worked closely with the school. It provides a social record of some of the things that occurred at NSG during this time, set against the context of a changing music education landscape. There may be things that other schools could adopt, but NSG is not offered as a blueprint for success. There are other primary, secondary, and special schools that can stake an equal claim to having either become a musical school or travelled a long way on this particular journey.

The book is divided into chapters that deal with separate issues and themes. It includes Chapter 6 on music across the curriculum contributed by Diana Pearman, a Deputy Head Teacher at NSG. This describes the way that NSG worked with the concept of using music as a learning tool in order to enhance other subjects. Chapter 5 is written by Sharon Green, looking at some of the aspects of how music can be taught in a more inclusive way in order to interest and motivate a wide range of students. This is an area that she has worked on with much success.

Although I hope the chapters are self-sufficient there are consistent themes that run through all of them and these are brought together in the conclusion. There are two particular strands which are especially prominent:

◆ the gap between school music and the musical interests of the majority of young people in schools
◆ the 'hidden curriculum' that shapes powerfully the experiences of all young people in education settings and leads to many young people feeling and in many senses being excluded.

The term 'hidden curriculum' refers to the actions and intentions of adults who work with young people in a variety of settings. In all the schools I have visited I have yet to encounter a teacher who overtly excludes students. Most adults talk about being inclusive. However, their actions and words often convey (often covertly) a different message. There is nearly always a group of 'musical' students who the teacher works with. It is the adult who makes this distinction. A result is that there is another group who, by default, are the 'non-musicians'. I have encountered very few schools, FE Colleges, or Local Authority Music Services who have thought this through or who cater effectively for all of their local community, although I know that there are some brilliant trailblazers. It is this unspoken and often unrealized attitude that makes change extremely difficult. We cannot change until we understand and acknowledge the nature of the issue. I believe that this exclusive (rather than inclusive) approach is a key barrier to creating a musical school. I know that many people will react to this statement by concluding that I am therefore attacking the notion of excellence. I am not. Anyone who knows me well would agree that I have done more than my fair share of working with high-standard instrumentalists, vocalists, and composers. I have won prizes on numerous occasions at national and international festivals and excelled as a performer. I have done these things because I know that there is a group of students who are enthusiastic, have particular needs, and require nurturing. I don't for one moment advocate that we abandon them or ignore their needs. I can recall a debate sparked in the UK national press about the Simon Bolivar Youth Orchestra of Venezuela's performance at the Proms in London in 2007. Everyone acknowledged that this orchestra, forged out of a project to work with under-privileged young people in Venezuelan slums, had given probably the most inspiring performance ever heard at a Prom. It sparked off an argument here about whether or not we give our students enough classical music to listen to. Although it prompted wide coverage in the press no one seemed to be able to see the significance of what this told us about our own education system and the barriers that keep us from this sort of inspiring approach, despite the many good things that go on in the UK.

I greatly enjoyed working at NSG and I hope that I helped to move things forward in a positive way during a period of enormous change. I know that I challenged what was happening and that this caused stress to some staff. My motivation was always the students. I feel that during this time music education in England was at an interesting stage and there were a number of good contemporary initiatives such as the Music Manifesto, Musical Futures, Youth Music, Standards Fund Grant, Wider Opportunities, and the Key Stage 3 Strategy (to name but a few). All of these had positive features and benefits. In particular I feel that there was growing evidence of a more inclusive and culturally diverse approach. This gives me hope. In fact I can remember feeling slightly jaded when attending an early Music Manifesto event, convinced that music education was never going to change and wondering if I should think about disengaging from it. I came away inspired. New developments and projects funded by central government are required to address issues of equality and diversity, but many traditional cultures and attitudes remain entrenched, particularly within formal education settings such as schools. I understand that the comments I am making will not lead to me receiving a high popularity rating amongst the music education community.

The message is hard and difficult to deal with. It is easier to work with a small group of motivated students than it is to address the needs and interests of all. By 'all' I mean those with difficult social backgrounds, special needs, looked-after children, and those about to be excluded. The Simon Bolivar Youth Orchestra gives us an insight into what is possible. Many musicians and teachers in the UK perform equally miraculous feats with limited resources and support. In reality, however, music education in the UK has got itself into a situation where we have persuaded others that there are young people called 'musicians' and that they should receive special treatment. It runs right through the education system. There is nothing wrong with this except that it creates many more students who by implication are non-musicians. The closer one examines this the more uncomfortable it becomes. My defence in raising the issue is that I am supporting the thousands of students every year who leave secondary schools loving music but just not getting what school music is about. It is one of the reasons that my definition of a musical school does not include just those with well-known bands and orchestras.

Chapter 1

What is a musical school?

It is our firm conviction that mankind will live the happier when it has learned to live with music more worthily. Whoever works to promote this end, in one way or another, has not lived in vain.

Zoltán Kodály

The purpose of this chapter is to define what is meant by the term 'musical school' and to examine some of the different interpretations that may be applied to this. I will use this chapter to outline my views in a general way before exploring them in more detail throughout this book. I will look at some of the features of traditional specialist music schools and public schools, since they are commonly thought of as being 'musical', and I will briefly explore their historical and cultural context. I will also consider how these schools and the newer Specialist Music Colleges (brought about through the British government's Specialist School scheme) match my template for what a musical school might look like.

What features might we find in a musical school?

If you think of the term 'musical school' what picture comes into your mind? Perhaps you think of a particular school. If so what are its distinctive features? It might be a school where a group of students are particularly engaged in making music through performing in a band, choir, or orchestra. Are these schools really musical? They might be, but there is also a possibility that they could be exclusive, culturally narrow, and in reality unmusical (even though many observers will feel that they are musical).

In *Music in the School* Janet Mills describes musical schools where

something significantly musical is being offered to whole cohorts of students, where students' experience of music is creative, and where the affirming and uplifting impact of making music spreads well beyond the school's music rooms.[1]

---

[1] J. Mills, *Music in the School* (Oxford: Oxford University Press, 2005), 129.

It is the term 'whole cohorts of students' that is particularly significant within this description. Janet Mills also reminds us that many of the schools that have traditionally been called musical actually provide a worthwhile experience for a minority of students and leave other students feeling 'hopeless'.

This view is supported by my own experience. I have visited hundreds of primary, secondary, and special schools as a teacher, adviser, and inspector over a period of about twenty-five years. During this time I have seen changes in the way music in schools is organized and I believe that in many ways the picture now is more positive than it was in the early 1980s. In other, significant, ways the picture has not changed at all. I believe that a number of different factors hinder music in schools, although some people, who have influence over these factors, may not appreciate or agree with the views I want to put forward. I will explore several of these factors in the course of the different chapters in this book.

As a starting point I will list the features that I might expect to find in a 'musical school'.

1. An inclusive policy and practice
2. Large numbers learning an instrument/voice
3. Musical excellence
4. Musical diversity
5. Effective use of music technology
6. Innovative teaching and learning
7. Attention given to student voice and views
8. A wide range of music extra-curricular activities
9. An innovative and effective curriculum
10. Strong engagement with the local community
11. Use of music across the curriculum to enhance learning

This may seem like a large and ambitious list. It is and I don't suppose that many schools exist that meet all of these criteria really well. Some, however, get close and I believe that the large majority of schools could improve their practice (and the experience of the young people they serve) through a mixture of aspiration and relatively simple solutions. For example, they might want to evaluate themselves against these criteria and see if they can improve on one key feature where they currently underachieve. I will therefore describe further what I mean by each of these criteria.

An inclusive policy and practice

This approach seeks to motivate and inspire 100 per cent of students and to also reach out beyond the school into the outside community. UK schools have tended to focus more effectively on a smaller number of students that they view as being 'gifted' in the area of music. In fact this sort of 'exclusive' approach becomes more prevalent as students get older (i.e. start at secondary school). It often seems to coincide with the stage in a student's life when they encounter specialist music teachers. At this stage the teacher seems to want to find the 'talented' students in order to work more intensively with them. However, the definition of talented students appears to be quite narrow and can result in the large majority of other students feeling that music at school is not for them because they do not have the right attributes—what Janet Mills describes as being left feeling hopeless.

This sort of approach seems to have led to a situation where music in schools (as a practical and participative activity) is only of direct relevance to a small number of students. This statement will leave some people feeling uncomfortable. I believe that there is a case to answer. In early years settings most children happily participate in music-making. In infant and primary years there is often a continued expectation that music is for everyone, although sadly a creeping view that it is more suited to the 'talented' students. More worryingly, it can become increasingly the territory of girls, the middle classes, and those who live in certain areas, or have supportive parents. Anecdotally and controversially I can suggest that it is often the domain of mainly white students from particular areas and demographic backgrounds. Look at the profile of our youth orchestras and professional ensembles for evidence. At secondary school the transformation into segregation is almost complete as the students who learn instruments become the 'musicians' and those who do not are the non-musicians. How many looked-after children learn an instrument? What sort of access to music do students in Pupil Referral Units have? How inclusive are our schools? Many are not as inclusive as they ought to be and more likely to exclude musically the further a student goes through his/her education.

Large numbers learning an instrument/voice

This might be above a certain percentage of the school population. More than 10 per cent of a cohort learning an instrument, especially at secondary school, is probably a significantly high proportion. This still leaves 90 per cent out of the equation. I feel that a musical school should aim to have 100 per cent of its students having had a real opportunity to learn an instrument, as well as the encouragement and support to carry on and make this a successful and rewarding experience. Opportunity is the important word here since not all may want to pursue learning an instrument within a formal setting such as a school. That is a choice which students should be able to make. The reality may be that the choice of instrument on offer is not inspiring, a selection procedure (often unwritten) is applied, and opportunities to link with community groups or informal learning outside school are not taken up. Many students I have talked to say that they would like to learn an instrument but did not have the chance. This is something they regret. By the time they are in year 8 at secondary school the door has almost certainly shut for the large majority. This is significant because many students will associate playing an instrument with being musical and therefore regard themselves as unmusical if they don't. They carry these perceptions into their roles as parents, teachers, and other aspects of their lives and so the situation is passed on to future generations.

Musical excellence

This refers to high-quality musical groups and the achievement of students both within the curriculum and in extra-curricular groups. Defining what is meant by the term quality is extremely difficult. For some this would mean taking part in national and international competitions with great success. It could also be perceived as success in a local music competition. Having a lot of students involved in music might be viewed as a quality feature, as might success in school examination results or instrumental examinations. I would suggest that a minimum baseline for a musical school would include a high-quality curriculum experience that is offered to all students. Others may view musical excellence in a more narrow way and link it with making a good impression on local stakeholders associated with the school. Excellence and quality are important, but they can also be synonyms for exclusion, selection, and narrowness. A musical school will therefore be striving for excellence and inclusion—a difficult but crucial balance to achieve.

Musical diversity

This means embracing a wide range of musical styles and cultures that reflect the interests of the student population, whilst introducing them to new horizons and developments. It includes the use of music from different countries and cultures presented in a positive, non-tokenistic, or superficial way. It will be made clear to students that there is no value judgement attached to music, either explicitly or implicitly. For example, a school may unknowingly suggest that western art music is the most important type of music (since this is the exclusive diet of extra-curricular activities at school). This hidden message may be promoted quite strongly to students even though the curriculum makes passing reference to other types of music. A school may feel that because the curriculum includes reference to calypso or raga it is culturally diverse. This may not be the case at all. It depends how these topics are presented and how seriously the school chooses to explore the perceptions that students pick up about styles and cultures. A musically diverse school will also reflect the background of the students—so in an area with a strong and vibrant local Bangladeshi community links will be made with community musicians, or a school that is close to a strong brass band tradition might use these resources effectively. There is the need to respond to the cultural interests of young people through the use of contemporary musical styles and cultures. The diversity issue is a huge one and much of it is revealed through the hidden assumptions and actions of adults. Many of these may be unintentional but they transmit strong messages to young people.

Effective use of music technology

This can improve the quality of musical outcomes, promote the value of music, and add excitement to music-making in contemporary styles. Technology can be used as a tool to improve communication in teaching and learning through the use of presentation software, overhead projectors, and electronic whiteboards. It can also be used as a method of developing an electronic learning space for e-portfolios and online learning. Music-specific software can be used to improve the quality of the experience and outcomes of young people. Using technology is not necessarily a good thing. Using it inappropriately can lead to a less effective learning experience for students. Contemporary music makes extensive use of technology. This is the musical world that young people inhabit and the impact of this on a school requires thought and skill in order to be used effectively.

Innovative teaching and learning

This includes consideration of current issues and developments (as well as reflection on traditional values) in order to maximize the achievement of students and contribute to the ethos of music in the school. Sometimes learning may be quite traditional but still very effective—leaving all students motivated, inspired, and wanting to carry on with the subject. Sometimes new ideas can be helpful in reshaping thinking. An ideal scenario is a school that has teachers who are reflective about their practice and want to research and explore new ideas in order to compare the results with traditional approaches.

Attention given to student voice and views

Students are the consumers of education and it is therefore crucial to respond to their interests. This might be through surveys, individual discussion, or online forums. This approach can be very valuable but does need to include all the school population, not just the students who are already positively engaged in music through or at the school.

A wide range of music extra-curricular activities that cater for a variety of needs and interests

A musical school will be able to get a good balance between these activities and the main curriculum (which is what all the students will experience). Effective schools will probably have a range of activities that cater for different tastes and styles—perhaps utilizing community musicians or other adults in order to ensure that music specialist staff have the capacity to concentrate on the curriculum as the main focus of their work or are given a lighter timetable in recognition of this commitment. The school will also provide good opportunities for all students to showcase their work, not just the high-status extra-curricular groups. The extra-curricular activity is the public-facing side of music in a school and is often seen, perhaps wrongly, as a barometer of the musicality of a school environment.

An innovative and effective curriculum that leads to good progression and clear pathways for students to pursue their studies

The curriculum includes the long-term routes that students take through learning. Ensuring that the routes offered through Key Stage 3 to Key Stage 4 and post-16 are seamless, flexible, appropriate, and suit a range of different interests/skills is essential. A musical school will offer courses that suit the needs and aspirations of all its students—there cannot be one model here since the nature of each school is different. Account will be taken of further and higher education pathways and the needs of future employers. The curriculum also includes the medium- and short-term planning that allows the learning to be interesting, relevant, and matched to the needs of the individual student (personalized). One approach may not suit all students. Planning will cater for the most able students as well as those who need specific help with aspects of their work, whose behaviour is problematic, or who have specific disabilities.

Strong engagement with the local community and national/international projects and initiatives

An increasingly important element in the development of schools is their place in the local community. They are viewed as hubs that provide universal services, such as education, but because schools link with nearly all students they are also good places to have access points for a range of other more specialist services. Schools are particularly well placed to link music with community groups, adults other than teachers, early years settings, and older people.

Use of music across the curriculum to enhance learning

Music can act as a learning tool and make a wide impact across the life of a school. Some research has demonstrated that music may be a powerful way of developing memory skills and that it has specific mood suppression or enhancing capabilities. These might also be used within a learning context. Music can help the learner to develop increased concentration, organization, and social skills. Employers report that these are skills that they see as being very important.

The list is not meant to be exhaustive and all these examples require further detail to provide clarity. There is also no implied order of priority in the list, although there is no doubt that different audiences will consciously, or subconsciously, apply value judgements to each of these statements. I know that I do. Does the list capture the essence of a musical school? It may do, since a school that manages to demonstrate all these attributes would be an exciting environment in which to learn. Realistically this sort of school might prove to be too great a challenge, especially in the secondary sector where the responsibility lies with one or two identified members of staff catering for large numbers of students. In primary schools and early years setting it is possible to achieve a culture where all staff are seen to have a role in music education. My key criterion for success would be number one in the list—a school that is inclusive and aspires to make all its students feel involved. I feel that although this is the most important, it is actually at odds with the approach that most schools, especially secondary schools, currently promote. This sounds like an accusation. It is not meant to be although I do sense a problem when many teachers and schools believe that they are inclusive but in reality are not. To test this out they only need to ask students. Not the minority who they work with closely but the majority who just don't see music in school as relevant enough to their lives. I will set out in this book some of the reasons why I feel that current practice often does not match what should be our collective aspiration.

I know there is something missing in these criteria. It is to do with the end result of all these various priorities. It is the motivation, interest, and enthusiasm felt by the students. So this could be another feature of a musical school. However, it needs to be for more than just a minority. It is currently more common to find this sort of buzz and interest in a small primary school than in a large secondary school, since the scale of many secondary schools often mitigates against a personalized approach. I don't underestimate the challenges faced by a secondary teacher. I know what it is like. However, I do feel that we have to understand that there is a challenge and that we should vow to try to make small changes that might have a big impact on a greater proportion of young people.

Schools that are described as musical

A school may already be deemed to be 'musical' by some of its stakeholders because it has one or two of the above features. Traditionally a school that achieves an aspect of musical excellence is often looked upon as being 'musical'—even though this may involve only a small proportion of the students (and may therefore leave the rest feeling 'hopeless'). For example, a string quartet might regularly perform at school open evenings and other events so parents and other visitors view the school as a place that is interested in and values music. The genre and the style of music reflects the ethos and aspirations of these parents, even though they may not be experts in this type of music. The reality might be that the four young people involved get most of their training and experience outside school, perhaps through private teachers. I have known several schools such as this and I am always amazed at how the perceptions of parents about a school and its musical ethos can be influenced by such an activity that interests and involves only a small proportion of the students. The truth is that there are multiple ideas and contradictions about what constitutes a musical school.

Interpretations of the term musical school

The term 'musical school' has particular and specific meanings for different audiences. For example:

◆ parents
◆ teachers
◆ governors
◆ senior managers
◆ students
◆ researchers
◆ musicians

Even these seemingly straightforward categories disguise a multitude of further layers. The term 'musician' might refer to a:

◆ nationally acclaimed classical performer who is consulted by central government
◆ locally based instrumental/vocal teacher
◆ part-time drummer in a jazz band
◆ music therapist
◆ DJ

The term student could encompass:

- a highly skilled and experienced A level student
- a year 7 student with little previous experience who listens to music avidly outside school
- a year 9 student for whom music is interesting as something to listen to outside school but who views music in school as a waste of time
- a year 10 student with multiple and profound special needs and a limited life expectancy

A parent in a socially affluent area may well have a different view from someone in a challenging urban environment, or a rural and culturally deprived setting. These ranges of experience (and consequent expectations) lead to multiple definitions that may be applied to what at first sight appears to be a simple term such as 'musical school'. None of these may coincide with my own view. It therefore seems important to explore this a little further in order to try to understand better the social and historical contexts which determine what a 'musical school' might look like.

The context of specialist music schools in England

If we talk of a 'musical school' many people may assume that we mean a specialist music school. England has a long tradition of specialist music schools, such as the Yehudi Menhuin School, Chetham's, or the Purcell School. There has also been a range of other provision such as the Pimlico Specialist Music Scheme (which is linked to a state-funded day school) and the Junior Saturday Centres at the various Conservatoires (where auditioned students participate in extra music tutoring outside school time). Many public schools have also used music as a mechanism to attract students, particularly through the breadth and quality of their extra-curricular activities. These schools include choir schools, which provide an education for young singers (often boys) who will sing in a linked cathedral or other church with a strong choral tradition. The boarding provision provided by public schools has often lent itself to the pursuit of musical activity, since students have concentrated periods of time together which make practice and ensemble rehearsal a useful and worthwhile use of time. These schools often have a 'Director of Music'. This post implies a particular emphasis on out-of-lesson performance activities, particularly in the western art tradition. Many parents appreciate this culture and welcome the recreational opportunities offered, as well as perhaps understanding the importance of learning an instrument for social networking, development of organizational skills, and team-building. Indeed these schools will be aware that engaging with this musical tradition makes the school more attractive to certain parents regardless of whether or not their children actually participate in musical activity. These schools are probably seen to supply high standards, quality, exclusivity, and a link with a long tradition of established practice. Most people associated with them would think of them as being musical schools.

The National Music and Dance scheme

This scheme provides central government funding for specific UK schools to educate students with 'exceptional talent' in music and dance. We will need to explore elsewhere the notion of what 'exceptional musical talent' actually is, or isn't, and how it gets defined.

Before 1973, support for students at these specialist schools was provided by local education authorities. In 1973, the Royal Ballet (Lower) School and the Yehudi Menuhin School were admitted to a fee remission scheme funded by the Department of Education in recognition of their position as Centres of Excellence for the Performing Arts. The fee remission income scale (i.e. the means test of parents) mirrored that of the old direct grant grammar-school scheme with some modification to account for the higher costs of boarding and specialist tuition.

Five UK specialist music schools were designated: Chetham's School of Music, Wells Cathedral School, the Purcell School, Yehudi Menuhin School, and St Mary's Music School (Edinburgh). Together with the Royal Ballet School, lower and upper divisions, they were allocated government-aided places. The scheme was expanded in 1996 by the admission of two new schools (Elmhurst School for Dance and Performing Arts and the Arts Educational School, Tring), and extra places were added at existing schools. In 2002, the scheme was renamed the Music and Dance Scheme and another dance school, the Hammond School, Chester, was admitted.

The reasoning appeared to be that there was a need to educate intensively those students who are thought to have this 'exceptional talent' in either music or dance. The assumption was that the education of these identified students needed to start at an early age and be carried out in an intensive way in order to maximize impact:

There is a need to educate and train, from an early age, children who are exceptionally talented in the two fields of artistic endeavour—music and ballet—if Britain is to maintain a world-class pool of talent for future generations. The need for early training, in particular the primary development of the physical and intellectual disciplines required of dancers and musicians, is recognised by many to be greater than for some other forms of artistic endeavour. The MDS enables exceptionally talented children between the ages of 8 and 19 to receive a good academic education alongside the best specialist music and dance/ballet training available. (DfES NMDS website 2006)

The music and dance scheme regularly produces a range of students who participate in high-profile televised competitions such as the BBC Young Musician of the Year.

The information about each of these schools suggests some common factors:

- early identification of those students who are thought to have exceptional musical talent (or dance where relevant)
- an intensive education in order to maximize the student's skills and potential—often using boarding provision
- an audition process that is designed to select the most suitable students
- independently run schools (privately funded) with very attractive buildings and an inspiring environment

They may also have other characteristics which are implied rather than being explicitly articulated:

- an emphasis on western art music—usually through the intensive study of one or more instruments
- a form of accelerated learning brought about by immersion in music/ballet and contact with more advanced students

The schools seem to raise at least one interesting question. Why music and dance? Why isn't there a specialist scheme for art or mathematics? An even more compelling case could be made for a specialist sports scheme. This might provide us with a Wimbledon winner of the future or help our rugby and football teams to excel.

Choir schools

As well as the independent, state-funded specialist music schools England also has a type of school known as a choir school. There are about 44 schools attached to cathedrals, churches, and college chapels around the country. More than 1,200 of the 21,500 boys and girls in the choir schools are choristers. The majority are Church of England foundations but the Roman Catholic, Scottish, and Welsh churches all participate in the scheme. Some take children from 7 to 13; others are junior schools with senior schools to 18. The majority are fee-paying but nine out of ten choristers qualify for financial help from the school or through the government's Choir Schools' Scholarship Scheme. This is also part of the Music and Dance Scheme. To become a chorister in such a school an audition is required. To get into St John's College School in Cambridge, for example, the boys have to take a voice trial:

The formal Voice trial takes the form of an audition, in which the children are given oral/aural tests, perform a prepared vocal piece of the candidate's choosing and play any instrument they may have studied. The audition is informal and relaxed in atmosphere. A singing coach is in attendance and at least part of the audition may take the form of a lesson rather than a formal test. The Headmaster is also in attendance to ensure that the children are comfortable with the process. (St John's College School website 2006)

I feel that some key questions emerge in relation to the National Music and Dance scheme. These questions are not meant to be pejorative. This type of education has existed for a long time and has been scrutinized on a number of occasions, so can stand such interrogation.

1. What is the process used to assess musical talent or potential referred to by many of these schools and is it subject to any scrutiny and evaluation? This is an important question because once the students have been selected their needs can be catered for relatively easily. Selection, however, leaves a far larger number of 'unselected' (or excluded) students. These schools therefore may be fantastic and probably offer a great experience for their students. I am not sure that they fit into my definition of a musical school.

2. The schools seem to centre on performance skills in western art music as their key criterion for defining musical talent? Is this the case? If so is this definition actually very limited and should it be expanded?

3. Is there any evidence to show that such talent can be identified in a consistent way and that the students identified make more progress in musical studies than they would have done in mainstream state-funded education? A corollary here could be a view that if this talent is a special need why can't provision be located in mainstream schools rather than students going to a special school?

4. How important is the element of boarding education provided by these schools or would suitable holiday and weekend tuition at a local centre be more cost-effective?

5. What exactly is the return for this investment in numbers of professional musicians or teachers produced and could this group be produced by a locally delivered system as part of a state-funded school system?

6. Why is it that music and dance are seen as areas that require this special provision. Why not art, maths, science, or sport?

Music schools around the world

The model of schools with a strong instrumental curriculum and an emphasis on music literacy (or study of musical theory) can be found in many countries around the world. As in the UK they are evident within both privately funded schools and state-funded provision. There are also commonly links to a Conservatoire-style higher-education system which students will aspire to access aged around 18. This is a higher-education institution where the principle study for students is music, rather than a university-style education where music students will be enrolled alongside students studying other subjects. The 'Conservatoire' is a powerful influence on music education for schools, higher education, and private teachers. In the UK it is associated with instrumental exams, such as the Associated Board practical exams, and naturally feeds into some successful students aspiring to study at a Conservatoire-style higher education setting. This is not unique. France, along with many other countries, has:

- music provided as a curriculum subject in schools
- state-funded schools that specialize in music
- privately funded schools that provide intensive music training
- local and national conservatoires (local provision mainly catering up to 18 and the national conservatoire, such as that in Paris, offering provision for those thought to require particular vocational training as a performer or teacher)

Schools with an enhanced music reputation can be found almost anywhere in the world:

The Various musical groups within the School perform regularly in the local community. Concerts are a regular feature of the School calendar, providing an opportunity for Students to gain experience in performing for an audience whilst at the same time enriching the cultural life of the School.

The Music facilities at the School are second to none.

The music block includes four music classrooms, a large open area, music staffroom, and a piano laboratory. A recently completed music center contains a modern administration area and library, 16 teaching/practice studios, recording facilities and ready access to a 700 seat auditorium. (Westbourne Grammar School, Melbourne, Australia website 2006)

In 1936, New York City Mayor Fiorello H. LaGuardia founded the High School of Music & Art in order to provide a facility where the most gifted and talented public school students of New York City could pursue their talents in art or music, while also completing a full academic program of instruction. In 1948, the School of Performing Arts was created to provide training in performance skills to students who wished to prepare for professional careers in dance, music or drama. (LaGuardia High School of Music & Art and Performing Arts New York website 2007)

There are some particularly famous examples of state-funded Hungarian schools which utilize the Kodály 'method' of musical education (this is not a method at all and an often misunderstood term, even though its roots lie with the British music educator John Curwen). This type of music provision is felt to be particularly beneficial from about 5 onwards. Music is seen as a language that is learned naturally through participation from an early age and the training provided often benefits all students (i.e. there is no prior test of musical ability applied). The results, however, are often quite spectacularly successful (in a musical sense). Young children who have been through this system can develop an extremely high level of aural acuity and are able to sight sing with a very high level of fluency. Many are able to transfer these skills successfully to learning an instrument. These schools also attract controversy about how desirable and cost-effective the provision is. This type of training in specific musical skills has sometimes been criticized for not offering sufficient musical creativity or flexibility. There are similar examples of specialist and intensive music education in most developed countries in the western world. Are these musical schools? Almost certainly in the eyes of the students, teachers, parents, governors, and other stakeholders associated with them. However, their existence may also contribute to other schools not being considered musical. Why? Mainly because specialist schools support the notion that you have to have a particular natural talent to be musical and that music is therefore not for everyone. You either have it or you don't. Quite what it is you have, in what quantity, and how it gets measured are important but unresolved questions. Given this culture many ordinary schools will give up the struggle to be musical before they have even started.

The Conservatoire-style higher-education system and instrumental examination schemes were all nineteenth-century developments. They still have a very strong and pervasive influence on music education in the UK and in many other countries around the world. This filters down to the type of music activities provided for secondary-age students because many class and instrumental teachers will have experienced this philosophy through their own studies or the values that they have received indirectly from their own teachers. It often includes an emphasis on learning an instrument in a western art style, the promotion of musical literacy through use of notation, and an emphasis on exams, tests, and competitions. This influence affects the value judgements that are made about music and school music education, which is then recycled by policy makers. I have noted already that music is often valued for its social and cultural capital and the support it can offer to a school's values. The role music plays in extra-curricular life and the fact that many socially advantaged and academically able students play instruments leads to music having an important function within the 'shop window' of a school. This use of music as a marketing tool and barometer of ethos is something that seems to be found fairly universally in schools in the UK and around the world.

In practice it seems that there are as many different permutations of musical school as there are schools. Table 1 shows that:

- there is a hierarchy and an elitism at work
- music is often seen as a special subject requiring intensive intervention but that this view almost always stems from a particular view of musical needs (identification of talent, nurturing and need for progression in a defined set of skills).

In practice there will be schools that have features of more than one of these categories.

Specialist Music Colleges in England—a new type of musical school?

The Specialist Schools scheme was originally introduced by the English government in 1994 and was subsequently enhanced due its perceived success in raising achievement. There are commentators who would argue that in its early days it was particularly successful at making some schools attract a more favourable student intake and therefore appear to be successful at raising achievement. Space does not permit me to explore this further here. A key element of the scheme was the idea of state-funded schools and academies

Table 1 Types of musical school

(a)	Elite, selective schools that provide intensive education in musical skills—these are usually based around western art music, instrumental provision, and theory of music. In these schools music is seen as being special and requiring a particular talent.
(b)	Schools that do not mainly select by musical talent but which have musical scholarships (through an audition) or other element that is partially selective and which provide a large amount of extra-curricular music activity, often have strong curriculum provision for students aged 14–19, and where music has a high profile.
(c)	State-funded schools that whilst not having a particular profile in music have an element of provision that is held in high esteem—a school band, string quartet, or jazz group for example. It may have quite good provision of instrumental tuition and a quite vibrant range of provision for 11–19-year-old students.
(d)	Schools that would like to offer more music provision but are unable to do so because they can not attract what they feel are suitable students, lack sufficient funds or find it difficult to recruit staff. They may suffer because of another musically successful school in the near vicinity.

(state-funded independent schools) electing to specialize in one or more subjects, whilst still delivering the national curriculum. A music specialism was introduced in September 2004. The first school in the country to be awarded Specialist Music College status was Northampton School for Girls (it started this status in September 2004).

This created an extra layer of school which specialized in music but had a 'comprehensive' intake. This placed them within category (b) in Table 1 but some may want to aspire towards category (a). The most striking features of this scheme were the scale of the project, the large amount of funding involved, and the potentially positive effect on the education of the young people involved. The scheme had some key components:

1. The use of business sponsorship—presumably to encourage a partnership between business and education
2. The use of specific targets as a lever for receiving the associated extra funding
3. Working with partner schools
4. Development of expertise in a subject which can be shared with others.

What does the application process tell us about the intended philosophy and impact of Specialist Music Colleges?

Guidance was published for schools intending to apply for this Specialist Music College status:

Music Colleges will raise standards of achievement and the quality of teaching and learning in music for all their students leading to whole-school improvement. They will encourage their students to develop a lifelong passion for, and appreciation of, music not only as composers and performers but also as audiences, technicians and critics.
Music Colleges will be inclusive by promoting enjoyment of many different musical forms and encouraging all students to participate in a wide variety of music-making. They will identify ways in which music can improve learning in other curriculum areas. They will be flexible in allowing some students to follow courses in music at their own pace. They will take a lead in using ICT as a means of enhancing learning in music and other subjects. They will enable students to work in school with professionals involved in music and to enjoy musical experiences outside the classroom. (DfES website 2006)

The aims and direction of Specialist Music Colleges appear to suggest a different focus and direction to those within the National Music and Dance scheme. Key elements were:

- an emphasis on whole-school improvement with general achievement targets and the idea that the specialist subject can help to improve other subjects

- a clear view that this applies to all students
- an emphasis on ICT

These foci may well be present within a school participating in the National Music and Dance Scheme. In fact these schools would almost certainly expect to embrace these attributes. However, such schools will have selected the students who participate in the scheme, which makes my definition of a musical school an uncomfortable fit in many ways for the specialist schools within the music and dance scheme. They are by their very nature selective rather than inclusive.

The potentially distinctive features of Specialist Music Colleges may, in practice, come down to the following:

1. Specialist Music Colleges do not need to select students on the basis of musical ability and will therefore work with a much broader spectrum of students. In fact these schools are allowed under English government legislation to select on 'aptitude' up to 10 per cent of students. Covert selection may also operate due to the fact that there is often a close correlation between able students and those who play instruments. This is a complex area requiring further exploration—I am not making a claim that learning an instrument leads to higher achievement, even though there have been researchers who have suggested that this is the case. There are almost certainly other factors at work, which ensure that the most able students are the ones who end up being interested in learning an instrument or being selected to have the chance to do so. Specialist Music Colleges are not required to select students on musical aptitude and it will be interesting to see how many actually did and the criteria that they used for this process. How many students ended up feeling 'hopeless' as a result of the selection procedures that were applied?

2. These schools ought to embrace a wider range of musical styles and cultures than those within the national music and dance scheme since they were not principally aiming to educate instrumentalists within the western art tradition. This, of course, will depend heavily on the particular interests and philosophy of key staff within each school and in reality they may merely be schools that selected and educated students that they viewed as being musically gifted and able. If this is the case they will not match my definition of what constitutes a musical school. They will also not match the original intention for this type of school.

The ethos of Specialist Music Colleges

Some Music Colleges may select students based on academic ability or some other characteristic (and may already have done so prior to achieving this status). This may be overtly or covertly. Some will be grammar schools or the most highly thought of and therefore popular school within their local area. I have also suggested that a certain style of music has a strong correlation in parents' minds with an exclusive, successful, and selective school. The model of a strong traditional music culture often correlates with high academic achievement. The reasons for this are complex but may stem from the following:

* playing an instrument often costs money and is therefore associated with the more socially advantaged
* academic selection and exclusivity is associated with western art music because of its formal traditions and status
* given a choice, instrumental teachers will choose to teach more able, socially adapted students (often girls) because to do otherwise would pose an unnecessary level of challenge.

It is not always clear in this chicken-and-egg scenario which comes first.

Academically selective school—attracts socially advantaged parents—embraces traditional values of western art music—this type of music becomes associated with particular social class and ethos—attracts socially advantaged parents—confirmed as academically selective school.

Specialist Music Colleges can use their status to confirm and re-enforce their reputation as a selective, academic, and socially exclusive school if they choose (either deliberately or unwittingly) to promote themselves in this way. Specialist Music Colleges can alter their profile, intake, and standing within the local community. When a school is over-subscribed it is inevitable that there will be some form of selection taking place. There has to be. Specialist Colleges are allowed to select up to 10 per cent based on aptitude in their specialism(s). Many schools select in other ways, some of which are hidden but very real to the end user (child or parent).

These statements require a small amount of further exploration. Parents like successful schools. If a school were to become a Specialist Music College it is possible that they could attract the most able and musically experienced students in the local area and give them an exceptionally effective education (musically, socially, and academically). The parents and students would be delighted by this and the school's popularity would be confirmed. The effect on the other schools, students, and parents in the area could be rather more negative, particularly where schools are in urban areas and where transport options mean that real choices can be made about which school a child should attend. This issue touches on one of the key challenges for the UK education system in the early twenty-first century. Political rhetoric was about choice—by parents of the school they want. The reality was that some schools are able to choose their intake and this leaves other schools and parents as potential losers in the scenario. The most effective choosers of education are usually the affluent, aspirational, and socially ambitious.

I think we are left with a key, although at this stage rhetorical question, about Specialist Music Colleges: Is it better for the musically interested students in an area to all attend one school or to be evenly distributed across all schools? The school that has all the musically active students will feel content, the other schools may resent this development because of the negative effect it has on them.

Characteristics of Specialist Music Colleges

The original Specialist Music College scheme set out some clear information and ideas about the ethos that these schools should aspire to. I think that the information is very good and provides a good starting point for a 'musical school' template. For example they should:

- have a significant (and increasing) number of students studying music as a subject in its own right or as part of a performing arts course
- encourage all learners to have an interest in a broad range of musical styles—both inside and outside school
- use the potential of music to enhance learning across the curriculum
- place high status on vocational courses in music, including music technology, recording, and mixing, which could appeal to a wider range of students
- make imaginative use of new technologies as a means of raising the quality of learning in music
- promote high levels of participation in extra-curricular music activities in their own and partner schools, including performance groups and instrumental tuition
- contribute to the Music Manifesto and support the delivery of wider opportunities for primary-school students to learn a musical instrument.
- extend learning opportunities in music through partnerships with local, regional, national, and international music-based industries and institutions
- promote enjoyment of many different musical forms and encourage all students to participate in a wide variety of music-making

- be lead practitioners in the use of ICT as a means of enhancing learning in music and other subjects
- work closely with their local primary schools to support access to instrumental and vocal tuition at Key Stage 2
- enable students to work in school with professionals involved in music and to enjoy musical experiences outside the classroom
- provide a varying and continuing programme of musical performances for the enjoyment of those within the school, other schools and the local community

I find this to be an impressive list because there is a clear focus on inclusion. A lot of thought has gone into it. A school could embrace many, if not all of the criteria used to describe a 'musical school' at the start of this chapter. A lot will depend on individual circumstances and the interest, skills, and vision of the staff who shape the Specialist Music College. There was, however, very little regulation of these schools and their specialism once they were designated. These schools received substantial extra funding but were mainly accountable for whole-school achievement targets in core subjects. Therefore although the guidance provided a good steer for these schools in how to plan their work in an inclusive and forward-thinking way there was nothing within the system that would hold these aspects of their work to account. I suspect that there was little guarantee that these schools would end up being what I would describe as 'musical schools', although I hope that some would.

In the next chapter I will describe some of the characteristics of one of these Specialist Music Colleges in more detail. The school is Northampton School for Girls—the first Specialist Music College in the country. The aim is to provide a case study example. There is no intention to suggest that:

- the school is, or ought to be, typical
- its practice is always exceptional
- it is has finished its developmental journey

I will try to test out the ways in which this school and other schools that I have encountered were, or were trying to be, a musical school.

Chapter 2

Specialist Music Colleges and the context of music education in 2004–2006

Nothing separates the generations more than music. By the time a child is eight or nine, he has developed a passion for his own music that is even stronger than his passions for procrastination and weird clothes.

Bill Cosby

The purpose of this chapter is to describe some of the features of the first Specialist Music College, Northampton School for Girls (NSG). In order to provide a context I will start by referring briefly to some of the other initiatives, developments, and projects affecting music education in England in the period between 2004 and 2006. I believe that this period was characterized by a rich and diverse range of developments.

The UK government funded either directly or indirectly a number of different music education projects in England at this time. Like most government initiatives they did not necessarily add up to a single, coherent view about music education because they came from different departments or were part of a variety of policy frameworks. Projects directly funded by central government included the following:

Wider opportunities

This gave funding to increase the numbers of students in Key Stage 2 able to take up a musical instrument. Several organizations were involved and the models were all different but had some common features. A key element was an enthusiasm to embrace large-group teaching (often with a whole class of children) and a clear message that instrumental playing opportunities were to be provided for all—hence the title. Further information about this project can be found in Chapter 7.

Music Manifesto

The Music Manifesto brought focus and direction to particular aspects of music education. A Music Manifesto Champion was appointed by the government and several high-profile figures from the music industry lent strong support. A series of reports were produced and plans were developed for activities designed to change the shape and direction of music education.

Standards fund

The UK government had given money every year to Local Authority Music Services to provide funding to support music education. It was up to the Local Authority services how to spend the money in line with local priorities.

Key Stage 3 Music strategy

The English National Strategies programme was a large-scale project designed to improve achievement in schools through a combination of resources, targets, and monitoring at a local and regional level. Although a government project, the delivery was awarded to a private company. The strategies project had started with primary-school education and had then moved into Key Stage 3— especially in the core subjects (English, maths, and science). It had gradually moved into Key Stage 4 and other subjects as well. In 2006 the project included music for the first time and a whole set of resources and potential training opportunities were provided for school teaching staff. However, unlike the training and resources designed for English, maths, and science, the music materials were viewed as being more optional and not widely distributed.

14–19

The 14–19 project was a massive development that sought to reform completely the curriculum offered to students in years 10 to 13. There were some key themes:

- developing courses that enabled students to move flexibly between different providers (such as schools and colleges)
- ensuring that every learner had the opportunity to access the complete range of courses in every geographical area of the country
- packaging courses into 'diplomas' that included a range of different qualifications and which strengthened vocational courses and work-related learning.

Many schools were already starting to look at long-term planning in order to put in place courses that would suit all learners and create good links with partner schools or colleges for delivery. A key theme in this project was the need for all students to be increasingly staying in some form of education or training until the age of 18 or 19.

QCA secondary curriculum reforms

The Qualification and Curriculum Authority was the government agency that dealt with the curriculum in schools. It was responsible for all curriculum content and for the regulation of the test and examination system. Students in years 7 to 9 often experienced a dip in attitudes and motivation and QCA revised the curriculum content for all subjects at Key Stage 3, Key Stage 4, and post-16. It also encouraged schools during the review period to experiment with a more flexible and innovative approach.

As well as these directly funded and initiated English government projects there were other interesting and important initiatives happening at the same time.

Youth Music-funded Action Zones

Youth Music was a national agency funded through receipts from the UK lottery. It set out key priorities and objectives for developments, particularly outside formal settings. One of the projects that it developed was called Youth Music Action Zones. This was a project in a particular area that was designed to develop music activity where it was felt that there was little currently happening.

Musical futures

This project was not funded by the UK government. It was supported by a private charity, the Paul Hamlyn Foundation. It developed a series of innovative activities that sought to meet the needs and aspirations of young people. The project was widely publicized and aligned itself with some aspects of government policy in order to complement mainstream views. For example, many of the projects developed were linked to the government theme of 'personalization'.

This overview of government-funded and other developments taking place in the English education system is not comprehensive. Hopefully it helps to establish that there was a wide range of activities taking place in music education and as a result I believe that it was quite a rich and interesting period for music education. I will now turn to a key development during this period—the establishment of Specialist Music Colleges.

What does music specialism look like in schools?

Northampton School for Girls was the first Specialist Music College in England. It achieved this status in September 2004. NSG was a large comprehensive school serving the town of Northampton. It admitted students using a fair-banding system to try to ensure a balanced intake. The school website gave an insight into what the school was trying to achieve:

As a Specialist Music College, NSG is at an exciting stage in its development as a leading provider of teaching and learning opportunities for both students and the local community. We are able to offer a unique experience to everyone who joins us.

We recognise that good quality education requires close co-operation between the school and the home. We are confident that we provide a creative and supportive environment where all our students can succeed in whatever areas they choose, enabling them to contribute in a major way to national and regional economic achievement and well being, as well as finding personal fulfilment. (NSG website 2006)

Apart from mentioning that it is a Specialist Music College the NSG website made little explicit reference to the values associated with this status. Few Specialist Music College websites did. They were more likely to describe the school in general terms:

Simon Langton Girls' Grammar School originated in the Middle Ages as an educational foundation for children in Canterbury, emerging as a separate school for girls in 1881. Our school motto 'Meliora Sequamur' (following the best) emphasises the school's continued commitment to excellence. Girls are following an 800 year old tradition in achieving high academic distinction, learning civilized and humane values and developing the personality and character to allow them to go on to play a leading role in the wider world. (School website 2006)

By August 2006 seventeen secondary schools in England had been granted Specialist Music college status. A further five schools had received Specialist status in music and one other subject. A relatively high proportion of the first seventeen Specialist Music Colleges were either single-sex, selective, or part of established foundations (or well-established traditions). It is possible that the first set of Music Colleges were not typical of all schools in the UK, representing a more selective and favourable group of schools. If so this might reflect the fact that music is often seen as being a high-status, exclusive activity, which is perhaps why some of these schools were attracted to this specialism in the first place.

Northampton School for Girls—the first Specialist Music College

I will look in more detail at Northampton School for Girls. The school is not presented here as an exemplar of best practice, although some of its work was undoubtedly very good, interesting, and innovative. I will attempt to give an insight into what the school was like in 2004, when it became a Specialist Music College and how it developed over the next two years. In order to do this I will first provide information about the profile of the school. About a year before applying to become a Specialist Music College the school was inspected by OFSTED. The report included a section describing the school:

The Northampton School for Girls is a comprehensive school for girls aged 13 to 18 years. It serves the borough of Northampton. Students come from all of the middle schools in the town. They reflect the very wide social, economic, ethnic and cultural diversity of Northampton. The school is of average size compared with other secondary schools in England. It has 1037 students, compared with 684 students at the time of the previous inspection in 1997.

The report also included an evaluation of how effective the school was:

The school provides a very good quality of education for girls of all social and ethnic backgrounds and levels of attainment. Achievement is high because teachers and students have high expectations of each other. (OFSTED Inspection report, February 2003)

In 2006, two years after becoming a Specialist Music College the school was inspected again and judged to be outstanding:

This is an outstanding school of which students, parents, staff and governors are rightly proud. The attention paid to students' individual needs is impressive and it helps promote outstanding achievement in both their academic and personal development. A student's comment sums up the views of many: 'This school allows you to be yourself and it helps you to achieve excellence'. The school is hugely popular. This is shown by the very large return of questionnaire responses from parents as part of this inspection, which was overwhelmingly in support of the school's work. There are many reasons for the school's success. The head teacher provides inspiring leadership. A governor observed, 'she has her eyes on the stars and feet right on the ground'. This means that the school's values are realised in practice.

The report made specific reference to the Specialist status:

The school's specialist status for music allows over 600 students to learn to play a musical instrument, with many learning to play more than one. The impact of the status is also very evident in other areas of the curriculum and benefits the wider community as well. For example, students assist in leading music workshops in primary schools, and the school's orchestra performs at local and national events. (OFSTED inspection report, September 2006)

The comment about the school's orchestra is slightly inaccurate but the sentiment about the quality of the school and the impact of the specialism seems fair. The two reports give a clear insight into a very successful and popular school. They also record progress over a three-year period. NSG was a very effective and improving school—the sort of school that I would have been very happy to send my daughter (if I had one). The music specialism was, not surprisingly, an area that needed to be developed and thought about further.

The NSG context

When NSG became a Specialist Music College the profile of schools in Northampton was as follows:

- one Academy (state-funded independent school)
- two 'faith' schools (one Church of England and one Catholic)
- two single-sex schools (including NSG)
- four other comprehensive schools

The boys' school and girls' school both took students from across the town and neither had a clear geographical 'catchment' area. As a result both schools relied on single-sex education, marketing, and their reputation to attract students. Parents saw both schools as very successful and they were very popular and over-subscribed. Both had moved from a position of relative unpopularity over the previous ten years and had changed their profile within the local community due to their success and their ability to inspire the confidence of local parents.

All Northampton schools

- were reorganized into a two-tier (primary, secondary) system with the assimilation of three year groups in September 2004; previously the schools had been part of a 'three-tier' lower-middle-upper system
- had a planned PFI (Privately Financed) building project (or similar sort of rebuild of the whole school)
- were initially operating across two sites as a result of reorganization.

These factors caused a significant amount of turbulence. NSG admitted 900 new students into the school in September 2004. These were from years 7, 8, and 9. In previous years the Upper School would have taken students into year 9 only. The Local Authority had taken the decision to assimilate students in this way in order to avoid changes in the education system being spread over too protracted a period of time. Any system involving such a large amount of change had an impact on the staff and students concerned.

What is perhaps less clear from this information is that NSG regarded itself as a very inclusive school and tried to resist the temptation to use its popularity to select the most able and socially advantaged girls in the town. In order to achieve this they subscribed to a 'fair-banding' system (meaning that the school would accept a proportion of students from different ability bands based on a standardized test) and used an independent person to match applicants to the school's criteria for entry. In 2004 the entry policy at NSG also included no selection by musical ability. However, in 2007 a decision was made to introduce a criterion of 10 per cent selection by musical aptitude into the admission policy. This was due to a number of factors related to admissions criteria being aligned between the boys' and girls' schools in Northampton. I feel that this was an extremely regrettable decision that was bound to have an overall negative impact on NSG's ability to maintain an approach that was musically inclusive.

Between 2004 and 2006 NSG was extremely vigilant about giving opportunities for all the girls in the school, regardless of their background. This philosophy of access and fairness was very strong and senior managers and governors all subscribed to it. In 2006 NSG had a year 7 intake with an average points score of 28.2. The Northamptonshire average was 27.3. The ability of the students on entry to the school had risen gradually over a number of years due to the popularity of the school. A key feature that had made the school successful and popular with parents was the well-developed care and guidance. The 'atmosphere' and the positive interactions with students immediately struck you when walking around the site. NSG had some difficult students but it promoted strongly the values of trust, respect, and self-esteem. Students were proud of the school and responded to this. This ethos flowed through many aspects of school life but was most forcefully felt when talking to the head teacher and deputies.

The staff knew the girls well and would take a lot of time, trouble, and effort to follow up and resolve problems. Mentoring was used very successfully in order to keep motivation high. The levels of guidance in the school were very good and were effective. Strengths in communication were reflected in contact with parents, which was always given a high priority. School leaders all promoted strongly the view that NSG was:

- a resource for the local community
- a comprehensive, non-selective school with a broad spectrum of students
- not distorting education in the local area but playing a strong role within it.

Despite this strong ethos and approach school leaders were not always able to apply this approach to music. Why was this? Principally because they, like many others, felt that music was different from other subjects and that there were musicians and non-musicians.

Benefits of Specialist College status

The Music College status brought some benefits:

- an extra £100,00 for a capital project
- recurrent funding of an extra £129 per student (this funding was identical for any Specialist College in 2004).

However, it also brought specific challenges:

1. The school had to raise £50,000 in sponsorship (although some of this was provided by the Specialist School's Trust).

2. The bid was a lengthy and time-consuming document to complete.

3. The targets required by the bid are very specific and offer a significant level of challenge.

4. The extra funding could not be built comfortably into the school's base budget because it was only available for four years unless a successful resubmission could be made. Therefore sensible decisions needed to be made about what was funded by the 'normal' budget and which development activities could be funded by the Specialist College budget.

Specialist College targets

As part of the Specialist Music College bid NSG, along with all other schools going through the same process, had to set a series of challenging targets. These were related to whole-school achievement, community development, and specialist subject targets (music and ICT). The music targets were:

1. To raise levels of attainment in music at all Key Stages 3, 4, and post-16 and to improve and increase curriculum provision.

2. To increase numbers making an active choice to study music at KS4 and further at KS5 and to be more inclusive of students from a wide range of backgrounds.

3. To increase and extend the range of opportunities for students within the music curriculum and in extra-curricular activities.

4. To increase access to the appropriate computer technology to enhance the teaching and learning of music and to emphasize the importance of music as a vocation.

5. To develop musical links with other areas of the curriculum and to highlight the ways in which music can improve teaching and learning.

6. To develop enrichment programmes which will enhance student's learning experiences through improved performance and use of technology.

The school was required to set various quantitative targets as part of the bid (see Table 2).

1. Maintain high-level achieving music level 5 or above, but increase percentage achieving level 6 or above to:
   35 per cent 2004
   40 per cent 2005

Table 2 Quantitative targets set by Northampton School for Girls as part of the bid to become a Specialist Music College

Music GCSE Year	No. of students	Grades A–C (%)	
2005	40	75	
2006	45	77	
2007	50	79	
2008	55	81	
Music AS/A2 Year	No. of students	Grades A–B (%)	Grades A–E (%)
2005	6	30	100
2006	8	35	100
2007	10	40	100
2008	12	45	100

    45 per cent 2006
    50 per cent 2007

2. To increase the proportion of the cohort opting to study music at KS4 to:
   16 per cent in 2004
   18 per cent in 2005
   20 per cent in 2006
   22 per cent in 2007

3. To develop an appropriate Music Technology course for introduction in September 2004/5

4. Set up a baseline test for students in year 7 to assess progress by the end of KS3.

5. Every music teacher's lessons to be observed at least once per term to ensure consistency of provision.

6. Increase the time allocation for the subject at KS3 from September 2004
   2 Music/1 Art in year 7
   2 Art/1 Music in year 8
   Guided choice for year 9: 2 Music/1 Art per week or 1 Music/2 Art

7. Develop exemplar material of A/A* material for use by gifted and talented students.

8. 2005 BTEC Performing Arts (Level 1) to be introduced.

9. To increase the peripatetic support in the school so that all year 7 students who wish to can learn to play a musical instrument.

10. Use of resident musicians for student workshops to engage the interest of and to extend the participation by a range of students from different cultural backgrounds.

11. Redesign reception, background music, video screen of performances.

12. Research into the effects of music therapy—to be provided for our students and then for other schools.

There were a wide range of other whole-school, community, and subject targets as well. These give a flavour of the significant expectations that went with the Specialist College status. However, the Specialist College programme was not strongly regulated and whole-school achievement targets were actually more significant than these individual subject targets. The reality was that many schools did not meet these specialist targets but if they were inspected by OFSTED and rated as good or better it did not matter. Therefore the focus of the original priorities set out by the Specialist College bid and the progress towards specialist targets became dissipated over time.

The musical context of NSG

In 2004, prior to opening as a Specialist Music College, NSG had a strong reputation within the local community for music. This was based on some key factors:

- a relatively large number of extra-curricular music groups
- the quality of the school choir
- good GCSE results
- the relative lack of these attributes in other schools in the town—apart from the boys' school
- a strong contribution to the community through a production company based at the school but involving a wide range of students.

The bid to become a Specialist College built on the strengths in the school and had some key elements that contributed to its success:

- effective and efficient bid-writing, particularly from the deputy head
- advice from a range of organizations, including the Local Authority
- strong support and astute thinking from the head teacher and governors

Like many schools it also had several areas that required further development in its specialist area—not surprising since the music staff up until designation consisted of one full-time person and another person teaching music part-time. This is a situation common in many secondary schools in the UK.

This lone person has the almost impossible of task of being a curriculum leader, running a wide range of extra-curricular activities, and managing extra instrumental tuition.

The bid clearly reflected the ethos of a comprehensive, non-selective school and meant that NSG seemed to be breaking new ground in taking this inclusive musical stance. The result of these positive factors was that the school was successful in its bid and opened in September 2004 as the first Specialist Music College in the country. Although other schools followed fairly quickly, being the first added an element of status and extra attention and responsibility. The school was noticed and often invited to contribute to national initiatives or debates on music education in schools.

In order to evaluate the key strengths and areas for development at NSG prior to this I will use my definition of a 'musical school' as a starting point. This does not provide the whole picture but a starting template.

An inclusive policy and practice

Musically, NSG was typical of most secondary schools in September 2004. The general policy and practices within the school were exceptionally inclusive. This was a strength. This approach had not been consistently applied to music education policy and practice. All students received their entitlement to music education in Key Stage 3 and were offered an option choice in years 10 and 11. Students were not discouraged or excluded from the curriculum. However, beneath this approach many schools structure their curriculum content and expectations so that it is clear that the students who are expected to participate in the music curriculum from Key Stage 4 onwards are those who are considered to be successful, often because they already play an instrument. This group are often thought of and described as 'the musicians'.

The logo of the Specialist Music Colleges (designed on behalf of the government-funded Specialist Schools' Trust) exemplifies this issue. The use of a treble clef and a musical stave immediately seems to set out an expectation of school music that is western, classical, and based around reading musical notation. It must put off a wide range of students who do not fall into these categories and makes a strong statement to a school's local community, government agencies, and other stakeholders. I feel that this choice of logo was a significant retrograde step in supporting a more inclusive ethos for music education.

Learning instruments

In September 2004 there were about 240 students learning an instrument at NSG. This represented about 15 per cent of the school population. There was an unwritten policy that students who already played on arrival at the school continued with musical instrument tuition. Locally there was a strong tradition in years 5–8 of learning instruments at middle schools and many students identified NSG as being a 'musical school' prior to it becoming a Specialist College. Very few received tuition at NSG unless they had been inducted into the system at their previous school. Instrumental tuition was provided almost exclusively by the Local Authority Music Service. There was not an agenda to increase the range or improve access to tuition at the school. There was also a small group of students who had lessons outside school (again provided by the LA Music Service) and who also played in county-funded groups. These students were generally of a higher standard—the Music Service encouraged them to have lessons at the Music Centre. They often participated in music-making at school but also had an important loyalty to the county-funded Music Service and its weekly activities. Music at school was something they supported but it was not a top priority for them.

Musical excellence

Musical excellence is a difficult area to evaluate since a lot will depend on the definition used. The school had a good-quality choir that was very highly regarded by the local community. It has also had a range of other extra-curricular groups which were of a good standard, although by no means exceptional. Compared to local secondary-school provision performance groups were above average. Compared to regional and national groups from other comprehensive schools that achieve recognition through competitions and awards NSG groups were generally below average. Performance in examination results was reasonable. GCSE results had been consistently above average over several years and a reasonable number of students got higher grades (although when compared to the performance of girls nationally performance was closer to average, since girls tend to do better). Achievement post-16 was about average but with small numbers. Overall this was an area with several strengths but where there was scope for further development.

Musical diversity

The profile of students at NSG was reasonably diverse. This was not fully reflected in musical activity—which was predominantly white. NSG was typical of many schools. Most do not analyse the uptake of instrumental/vocal tuition and compare this information to check whether it is typical of the overall school population. Many might find the results of such a comparison uncomfortable. There are also issues in schools across the country about the participation of Muslim students learning instruments and participating in music groups, especially where the local religious ethos is very strong, since some religious leaders can actively discourage participation in music for these students. This is a particular feature that I have encountered quite strongly in some schools where there is a high proportion of Muslim students.

I enjoyed music. Got the music award in grade eight. Played in the school band. Sang in the school and the church choirs. Sang on my way to and from school, at home, and before I fell asleep at night. Learned to whistle (after much effort), and would whistle anything from Bach's Hallelujah Chorus to commercials on TV. Liked to play the kazoo. Tried to teach myself guitar.

And then, I became a Muslim.

Suddenly, music was no longer an innocent expression of joy. It became a dubious thing at best, especially for women. Not only must the words of the songs you sing pass a number of moral and doctrinal tests, and no musical accompaniment is allowed except the daff (hand-drum), in the opinion of a great many scholars, but a woman's singing voice can't be heard by any man not closely related to her.

If that were not enough, the cultural stuff put upon us was even more stringent. 'Good' women don't play musical instruments. And even whistling while doing the dishes was frowned upon, as it allegedly attracts demons. I tried to conform; I really did. I didn't listen to the radio, even when I drove. I tried hard to like nasheeds, and to only sing them. I bought a daff. I tried not to whistle.

I attended all Muslim events which might have singing at them, such as celebrations of the Prophet's birthday. I would sing along (I couldn't help myself), but hide the lower half of my face with my arm, so that no one would know I was singing and be offended.

It was like trying to make oneself believe that an ugly, concrete warehouse which is being used as a mosque is more beautiful than an old gothic cathedral. It isn't true. And the ugliness, with its attendant lies, smothers you in the end. Art and music, to be truly beautiful, can't be held hostage to ideological programmes.

Why, I wonder, did God create some of us musical? In order to test us, to see if we would presume to make music, and then punish us? (Posted on internet chat room June 2006)

This culture of faith-dictated anti-music views was not overtly present at NSG. However participation rates in instrumental tuition did not match the overall profile of the school population—with white girls being by far the largest group and other ethnic groups being under-represented. NSG's music groups also catered predominantly for western art style performers. The choir, band, string group, guitar group, and jazz group were the ensembles with the largest numbers. There were also two 'rock' groups (although by their nature these included only a few students).

Most schools have music groups that reflect a particular style of western music-making and contain students who have taken up an instrument. The process by which they started playing is a significant factor and as a result of selection these students can often be white and middle class. This is, of course, a generalization and the issue will be explored further in a later chapter. During a period when I was inspecting a lot of schools I undertook an informal analysis of the first names of students learning instruments in about seventy schools. This analysis demonstrated strongly that if your name was Sophie, Lucy, James, or Anthony you were much likely to learn an instrument than Kylie, Chelsea, Wayne, or Dwain. Is this because these students did not want to learn an instrument, or because some sort of filter was being applied?

NSG was also typical in that musicals and shows often attract a different and more diverse student clientele. The students who participated in these activities included a number of girls who were not involved in other ways. This probably resulted from the fact that these students identified more comfortably with the style of music used in shows and also did not perceive the need for a prior commitment to western art music styles of performance.

Effective use of music technology

In July 2004 NSG had one 'stand alone' computer equipped with a music software program for writing scores. This was used by a small number of A level students. There were also some electronic keyboards (extensively used with year 9) and a high-quality portable recording desk. There were no local 'online' resources for students to use—although they may have accessed the internet from other locations in the school, such as the library, for research purposes. The effective use of music technology was an area requiring extensive development and the school recognized this need.

Innovative teaching and learning

In July 2004 NSG had one full-time music teacher and another member of staff who taught a small amount of music. In many schools the outcome of this can be that the music department has a very specific focus on managing extra-curricular provision and through no fault of its own has insufficient energy available to engage with developments in teaching and learning.

Attention given to student voice and views

Like most schools NSG had a group of committed students who identified themselves closely with music and participated enthusiastically in activities. There was a close correlation with uptake of instrumental tuition and participation in extra-curricular groups. Informal discussions with this group of students about views and preferences were fairly common. Like most similar schools the views of the remainder of the students were less clear and less researched.

Use of music across the curriculum to enhance learning

NSG had a strong track record of considering learning styles and the consequent teaching strategies that might be used. For example the terms 'visual learner' or 'kinaesthetic learner' would have been familiar to many staff at the school. The concept of music as a specific tool for learning across the curriculum was not something that had been developed prior to September 2004. It was, however, a very strong feature of the NSG bid for specialist music status and championed by one of the deputy head teachers.

A wide range of music extra-curricular activities

NSG had a relatively large number of extra-curricular music activities taking place. They included

◆ Choir

◆ Band

◆ String group

◆ Jazz group

◆ Two rock groups

◆ Theory group

The majority of these groups were run by visiting instrumental teachers. Whilst this was an area of relative strength there was scope to increase the range and diversity of the groups still further.

An innovative and effective curriculum

The NSG music curriculum was similar to that in most English schools. Students received a core entitlement in Key Stage 3, a GCSE option, and an A level option. The content of the curriculum was reasonably traditional in scope and style. This was an area that required significant development.

Strong engagement with the local community

NSG had some strong links with its local community. The fact that there was a 750-seat theatre on site meant that members of the public knew of the school and many would have visited the theatre in the past. Other, more recent, provision within the town had meant that by September 2004 the theatre was relatively little used; this was an area that needed further development. The school had a strong link with a community theatre production company that resulted in an annual production involving students from the school and outside performers as well. This was a strong feature of the life of the school and added significant strength to its bid for specialist status.

What were the immediate enhancements made at the school and why were they planned?

When NSG opened as a Specialist Music College some key extra factors immediately contributed to the musical profile of the school:

1. The appointment of two new full-time members of music staff—this brought a new dimension to the teaching and some new ideas and energy.

2. The appointment of a full-time music technician—this was a key factor in levering change due to the focus this gave to the development of ICT within music. By the end of the second year NSG had two full-time music technicians and another general ICT technician who had a degree in music. A striking feature of the appointment process for these posts was the number and quality of adults in the local community who were not qualified teachers but who had very good levels of skills in music-making, ICT, and often a combination of both. With the development of a children's workforce and reforms to teachers' roles and responsibilities this group of adults provide a potentially invaluable resource for schools.

3. The appointment of a Music College administrator—this brought a focus to many aspects of the Music College, especially the interface with the local community.

4. My secondment for two days a week—this brought contact with a wide range of outside views, an element of challenge and the development of new ideas—particularly in the interface with the local community.

5. Being the first Music College meant that the head teacher and other staff were often involved in activities and discussions with national initiatives.

Other potential contributors to change were: the planned development of a new suite of music accommodation as part of the PFI building project (scheduled for September 2008) and the improvement of the acoustic, equipment, and infrastructure of Spinney Hill Theatre. The Theatre is a 700-seat auditorium which was used to a limited degree by local community groups. It is an extremely useful space with especially good sight lines for the audience, a large stage area, and a separate entrance (meaning that it can operate independently of the school if required). The theatre had been quite a high-profile venue for concerts but although the acoustic was very good for groups requiring amplification it was extremely dry and unfriendly for acoustic performances. However the theatre offered a key possibility for the Specialist Music College in working with the local community and the sort of opportunities that could be made available.

Additionally a very significant factor was the development of the music technology infrastructure within the Music College—this is dealt with in Chapter 8. The ICT developments and set-up were one of the really key factors in changing the culture and interface of music teaching in the school very quickly.

What was the impact of the specialism after two years?

Most outside visitors and observers were impressed by the progress made by NSG in its first two years as a Specialist Music College. A progress report at the end of the two years might look like this:

Overall NSG has made good progress in several areas over the last two years. In some areas progress has been outstanding. This is despite the fact that the school had to respond to a major reorganization of education, which resulted in the assimilation of three year groups, the development of two sites, and induction of an extra fifty teachers. Additionally school leaders have had to cope with the planning of a new school building, negotiations with architects, and accommodation of building works on the main school site. The development of the music college ethos and direction during this period of turbulence has been exceptional.

An inclusive policy and practice

The issue of inclusion was addressed consistently when dealing with the curriculum, extra-curricular activities, and access to instrumental teaching. The issues were better understood at a senior level and expectations started to come more in line with the overall expectations for the school. For example, the curriculum was revised at Key Stage 3 on a regular basis and Key Stage 4 options that were suitable for a wider range of student's interests were investigated. Overall progress in this area was sound but NSG still had a long way to go at music department level.

Large numbers learning an instrument/voice

The policy on access to instrumental tuition was revised and updated. More students were given the opportunity to learn an instrument with a visiting tutor or as part of an online learning project and rock school. The numbers learning increased sharply from 300 to 625. There was some resistance to this development within school.

Musical excellence

The school maintained its tradition of achievement with musical groups and promoted high-quality events such as the celebration day events involving professional musicians and a performance at St John Smith's Square in

London. Locally the school achieved a reasonable level of excellence but did not develop a more regional or national reputation.

Musical diversity

Diversity was promoted in the curriculum through the range of topics that were covered, although like most schools the curriculum tended to promote most heavily western art music. More white girls learned musical instruments than was representative of the school population.

Effective use of music technology

The rate of development in the use of music technology was phenomenal. This one factor had a profound effect on the ethos and culture of music in the school. The use of a virtual learning environment was developed with post-16 courses being accessed by students consistently and effectively. The pedagogy of using music software as a tool to support music teaching was still underdeveloped.

Innovative teaching and learning

The development of ICT, resources and facilities had a strong impact on teaching styles, content, and methodology on the main school site. The quality of teaching on the lower school site was often good with attention given to the planning of effective lessons, especially with years 7 and 8. Good use was made of national strategy materials and developments. ICT was underused in years 7 and 8. Overall, however, the development of innovative teaching and learning was slow because it was not discussed sufficiently due to other pressures.

Attention given to student voice and views

The attention given to student voice and views across the school was very good. Students had opportunities to record their views in a wide range of surveys and interviews. Students were proud of the school and the attention given to their views was a key factor in making them feel that they had a say in the direction that it followed. In music this remained underdeveloped.

A wide range of music extra-curricular activities

The school offered a very good range of activities. They catered for a wide range of needs and interests. Over the two-year period the opportunities for students were being extended and developed. The range of projects and activities with visiting artists was exceptional. More needed to be done to include a wider range of students.

An innovative and effective curriculum

The curriculum was developed to include a greater element of choice at the end of year 8. The development of further curriculum pathways at Key Stage 4 was explored. The Music Technology course for post-16 students enabled a wide range of students without formal performance skills to access a course that met their needs and aspirations. An innovative development was the use of a music therapist working with identified vulnerable students.

Strong engagement with the local community

The engagement with the local community was exceptional. NSG sought to work with a wide range of groups. These included

- local schools, including Special Schools
- early years
- community groups
- professional artists
- local service providers
- regional and national service providers
- students excluded from school

Access to information, resources, and expertise was made freely available to a wide range of organizations and individuals. NSG contributed to local and national developments through representation at a wide range of events and activities. NSG sought through its actions to support the wider local community and make a strong contribution to the development of music education.

Use of music across the curriculum to enhance learning

The school consistently promoted the use of music as a tool for learning. All staff attended training and had access to the necessary resources and materials. A few staff explored this effectively and incorporated a range of activities into their teaching routines. All staff sought to use music as a learning tool during the annual celebration day. Students reported that the use of music across the curriculum increased substantially over the two-year period.

How does this fit with the aims of Specialist Music Colleges?

The guidance documentation for Specialist Music Colleges is excellent. It encouraged these schools to take an inclusive and broad approach to music education. Once they had achieved this status it is very much up to them how they choose to develop. This diversity and independence can be a strength where a school has a clear vision about what it wants to achieve and its vision is actually visionary. However becoming a Specialist Music College does not guarantee becoming a musical school. Redesignation mostly depends on whether or not a school reaches its agreed whole-school targets (GCSE and Key Stage 3 examination and test results for all subjects). What it has done musically will not really enter into the equation.

Was NSG a musical school? I believe that some aspects of its work demonstrated that it was but it had several areas that needed to be developed further. I think I could answer the question best by saying that it had started to become a musical school and that in many respects it had made good progress. It would be fair to say that it had a long way to go and that there were many other schools around at the time, whether Music Colleges or not, with equally good or better practice. It was certainly a very good school and one that I would have been very happy to send a child to. It had senior managers who had the vision and energy to carry it forwards. They were also very strongly committed to being inclusive and this was one of the school's greatest strengths. How it continued to develop would depend on government policies and the priorities of new senior managers who take over the shape and direction of the school. They will need to ensure that it continues to develop policies and practices that are musically inclusive and which cater for a wide range of students. More than this they will need to have the knowledge and courage that will enable them to challenge some of the assumptions, custom, and practice as well as breaking the barriers that stop all students participating in music. A school such as NSG will need at least one person within the leadership team who has the passion and energy to challenge the status quo, commonly held views, and the tenacity not to accept anything else. The key driving factor will always be the ethos that is created by leaders at all levels. This ethos will be experienced by all the students, not just those who are interested in and engage with school music. The next chapter will examine the views and experiences of the students at NSG and in schools generally.

Chapter 3

The views of students, staff, and other stakeholders about music

Music means a lot to me. I've always said, if you can choose to see, hear, taste, or smell I would choose to hear. I have many memories with some sort of music played in the background that I remember to this day and I will remember for many years to come.

NSG Year 8 student

The purpose of this chapter is to explore how students, staff, and other adults working with schools feel about music. This means music they listen to and use for relaxation or stimulation as well as music they encounter in school. There is an important distinction between these two areas and I will explore how they link together and whether school music matches the interests and aspirations of young people.

In addressing these questions I will consider the views some of the stakeholders involved with Northampton School for Girls. This is set against a wider agenda of what was happening in schools generally during 2004–6. Much of the information is based on a survey carried out with 1,344 students at NSG in June 2005. They completed a questionnaire asking for their views about music in and out of school. These were given out during tutor time and teaching staff supervised the activity to ensure that students understood what to do. Staff were given written instructions and a briefing on how to organize this session. This meant that it was done individually and with appropriate care. All the questionnaires contained legible, considered responses. Open-ended questions were often completed with an impressive amount of detail and thought. The large number of responses gave a very robust picture of the views of the students. Staff also completed a questionnaire and there was a high response rate from both teaching and support staff.

The responses were analysed qualitatively and quantitatively. The statistical analysis was carried out at the Royal College of Music using SPSS software by Louise Oakes. Janet Mills very kindly supervised this process. This information, coupled with the structured and unstructured conversations I carried out with staff and students over a two-year period provided a rich insight into the views of a wide cross-section of stakeholders associated with a school at a very significant point in its development. Before starting this process I believed strongly that the music specialism might come through in students' views, although I was also aware that a significant proportion of the students (years 10–13) would still be able to remember the school prior to September 2004 (before reorganization and designation as a Specialist Music College). I was interested to find out what impact this event had made on them.

The second part of the survey explored students' views about music as a curriculum subject. They were asked questions about favourite subject(s) and I was interested to see where music featured. I was aware that a significant number of students had chosen to come to the school because of its reputation for music—even before its designation as a Specialist College. I therefore expected that music might be quite popular, especially because at this stage in the year the students had experienced several events related to the designation as a Specialist College which had raised the profile of music within the school.

Teenagers' views on music outside school

Students often have strong views about music. Music has an important link to their cultural identity and developing sense of self. It is often associated with particular images, clothing styles, and values. It can promote both conformity and individuality, according to a student's particular needs. As students mature and develop into adolescence they start to feel the need to move away from their parents' cultural values in order to develop a sense of independence. Often students will not be aware that some of the cultural reference points they choose are developed and promoted by media marketing specialists whose aim is to sell them things. Popular music started off as something that was noticeably distant from the views and tastes of adults in the post-war generation. Its birth belonged to the 'baby boomers'—the first generation to have significant disposable income. Their strong response to a new type of music reflected a sense of independent cultural values and rebellion from their parents. As musical styles and tastes have become more diverse it has probably been increasingly more difficult for young people to find something that is different, radical, and shocking. It is hard to rebel against a generation who invented the idea of rebellion. Modern tastes are actually quite eclectic. Young people often have a wide range of interests and many feel no strong desire to listen to the latest 'chart' music released by the recording industry. Music is now available via the internet and much of it is discounted and readily accessible. This has the effect of making choices and tastes more personalized and social groups operate over greater distances. This global communication provides young people with numerous forums for discussing music:

Bands like Nickelback and Hinder are ruining rock and making it all sound the same. Try listening to some more industrial music, it's not exactly rock but it's not the same thing over and over again. I think you have the wrong idea about rock music, although I will agree that I hate seeing these 15 year old girls running around saying they love rock music and that their favourite band is Hinder.

I guess it's just a matter of opinion. Open your horizons a bit more and don't just stick with rock and metal. Try industrial, EBM, goth, alternative . . . etc.

Tiesto, Paul van Dyk, Luca Agnelli (may be hard to find . . . let me know and I can send you a couple songs), Benny Benassi, Prodigy (Spitfire is a good song), k90, Motorcycle (as the rush comes is a good one), Fatboy Slim, Armin Van Buuren, Deep Dish, Paul Oakenfold, Darude.

(posted by young people in internet forums 2007)

Although there was less conformity to particular musical styles in 2004–6, music remained a very popular leisure activity for young people. Music is written in a format that will appeal to them and the music industry makes a lot of money out of this age group. For the large majority music is defined as something you listen to, rather than participate in as a performer or composer. It is often associated with other themes such as parties, fashion, and the media. It may be thought of as being glamorous and offers a glimpse of a world that a young person may aspire to. The focus of this market has increasingly shifted downwards in age as older students are less influenced by 'chart' music and are likely to develop more specific and focused tastes. Children aged 7 or 8 are increasingly aware of some of the images and styles that go with commercial music.

The views of NSG students about music outside school

The quote from a year 8 student that starts this chapter is very typical of the response given by almost all students at NSG. In this section of the survey students often talked about music in general and not music in school, even though the open-ended nature of the questions gave them every opportunity to refer to music-making in school if they wanted to. Many of their views matched my expectations but their passion for music surprised me. In the survey an overwhelming number of students wrote effusively about music and what it meant to them.

Music is very important to me as there are so many different pieces and artists that I really enjoy listening to. It depends what mood I am in and what it is I am doing at the time. (NSG year 12 student)

The type of music described by students was usually 'popular' music. Terminology is difficult because students had very specific tastes. Terms such as 'R and B' may mean something to them for a period of a year or two and then be quickly superseded by something different, but equally specific. 'R and B', for example, can describe rhythm and blues, but this is not what a teenager in 2005 meant by the term. This use of terminology is a hugely complex area that will take much space to disentangle and will change very quickly. For this reason I do not intend to devote any time trying to get to definitive descriptions. I use the tem 'popular' as a shorthand to describe music that students at NSG were listening to and which was in a contemporary and popular style, rather than a 'classical' style (another problematic term). The term popular covers a huge range of artists, bands, and styles. This may not be music that is found in the charts. It will almost certainly not be what the students themselves would describe as 'popular' because they have their own very specific vocabulary. It is their music, it is not classical, and has popular appeal.

As students got older they tended to be more selective about particular artist(s) they wanted to listen to and might associate themselves with a particular fashion or social group defined around that style of music. For younger students (years 7, 8, and possibly year 9) listening to music was often related to the physical sensations of dancing or the social aspects of attending a party. Teenagers responded well to fast-tempo music that enabled them to expel energy through dance and movement. It is an active, kinaesthetic experience. Live music is also an important feature:

Although we were quite far from the stage we still heard and saw many stars. To be a part of that atmosphere was brilliant. Needless to say I had a sore throat the next day from all the shouting and screaming I did. (NSG year 11 student)

The lively, active, and kinaesthetic strands are important for us to consider when we evaluate how music in schools matches the interests and preoccupations of this group of students. Is the curriculum for years 7, 8, and 9 lively, participative, and utilizing the high-energy styles that they respond to so strongly? Rarely, in my experience. There are several reasons for this:

- limitations imposed by classroom spaces and design
- the backgrounds and enthusiasms of many music teachers
- the different social and physiological context of classical music styles that are often used in classrooms.

Although I expected students to feel enthusiastic about music outside school the depth of a very large number of their responses surprised me.

We always have music on in our house and I couldn't have it any other way, it's a way of life, it makes me, me. It helps people be who they really are and it touches me deep down inside at a place that nothing else does. I couldn't live without it. (NSG year 12 student)

The music industry is very well organized and sophisticated and tries to ensure that there is music available to suit the needs and tastes of a wide range of listeners. Teenagers are a particularly rich vein of potential consumers because they have a reasonable amount of money to spend on pleasure for themselves. They do not have cars to run, children to feed, or mortgages to pay. They are often experiencing intense emotional development caused by the release of hormones brought about by puberty. The themes of love and loss found in most popular music meets their preoccupations perfectly. They are also at a stage in their life where they will respond strongly, although perhaps subconsciously, to strong sexual imagery and an overt emphasis on glamour, alienation, or individuality used in many popular music videos.

Music to me means everything. Music inspires me to think about other people. It's a way that I can express myself and find my real feeling deep down inside me I wish other people would look at music in the same way that I do. So they can really see what is going on in the world. In every song there is a hidden message. (NSG year 7 student)

There seems to be a large gap between this incredible enthusiasm for music and what they look upon as school music. A few of the students spoke of their own involvement in playing music as a positive feature of their lives outside school. In the survey this was a surprisingly small number. In the UK about 10 per cent of the school population participate in school music-making (i.e. specifically playing an instrument in an ensemble). At NSG the proportion learning an instrument in 2004 was about average. However, only four students out of the 1,344 who completed the survey mentioned being involved in music as a practical activity. This seems surprisingly low, especially in a Specialist Music College. To this small group of students music had some different nuances:

Music is my life. I couldn't live without it. I play piano, saxophone, clarinet, guitar (both electronic and acoustic). I sing. I've written songs before. I love my guitar and play it everyday. I love to play at my music school every Saturday. I would love to continue playing my instruments as they mean a lot to me. I can't explain how important it is to life. (NSG year 10 student)

I love to play music where everyone is just having such a good time. You can just forget about everything and just get wrapped up in the music. Its also seeing an audience completely enthralled by the music. Its also the buzz I get after I've played with the concert band and standing up with everyone clapping. (NSG Year 13 student)

Another student mentioned her engagement with a wide range of music outside school:

Music means money! I teach piano so I get a fair amount of money out of it. I really enjoy music, I don't know what I would do without it. I play piano, flute, piccolo, clarinet, violin, keyboard, organ and saxophone (this takes up a lot of time). I enjoy listening to a wide variety of artists, bands and singers. I enjoy music from classical to pop to Rand B, heavy metal and rock. I enjoy being able to play a whole variety of instruments and a whole variety of music. I remember playing at the Royal Festival Hall in London in year 7 at Middle School with my school band. I played a piccolo solo at the beginning of Lord of the Dance. My grandma was in the audience and I remember looking over and seeing a tear in her eye. I remember the first time I went to teach the piano it was 3 years ago. There were 3 children waiting to be taught. I was made very welcome and I still teach them through their grades 1, 2, 3 and 4 exam. I am very proud of that. (NSG year 11 student)

In her commentary this student later made it quite clear that she did not participate in school music despite her experience and enthusiasm. A few students talked about playing an instrument and the slightly negative realities of performing in a concert or exam:

I had to do a performance for my exam. Me and a old friend played a juet [sic]. We came last but we still tried. (NSG year 7 student)

Others wrote tellingly about being been excluded from active music-making through lack of opportunity:

When my mum plays the piano it gives me a sense of warmth. I would love to be able play an instrument—but no music teacher encouraged me to take one up when I was in main school. She told me it was too late and I was too old. I was 14. My mum started playing when she was 15. (NSG year 12 student)

A few students mentioned the use of music in worship. They responded to the way that music was used to enhance ceremony. Worship included a range of faiths.

In Hinduism music is used a lot. It is used in many different festivals and occasions, Navrati—9 days where we do garba (traditional dancing style). In the mandir/temple we have people who are singing bhajans (traditional songs). (NSG year 12 student)

As well as their strong personal response to music many students were also very aware of its power to mark important occasions in life or as a link to a particular memory.

Music is very important to me because there are certain songs that mean things to me. And there are songs that remind me of times I've been through. (NSG year 10 student)

I don't play music but I do remember one day I was in front of the mirror and me and my sister decided to make up an alternative to Back Street Boys an Indian song kabhi kushi kabhi gham meaning some times happy sometimes sad. The reason it is a special memory because I had so much fun back then and now my sisters are busy with studies. (NSG year 10 student)

Music helps me to explain my feelings and it can calm me down. Some music reminds me of people I love and people I can't see like my dead granddad. Without music I'd feel lonely. (NSG year 9 student)

The views of staff about music and how it affects the Specialist College

If there is a vision for the Music College at some time in the future then it might be a reception area that welcomes you to the sound beams of the latest concert, or Jazz evening or resident musician's workshop or summer school while the plasma screen displays the associated images. In the open area in the centre of the school students are giving impromptu performances on the steps of the area leading up to the Theatre, or practising their instruments in any area of the school or it is lunchtime and the senior citizens/other members of the local community have arrived for their weekly concert in the theatre organized by the students. Around the school lessons are in full swing, the performing arts block is alive with music in Dance, Drama, and Music lessons, in Technology music signals the start and end of the sessions and permeates the whole centre, in Science students are gyrating to music in order to comprehend the structure of a molecule, in History the songs of the Trenches accompany the World War One lesson and so it goes on and on. (Deputy Head Teacher NSG)

Staff (the term is used here to describe teaching and non-teaching staff) at NSG had equally strong and positive views about music. Many recognized the importance of music in marking important life events:

Music brings back memorys [*sic*] of events in time as we go through the journey of life.

Some were more analytical:

I've never been sure if I liked music more than art. Music-wise I am a child of the 60s and I've never really grown out of liking lyrics and listening to formats and waiting for the middle 8 and music scaffolding in general. Then I started to realize that lyrics could be categorized into gaining or losing or got 'love' which spoilt it a bit. I played the piano as a child then taught myself the guitar in the late 60s and have been playing and singing ever since. It helps me when I'm feeling happy or very lonely and depressed—it's always there for me and is better than a friend. When home in the 1980s with babies I learnt to play the clarinet and got up to and passed grade V—I got to quite like Mozart at that point. When feeling energetic at a party I'll get up and embarrass my children as I mime along playing air guitar. I simply love it.

I like discovering fresh new music—professional, semi-professional, and amateur, per-formed by musicians of all ages. This mostly takes the form of some sort of guitar-based music. Music is really important to my family too. Time is spent every day composing music, playing music, and listening to and talking about music in our house.

Most associated music with a particular memory, incident or phase of their lives:

As a child of the seventies music was the backdrop to my teenage and early twenties existence. Top of the pops, New Musical Express, Sounds were an integral part of youth culture at the time. I remember my first concert was Christmas 1971 when I paid 50p! Yes 50p! to see the Lindisfarne Christmas Concert. Fog on the Tyne! Lady Eleanor! Clear White Light! What classics, what memories!

I enjoy music to motivate me and to calm me. I enjoy dancing and express myself freely through music. A favourite memory is somewhat melancholy but uplifting at the same time. It was a large congregation singing Blake's Jerusalem at a young man's funeral. Everyone sang with passion and the atmosphere was fantastic.

Music was important at school concerts when I sang in the choir and played the French Horn in the School orchestra.

Rolling Stones 'Satisfaction'. First song played on our new record player in the kitchen of the home I grew up in. A family moment. . . . Dad encouraging my brother's musical taste! Me looking on as younger sister in awe!

Staff generally liked music a lot and considered it to be very important. They enjoyed listening to it and associated music with particular memories, events in their life, or good/difficult occasions. Many also thought that music could affect the way they felt. This ranged from playing music that was in sympathy with their prevailing mood to choosing music that would deliberately change it—for example playing an upbeat piece prior to going out or a relaxing piece at the end of the day. Two staff had a negative perspective about music:

As I am not a music person I do not have any memories particularly associated with music.

I rarely have it on and will often turn or ask the children to turn theirs down. Prefer silence when walking/running. Do not play any—will not turn on at home.

Three out of 1,344 students also felt that music was something that they were not involved in, did not enjoy, and had no interest in.

Some staff felt positive about music generally but more negative about music in school. There were a few who felt that the Music College status had resulted in a lot of resources, time, and attention being given to music at the expense of other subjects. One music teacher felt that although the benefits of being a Music College were enormous it brought extra responsibility, work, and expectations as well. Fear of change and increased workload were inevitable concerns but senior leaders felt able to rise to the challenge:

One of the best early decisions was for the Head to negotiate with the LEA the release of one of their Inspectors who was to work with us two days per week. This was an absolutely crucial decision in the early success of the college as the Senior team was still grappling with the demands of our transition to a secondary school due to coincide with the launch of the Music College in September 2004. This combination of events was intentional and provided us with the perfect way of bringing the two sites and teams of people together, as there were 43 new teaching and support staff many of whom had been recruited from the Middle schools. (Deputy Head Teacher)

What is interesting and ultimately challenging is that none of the staff or students in the survey identified music at school as being a powerful memory or feature of their life—apart from a handful who mentioned performing in extra-curricular activities. Class music lessons did not feature in their views about music at all.

Subject preferences at NSG

Students were asked about their preferences for subjects by indicating their favourite and least favourite three subjects. They were then were asked some supplementary questions about other aspects of their views about school:

1. What is it about your favourite subject(s) that makes you like it?

   Commentary   *In this question I wanted to get some idea of which subjects the students liked and did not like. I also wanted to explore some of the reasons for this. I gave them a choice of more than one subject because I felt that this would give a greater feel for particular groups of subjects that were popular, or not. I felt that there was a good chance that music would make it into the top three choices but that it was less likely to appear as a favourite choice if students only had one choice.*

2. What was your main reason for coming to this school?

Proximity to school	
Recommendation of Friend	
General reputation of school	
Wanting single-sex education	
Reputation for music	
Other—please say what the reason is.	

   Commentary   *I was interested in all answers here but was particularly keen to see how far music made an impact on the choice made by the students—I was aware that the strong music reputation of the school had been an attraction for some students prior to it becoming a Specialist Music College.*

3. NSG is a Specialist Music College. When you heard this what did you expect?

   Commentary   *I was interested to know their views on the news about the Specialist status and if they had thought about the impact that this might make on them.*

4. Have things been different to your expectations or the same?

Commentary   *They were asked to tick one box and then go on to make a comment that gave further information about their views.*

5. Describe how you feel the school is the same or different to what you expected.

6. Describe your musical experience and background by ticking the box that most closely describes you

I am not involved in music-making at school or outside school other than class music lessons.	
I am not involved in music-making at school or outside school although I enjoy listening to music on CD/TV etc.	
I am learning to play an instrument either in school or out of school but I am not involved in any school music groups.	
I am learning to play an instrument either in school or out of school and I am involved in school music groups.	
I am learning to play an instrument either in school or out of school, I am involved in school music groups and I play in other groups outside school during the evenings or weekends.	
Other—please describe yourself.	

Commentary   *This section was included in order to analyse their perceptions depending on whether or not they participated in musical activity in or out of school. It offered an opportunity to profile the students.*

7. Are there any things that you would like to suggest about what NSG ought to do as a Specialist Music College?

8. What do you like most about NSG?

9. If you could change anything about NSG what would it be?
   Commentary   *The last three questions were used to get general views about the school.*

Students were also given the opportunity to write more open-ended comments about how they felt about music in school.

Analysis of the attitudes to the subjects section of the survey

The proportion from each year group completing the questionnaire was representative of the overall school population.

Students were asked about their attitudes towards NSG becoming a Specialist Music College. The proportion who found that things were the same was very close to the percentage who found that they were different. This survey was completed after about eight months as a Specialist Music College. I expected that there would be a greater number who felt that things had changed than was actually the case. When asked to describe ways in which they felt the school had changed, they were given free space to write, and the responses were coded into categories. This question generated a mixed response, with no category being mentioned by more than 6 per cent of students. There was no clear view about how the school had changed, and the impact of being a Specialist Music College was not a strong feature in their views.

In response to the question, 'What was your main reason for coming to this school?' 7 per cent of students chose the school's reputation for music. However, the most popular response was the general reputation of NSG, which attracted 48 per cent of students. The students were asked about their musical background and level of involvement in music outside classes. This showed that 41 per cent of NSG students had some musical training outside school music classes. This was a surprisingly high number. A total of 270 students learned an instrument but did not participate in school music groups (presumably because they had not reached the right standard), 47 had started an instrument but given up, and 20 learned an instrument regularly to a high standard but did not participate in music at school.

At the end of the questionnaire, students were asked what they liked and what they would change about NSG. Again, these produced mixed responses with no overall strong view. The most popular aspect of the school was the social life, commented on by 9 per cent of students. The most frequently mentioned thing that students would change was the toilets, mentioned by 82 students, followed by extra-curricular activities and rules on jewellery.

The responses to what students liked best about NSG were analysed by year group. There was a significant variation of opinion. In year 7, the things students liked most were the teachers, swimming, and the uniform. Year 9 students rated lockers (11.5 per cent) and understanding (10 per cent) as the best things. Amongst year 11 students the most popular aspect of the school was the freedom they had, this was mentioned by 19 per cent of the year; they also liked the social life, included by 14 per cent. The year 13 students chose jewellery (10.3 per cent), freedom (8.6 per cent), and physical education (8.6 per cent) as their favourite things.

Analysis of the popularity of subjects

Each student was asked to rate a maximum of three subjects for each category, so each subject was not rated by every student. In order to assess the relative popularity of subjects, taking into account the fact that some were studied by fewer students and therefore would have attracted a smaller number of negative or positive ratings, a Scaled Popularity Factor (SPF) was used. Amongst the top 'most favourite subjects' were art (20.6 per cent), drama (18.8 per cent), and PE (17.5 per cent). These subjects also had low scores for 'least favourite subject'. Some subjects gained almost equal numbers of positive and negative listings, and others were mentioned by only a small number of students.

Comparisons were made between students who learned a musical instrument, and those who did not. Of students who studied an instrument, 25 per cent rated music as one of their favourite subjects, compared to 12 per cent across the whole school. The most popular reason for choosing a favourite subject was that lessons were enjoyable. A total of 160 students listed music as one of their top three subjects.

Art was the most popular subject (rated +0.61 on a scale of −1 to +1 based on students listing it as most or least favourite). Drama was the second favourite with a rating of +0.57. Drama was chosen by 527 students in their favourite subjects list (3.29 times as many as those who chose music). Maths was the most unpopular subject, given −0.7 on the same scale, and science scored −0.52 (making it second least popular). Music was listed by 160 students as one of their top three subjects but students who studied a musical instrument were much more likely to rate music as one of their favourite subjects. Analysing students' responses showed that they were more likely to choose a subject with practical, kinaesthetic activity (art, drama, and PE) as their favourite than an 'academic' subject with a higher proportion of writing, a tendency to sit down to complete written tasks, and which they therefore were more likely to consider 'boring'. These results raise particular questions and challenges. For example:

1. Should science and maths be taught in a more practical way in order to appear less boring?

2. If so, would this lead to insufficient rigour, challenge, and possible low achievement?

3. If music were more practical and kinaesthetic would it be rated more highly by a large proportion of the students?

4. Students' main focus when completing this part of the survey was how enjoyable they felt a lesson was (or not). How can music be made more enjoyable for a wider range of students?

Students mainly chose to come to NSG because of the general reputation of the school. Music did feature as a reason for selecting the school and some

THE ATTITUDES OF STUDENTS TO MUSIC | 57

students did rate it as a popular subject. Many did not, despite the fact that it was a Specialist Music College. A later survey may find a change in these perceptions. Students were much more likely to elect to come to the school because of its general reputation for high standards, friendliness, and behaviour than for its reputation for music.

What else do we know about the attitudes of students to music?

NSG included a large and wide cross-section of students from a range of different backgrounds. I suspect that the views of students at NSG were typical of most young people in the UK at the time, although I also suspect that there would be regional, social, and cultural differences that might have a big impact on an individual school. The 2006 Music Manifesto report set out some ideas about young people and their interaction with music:

Young people's vitality, passion and creative determination to make music, with or without the support of the education system, is a clue to its value to them and its potential for the education system. We have an opportunity to use music making to provide the wider creative skills—such as team work, creative development and risk taking—that our young people are going to need desperately as they navigate the hard realities of an unpredictable century. And the young are already motivated to work hard to achieve these skills through music—what other subject can claim this?

This comment suggests that we ought to take an approach to the curriculum that promotes general skills rather than specific aspects of music content. It may just reflect the current views being promoted by central government and which were about to feature in the 2007 QCA National Curriculum reforms.

Schools and music providers need to connect their music provision more meaningfully with young people's own interests, passions and motivations.

This suggests that the curriculum does not currently connect sufficiently with a large group of students. I agree with this and it reflects the views of students at NSG.

The transition from primary to secondary school is a crucial moment for children's interest in music. During their KS3 years, too few pupils are able to sustain progress made in primary school or to consolidate their skills beyond their lessons. During this period many abandon instrumental tuition because of peer pressure, the more challenging atmosphere of a secondary school, or the school's lack of support. Many pupils maintain their interest in music outside school, but they often find that lack of facilities and learning opportunities inhibit their ability to progress as far as they would wish. There is no national research on the availability of out-of-school-hours music provision.[1]

---

[1] *Making Every Child's Music Matter*, Music Manifesto Report no. 2 (London: HMSO, 2006).

I think that these comments are very accurate and give a good steer for the ways that central government projects and resources should be targeted. However a crucial factor, which I will return to, is the understanding, motivation, and engagement of music teachers so that they develop an agenda that is more inclusive and responsive. This is a huge issue because the experiences of young people are not decided by comments made in the Music Manifesto document, which will come and go, but by the transactions that take place in school classrooms across the country. Changing the hearts and minds of this group of professional staff is crucial.

In January 2006 the music industry carried out a survey on attitudes to music. It found that 21 per cent of the population played an instrument and 11.25 million households owned one. Eighteen million players aged over 12 had stopped playing and nearly nine million of these would like to start playing again! Of those who had never played, seven million said they would like to learn a musical instrument. That is thirteen million people who would like to learn an instrument but currently do not, many of these of school age. The most popular instruments were guitars (37 per cent) and pianos/keyboards (35 per cent). Of the respondents 90 per cent felt that playing a musical instrument was fun, relaxing, and a good means of expression; 94 per cent thought that music helped a child's creativity; and 84 per cent felt it helped intellectual development.

At a Music Manifesto event in London on 18 May 2005 the composer and broadcaster Howard Goodall set out his views about music and young people. This was based on informal research he had carried out visiting a number of schools that he felt had achieved great success in engaging young people with music-making. These schools were therefore not necessarily typical of the UK education system but his views offer an interesting insight into the thoughts of the young people he encountered.

Diversity is the normal state for young people in Britain today, it is their cultural and social norm and their everyday musical state as well. They don't really get this idea that there was once a time when you only played one sort of music. If you ask them who their favourite composers are, they will give you—without hesitation or qualification—lists of names that are picked from every corner of the musical firmament. I wrote down a few from the other day from some 16-year-old girls, they said Bach, Tchaikovsky, Coldplay, Frank Sinatra, Purcell, Blue. Or one marvellous response was 'Eliza Fitzgerald, Mozart and Eddie Mercury'. When asked what piece of music might be set for analysis at GCSE, one student suggested Queen's Bohemian Rhapsody and the 1812 Overture.

These views seem to confirm those of NSG students, although the students in his survey were more engaged with classical music than the general school population because of the type of schools he visited.

He did find a similar level of passion and enthusiasm:

It struck me powerfully during my discussions with young musicians that for them, music is an emotional, not a cerebral activity. Almost without exception, when they talk about music they talk about its sensual and spiritual power, its 'wow factor', its ability to move one to tears or make one want to get up and dance. Boys, especially, refer to the sheer muscular power and physical energy of pieces like Orff's Carmina Burana. They describe it as having an almost tangible effect on one's body. Whilst they might be amused, tickled or intrigued by the challenges and the concepts of the experimental music of the mid-20th century, something—incidentally—all GCSE students are famil-iar with these days, they don't actually hear it as music. For them, what John Cage or Pierre Boulez does is of tangential, non-musical interest—like a science experiment. It does not engage with their senses or their emotions at all. To some extent this explains their passionate distaste—one might even say loathing—for avant-garde modernism.

Howard Goodall's sample included a range of students who were much more likely to participate in music-making in and out of school. The students were very aware of the positive benefits that they felt this brought:

When asked what they got out of participating in music-making themselves the imme-diate response was always that music was a great social activity. Being in an orchestra, a choir, a band is always linked with friendship and a lot of fun. This may seem like a trivial detail but to young people it is of tremendous importance, especially as these days, thank goodness, they are pretty well all doing it because they want and choose to, in their free time. In terms of recruitment and involvement, an emphasis on the social rewards of playing music may be the most powerful lure that any teacher or group leader may have at their disposal.

In a school with a strong musical tradition the balance of perceptions can shift. In a school that he visited, classical music was a very strong feature of the life of the school and the students who attend it. Despite this the large major-ity of students in this school, and certainly in most schools in the UK are more engaged by popular music. This once again raises the issue of students' love of music set against their perceptions of school music, even in what many would think of as a 'musical school'.

One of the things that happened at this school was that one of the girls, aged 15, said that her favourite composers were Debussy, Bach and Mozart, adding apologetically, that 'I don't really like pop music which shows just how much of a loser I am'. This made me pause to reflect on why she felt she should say this rather sad statement. (Howard Goodall—extracts from speech to the Music Manifesto signatories, London 18 May 2005)

The 'Musical Futures' project approached music-making with young people in 2007 from a particular standpoint and provided an interesting perspective on students' views.

300 Year 8 students took part in an exercise to identify a range of music projects they would wish to see in their schools. For at least two of the three groups this required imagination, since they have been without a full-time music teacher for some years.

These were schools at the opposite end of the musical spectrum visited by Howard Goodall. They lacked resources, traditions, and expertise. The solution proposed by the project was as follows:

> This highly-enriched curriculum involves all children in skills sessions on bass, guitar, keyboards and drums, forming cover bands, writing minimalist music soundtracks, improvising jazz pieces, sampling and sequencing music, taiko drumming and samba workshops, song-writing and recording studio sessions. The project-based delivery (as opposed to a series of lessons) meets another of their stated desires: that the music made should be 'real', with authentic end products.[2]

I am not going to try to evaluate the success of this project. The literature associated with it suggests that the leaders tried to understand the interests of a wide range of students and respond to them. There will no doubt be discussions about delivery models and practical details but I suspect that the students involved mostly felt engaged with the stated aims of the project because it responded to their needs—practical, kinaesthetic activities in a popular and contemporary style. Careful planning will be needed to ensure that this does not remain at the level of an isolated activity that does not develop students' attitudes and skills over a longer period of time.

Many secondary schools in 2007 were turning to more open-ended and project-based activities in order to negate the perceived pitfalls of the National Curriculum. 'Opening Minds' was an RSA curriculum approach based on competencies categorized into:

- learning
- citizenship
- relating to people
- managing situations
- managing information

This sprang from a conviction that the way young people were being educated was becoming increasingly distant from their real needs. It was felt that there was a mismatch between the content of the National Curriculum and what education ought to offer students and employers. In particular, the information-driven curriculum was unlikely to equip young people adequately for life in the new century. Instead, it was suggested that the curriculum should develop the competences and skills needed to survive and succeed in their future world. The themes of curriculum content and relevance

---

[2] *Musical Futures: Paul Hamlyn Foundation Special Project* (London: Paul Hamlyn, 2006).

appeared consistently in 2007 and one outcome was a revision of the National Curriculum content in order to make it freer and more flexible, although much content remained. Students I spoke to wanted a curriculum that matched their musical interests. This is set against other drivers such as employers—requiring particular skills (but not necessarily knowledge) and several influential higher-education organizations which want to retain some of the traditional activities they can build upon for academically orientated courses. This leads to confusion and lack of direction. I will pick up these and other issues in Chapter 4.

What conclusions can we reach about attitudes to music?

The views of students and staff at NSG were clear and I am confident that they were representative of students at this school. I suspect they were also representative of many students in 2005. Students liked music a lot. In fact they were really passionate about it. When talking about music the vast majority referred to the activities of listening to music, dancing to it, and absorbing it as part of the tapestry of their lives. They associated it strongly with some key moments in their lives, sometimes sad and sometimes joyful. They believed that it can be used as a mood enhancer or sometimes as an aid to changing moods. They would spend a lot of their disposable income buying or downloading music and a staggeringly high amount going to concerts or buying merchandise. They responded strongly to the imagery of pop music, the marketing and glamorous lifestyle promoted by music companies. They liked the themes of 'pop' music—love, betrayal, and loss—because this mirrored the strong preoccupations of their own lives. They also responded strongly to their changing bodies, the onset of puberty, and the strong sexual connotations of 'pop' music (even though this was almost always at a subconscious level). There was also a small group of students who were preoccupied with 'classical' music and quite single-minded about their engagement with this genre. NSG is a girls' school. Was this significant in shaping the student's views? I am not in a position to give a definitive answer to this question. However, my experience of young people over twenty-five years of teaching and visiting hundreds of schools suggests to me that the characteristics I have described are fairly universal. I suspect that these views were representative of the majority of secondary-age students in the UK. I think that primary-age students are generally more open-minded in their musical tastes but start to respond to influences around them from the age of about 8 onwards. For some it will be younger or older than this. Each school has a general ethos and a musical ethos which is the result of a number of complex factors. However primary-age children are at an ideal age to influence and engage in musical activity of all descriptions because they are more open-minded, less socially segregated, and more willing to try things.

Music often has a different status in school than it does outside school. Many students did not relate to music in school. Probably as many as 90 per cent in most schools see music as a peripheral activity that they might have wanted to engage with—for example, through learning an instrument—but which was not for them because they are not 'musical'. This definition was imposed by adults around them. School music does not link with their huge love of music. Of course there were exceptions. There are students who become highly engaged in music-making through participation in a school band or group and they develop a strong affinity with this type of music-making. Many of their peers don't and this seems to me to be a real tragedy.

Most students like 'popular' music (although I have acknowledged that what this means is difficult to pin down since definitions and styles are constantly shifting and changing). They like to feel part of a particular musical style or community but are less conscious about the need to fit in with their peers' musical taste and as a result musical tastes are quite eclectic. The internet provides them with a global perspective. They like music that is fast in tempo, upbeat, and which sounds contemporary. For the vast majority this does not include western art music, which sounds alien, culturally obscure, and does not match their experience or aspirations. School music is also predominantly white and socially slanted towards the middle class. The music students listen to is often heavily influenced by black culture and comfortably accommodates references from a wide range of different styles and sources. Modern technology gives students easy ways to listen to, compose, and perform music in a style that they are comfortable with. Music in school is often not like this. Students feel it is focused on dead composers with obscure names and lifestyles. If you live in a tough urban environment what on earth can it feel like to write about the life of J.S. Bach, to listen to the music of Pachelbel, or to learn that Every Good Boy Deserves Favour? Is it any wonder that school music tends to end up as something that those who have instrumental lessons engage with and the majority do not relate to at all, certainly not linking it to their own passionate feelings about music? The few who do find their way into this secret garden seem to represent the middle-class minority and feel themselves in danger of being a 'bit sad' because their interest is not shared by the majority. These are the students who might end up taking A level music and ultimately becoming music teachers.

We also know that many students would like to play an instrument—especially the drums, guitar, or perhaps keyboard. However, they currently do not have sufficient opportunity. We know that some students start to play and then give up for various reasons. Quite a few of these regret it and would like the opportunity to have another go or perhaps try a different instrument. We also know that the number of households in the UK owning instruments is quite high. All of these factors suggest a level of untapped potential in engaging young people with music in schools.

We seem to have a situation in England where music is in danger of being viewed as a peripheral and marginal activity for young people because the content of the curriculum and the hidden curriculum messages that are promoted in schools mean that many see themselves as not being 'musical'. They are not involved because music in school is something like a foreign language—it is OK if you can speak it but hard to understand if you sit outside it. Schools with these characteristics cannot be musical because they do not cater sufficiently for the interests of a very large proportion of the school population.

My conclusions then are uncomfortable. They suggest that curriculum music in schools is white, western, classical, and not matched to the musical interests of the large majority of young people. Sometimes these influences are 'hidden' because the school curriculum appears to include music from different cultures. It may even include elements of popular music but done in such a way that students do not develop a real sense that music is for them and that they might be able to continue with it when they get into year 10. Sometimes messages are more overt. I once visited a school where all the 'musicians' in year 9 were segregated and given an ensemble performance session every week. All the 'non-musicians' were sent to a basement room where they could play keyboards. However, they needed headphones for this and had to remember to bring their own or they would have to write out facts about Bach's life and grandchildren for the whole lesson. The school was widely regarded as the most 'musical' school in the area because of the quality of its extra-curricular groups. It did not meet my definition of a musical school but would not have wanted to change. I believe that a key component of a musical school is that it should understand the musical interests of its students and try to meet their needs. Additionally it should set out to educate them beyond their immediate interests, but to do this they need to be motivated and engaged.

It seems to me that we have to think of a more effective way to meet the needs of both the musically experienced and able students (who will be the minority) and the far larger majority who, for whatever reason, feel that music in school is not for them. The students who receive instrumental lessons need to develop a wider repertoire of skills than individual and ensemble performance skills in a white, western classical style (using standard musical notation). We need to offer them excitement and challenge in order to stretch their horizons. This would include a wider range of styles, more improvisation skills and greater emphasis on the management/organization of groups so that they can start to take responsibility and learn what this feels like. We also need to find an alternative approach for the majority in order to engage them and make them enthusiastic about music in school—at least as enthusiastic as they are about art, drama, or PE. I am sure we can learn from art and drama in particular, which seem to have escaped the demons of the great classics and found a mode of engagement that switches young people on. The school that manages to achieve this, or get a long way towards this goal will be well on the way to becoming a musical school. I have to admit that achieving this task is difficult and many will want to shy away from it. Until we can change the climate in music education there will not be much support for this approach. I can remember an occasion when I managed to involve a whole year group in a range of activities that led to a public performance as part of an arts evening. Several parents admitted to me that they were perplexed by the amount of enthusiasm their son/daughter had shown for music, because they did not consider them to be musical. This I could cope with. It was harder for me to realize that the Deputy Head Teacher was scathing about the evening because it did not fit his picture of what a musical evening might look like. He was an amateur musician with fairly fixed views but these were influential and made me realize that involving and enthusing all students may not lead to instant enthusiasm from senior staff. He was, however, more impressed by the outstanding performance of the *Messiah* that I put on at the end of term.

Chapter 4

The curriculum—background and theory

Now, what is music? This question occupied me for hours before I fell asleep last night. Music is a strange thing. I would say it is a miracle. For it stands halfway between thought and phenomenon, between spirit and matter, a sort of nebulous mediator, like and unlike each of the things it mediates—spirit that requires manifestation in time, amid matter that can do without space. We do not know what music is.

Heinrich Heine

I am using the term 'curriculum' to describe all the experiences and opportunities that young people access through contact with a school, or other educational setting. There are four key elements that I want to focus on:

1. Class music lessons—received by all students (unless a school decides not to make music available to all)

2. Instrumental music lessons

3. Extra-curricular music activity—usually provided for a minority of students who receive extra instrumental lessons (or for a group of students who opt into these extra activities)

4. The hidden curriculum, which I refer to in most sections of this book. This important element includes the ways that adults make assumptions about students and transmit particular messages about their expectations of them.

The hidden curriculum

The term 'Hidden Curriculum' was first used by the sociologist Philip Jackson in 1968, although the concept had been in existence before this time. Jackson argued that what is learned in schools is more than the sum total of the curriculum. He suggested that schools should be understood as a socialization process where students pick up messages, not just from things that they are explicitly taught. This hidden element of a school will impact on all students—it is often described as its 'ethos'. This comes from a variety of sources. Key elements are usually provided by the head teacher (and other senior managers), the teachers (whose approach is shaped by their own experiences), and school traditions, which sometimes linger, even though personnel change. Some of this ethos can also stem from the design of a school building and the facilities that are available to students. I cover design issues in Chapter 9.

What are the hidden factors?

The hidden curriculum affects music education in numerous ways. For example:

+ Teachers may respond more positively to students who they feel are 'interested' in music. This may result in more positive messages being given to boys or to girls. It may also result in particular social groups being supported and encouraged more than others. Of course, teachers may not realize that they are doing this, since their behaviour reflects an unconscious outcome of their own background and experiences.

+ Senior managers may believe that music is a talent that you have or do not have and construct option choices accordingly (they may be supported in these actions by music teachers who also believe these things, or find them convenient in terms of organization and management). Senior staff may therefore transmit strong messages about desirable musical styles, about students with 'talent' and these factors may affect a number of the decisions that they make or support. A musical school will require either enlightened managers or those who are prepared to challenge the status quo, because they realize that music should not be approached differently from other subjects, even when this is at odds with what music staff say!

+ The interests of teachers and other staff may be promoted strongly even though they do not match those of students—because teachers may not consider sufficiently all students in a school (rather than a select few).

+ Technology may not be used effectively because it is not approved of or because the teacher is consciously or subconsciously aware that his/her skill level may not match those of the students. This may make the teacher feel vulnerable and want to control the access offered to these types of resources.

+ A visiting orchestra, or other group of musicians, may choose to work with those who already play an instrument because these students seem keen, easy to manage, and results are tangible.

There are many other examples of the ways in which the hidden curriculum has a strong and pervasive influence on schools, Music Services, and a range of education activities involving young people. However, putting together the information for this book has made me realize, even more strongly than I did before, that this hidden curriculum and the attitudes of adults who work with young people's musical interests are the two most significant barriers to creating a musical school. Unless staff, at all levels, can share a single vision which enables all young people to feel engaged, motivated, and musically valued we only manage to maintain the current situation where too many schools are unmusical. Staff need to subscribe to a determination to take the radical, difficult, and complex decisions that will lead to positive change for the benefit of all young people. That is a hard culture change to achieve.

The hidden curriculum is developed in this book as it arises in each chapter. I feel that it is an extremely powerful agent in shaping provision, providing resistance to change, and defining a musical school. I remember a job interview once where I was asked which was most important: the curriculum or extra-curricular activities. I initially replied that both were important. Pressed to make a choice on the issue I said that the curriculum was the most important feature because it affected all the students in a school. Instinctively I knew that this was not necessarily the answer the governors wanted to hear and we had a lively debate, which gave me a good insight into their perceptions. This dilemma is faced every day in schools across the world. Is music a subject that should be made available to all students or is it something that is best suited to a smaller group of 'talented' students who we consciously or unconsciously select? Is there actually any method of selection that is meaningful, culturally diverse, and supported by research evidence? I believe that there is absolutely no such selection process, that any suggestion that there is flies in the face of the evidence, and that we should question our motives in ever wanting to apply it. I feel very strongly about this on behalf of the countless students who have been put off music at school by being made to feel excluded in this way. I believe that these fundamental questions and how a school, or other setting, deals with them goes to the heart of defining what a musical school is like.

Regrettably, class music and extra-curricular/instrumental music are dealt with in separate chapters in this book due to the amount of space required for each topic. This chapter is principally about whole-class lessons. However, I believe that musical activities should always be as integrated as possible. Treating them separately mitigates against developing a musical school. I feel that although schools often congratulate themselves on their ability to provide extra-curricular opportunities, they do not, on their own, characterize a musical school, although many stakeholders regard them as being the key element that makes their school musical (thus making a strong contribution to the hidden curriculum experienced by the students). I also believe that music education has suffered because class music and extra-curricular music have been too separate and that more status is often given to music as an additional, out-of-class activity, even though this does not involve all students. So that there be no confusion let me state clearly that I believe strongly that we need to develop activities that motivate and inspire our most experienced musicians. They are important and deserve to be developed fully. I can give quite unequivocal evidence of having done this successfully over many years. I am not suggesting for one moment that we should be dumbing everything down or that we should not be stretching those students who need it. Being inclusive means catering for excellence as well as a wide range of other skill levels and interests. So I am not just pointing a finger and saying, 'come on you should all do better'. I am trying to say, 'I think there is an issue here and any school that wants to describe itself as "musical" needs to at least acknowledge it.' Then we can all work together to try to address the issue.

The changing curriculum

The curriculum is constantly in a state of flux. It has to respond to the changing and often competing needs of students, parents, and employers. Politicians also shape it. They come and go but the direction they provide often outlasts their term of office. In 2007 the Qualifications and Curriculum Authority (QCA), responsible for the curriculum in England, announced a consultation on changes to the Key Stage 3 curriculum (provided for students in years 7 to 9). This followed a fairly regular series of revisions of the original 1988 National Curriculum guidance information for this (and other age groups). Prior to the introduction of the National Curriculum each school had the freedom to choose its own curriculum content until students reached the stage of taking public examinations aged 15+ (when a common syllabus or 'specification' had to be followed). This represented a high level of autonomy for schools and teachers. Politicians did not trust this and so started to dictate what was taught, resulting in a curriculum that had large amounts of centrally outlined content. This National Curriculum was introduced in 1988. The rationale was that:

- all pupils should be entitled to a broad and balanced curriculum
- because individual schools had complete autonomy over curriculum issues many did not provide an 'entitlement' to a broad and balanced range of subjects
- the state should provide a framework to ensure a consistent student experience and opportunity.

In 1988, there was some support for the idea that all students were 'entitled' to receive the same curriculum experience, rather than schools deciding what was best for students. Although there was a significant element of opposition from the teaching profession to this perceived loss of freedom, the National Curriculum had some possible advantages:

- teachers felt that they could teach what was expected and feel that they must therefore be doing the 'right' thing
- training and resources could focus on supporting some defined content
- it was possible to measure provision in a more systematic way across a range of schools and settings
- all students had an 'entitlement' to receive the same experience. None could be written off by schools who had to provide the same for everyone.

However, an outcome which emerged over time (although one that education professionals might have predicted) was that students' motivation and engagement dipped in years 7 to 9, although it often improved when they reached public examinations in year 10, when they chose more elements of the curriculum and could see a fixed point in sight—the terminal examination. The number of students choosing music at this stage was relatively small, certainly compared to art or drama. The accompanying targets and league tables meant that many primary-school students probably received an increasingly impoverished arts curriculum as class teachers were asked to focus more and more on English and maths.

Once students started year 7 they faced three years of a similar sort of diet with a heavy emphasis on core subjects (English, maths, and science). If they had not succeeded in primary school they were unlikely to become motivated by the transfer to secondary school, especially as they did not have the benefit of one teacher who knew them very well. By 2007 the wheel had started to return to a pre-National Curriculum culture. Reforms meant that subject content was broken down into less prescriptive chunks and schools were encouraged to be more flexible and creative in how they approached Key Stage 3. Any teacher under the age of 30 had not experienced a secondary curriculum outside that prescribed by the National Curriculum. Many found this difficult. In reality they had always had considerable curriculum flexibility but most schools felt safe within constraints set out by central government. Curriculum innovation and experimentation were probably seen as dangerous and a bit risky. Gradually the idea of project-based work across subject areas started to regain popularity, following a period where it had been dismissed as contributing to low standards. Schools were encouraged to consider shortening the Key Stage 3 curriculum and to plan ways in which students could start exam courses earlier (if this suited their skills and abilities).

There is perhaps a continuum of approach reflected in these changes. Each has particular strengths and weaknesses, which ultimately lead to a change in direction. Each approach contains the seeds of its own dissolution. In musical terms it might look like the diagram in Fig. 1.

Other government-led policies and how they are resisted or embraced

I could choose any number of government-led agendas and policies and show how they did or did not impact on the curriculum experience of young people. I will choose one example in order to illustrate a general theme. In 2007

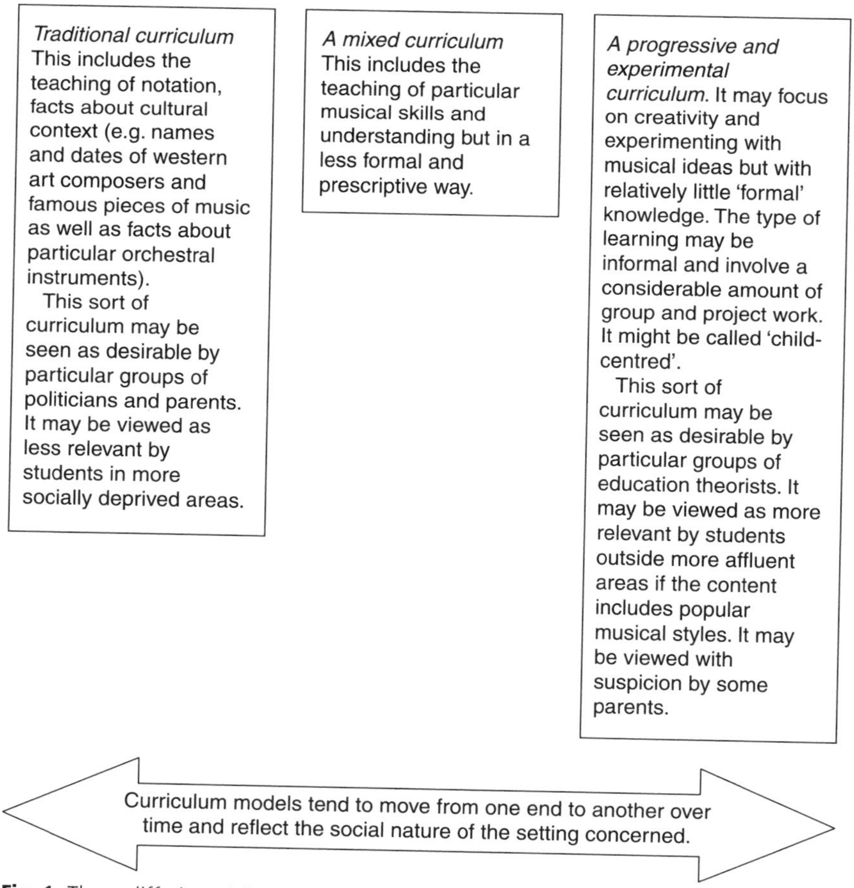

Traditional curriculum
This includes the teaching of notation, facts about cultural context (e.g. names and dates of western art composers and famous pieces of music as well as facts about particular orchestral instruments).
  This sort of curriculum may be seen as desirable by particular groups of politicians and parents. It may be viewed as less relevant by students in more socially deprived areas.

A mixed curriculum
This includes the teaching of particular musical skills and understanding but in a less formal and prescriptive way.

A progressive and experimental curriculum. It may focus on creativity and experimenting with musical ideas but with relatively little 'formal' knowledge. The type of learning may be informal and involve a considerable amount of group and project work. It might be called 'child-centred'.
  This sort of curriculum may be seen as desirable by particular groups of education theorists. It may be viewed as more relevant by students outside more affluent areas if the content includes popular musical styles. It may be viewed with suspicion by some parents.

Curriculum models tend to move from one end to another over time and reflect the social nature of the setting concerned.

Fig. 1 Three differing philosophical approaches to a music curriculum

the government suggested that the curriculum should be 'personalized'. There were differing descriptions of what this meant. One definition held that personalized learning included the key elements of:

1. Assessment for learning—giving clear feedback to pupils so there is clarity on what they needed to improve and how best they could do so. There was also a clear link made between student learning and lesson planning.

2. Effective teaching and learning strategies—a wide repertoire of teaching skills and management of learning. This required a range of whole-class, group, individual teaching, and ICT strategies to transmit knowledge, to instil key learning skills and accommodate different paces of learning.

3. Curriculum entitlement and choice—a curriculum entitlement and choice that gave breadth of study, personal relevance, and flexible learning pathways through the education system. The National Curriculum was considered a vital foundation for all 5 to 14-year-olds. New GCSEs in subjects like Engineering, ICT, Health and Social Care were planned in order to broaden the options available to students.

4. School organization—school leaders and teachers needed to think creatively about school organization in order to best support high-quality teaching and learning and to ensure that pupil performance and pupil welfare were mutually supportive.

5. Strong partnership with parents and carers, so that they become more closely involved in their child's learning and helped improve behaviour and attendance.

These themes are picked up by Sharon Green in Chapter 5. Most people will feel that these 'new' ideas represent common sense and will detect little difference from the work done by many schools over a long period of time. Government-led initiatives and developments can seem important, even though they can also be short-lived and possibly ill-conceived. Many activities and commercial products will have been developed or rebranded to meet the 'personalization' agenda of 2007. However, the teachers, schools, and much of the curriculum will probably have remained essentially the same because teachers, like most adults, have an in-built resistance to change and tend to preserve approaches that they have used for a long time. For example:

◆ The actual content of the curriculum and the time available for music did not change greatly so what could be achieved by teachers was constrained.

◆ Music is always in danger of becoming an optional activity in Key Stage 3 and a minority activity in Key Stage 4/post-16—because it can be seen by students and senior staff as the preoccupation of a small group of talented students (although music teachers are most responsible for promoting this view).

♦ With no extra resources, training, or support music teachers will tend to stick with what they know. Who can blame them? What they know is learned through their own experiences of music education or in schools that are influenced by long traditions. This sort of culture is deep-rooted and not likely to be influenced by central government suggestions that come and go on a regular basis.

♦ Support for class music dwindled sharply between 1995 and 2007 as a result of a central government financial squeeze on Local Authorities and schools being given greater autonomy. Many, although not all, LA Music Services tended to promote a traditional, instrumental-led curriculum.

In secondary schools a big challenge is how to make sense of a 55-minute lesson, once a week with a group of 30+ students. This provides limits on the sort of transactions that can take place. Compare this to what could be achieved teaching a group for one day a week, or with four hours each day. The organization and structure of the secondary curriculum is traditionally compartmentalized into short but regular sections. A curriculum that is creative and innovative may need to be flexible and able to make links with other curriculum areas. It is the sort of curriculum that many primary schools are able to provide very well because students stay in one place with one teacher and s/he can decide how best to organize things. A secondary topic-based, integrated approach can provide greater flexibility but might also neglect facts and information often felt to be important. Can musical activities that cater for the needs of all be planned in this context?

Music education is caught between two main types of curriculum. One is prescriptive and centralized, the other is local and flexible (with all the shades that lie between). The organization of learning in secondary schools is a barrier. Government agendas that set off firmly in one direction but divert as new politicians come and go provide a dynamic set of challenges. We also seem unsure whose needs we are trying to meet. Is it employers, is it education for life (to pass on essential cultural information), or is it both of these things? Is it something else altogether? Have we all got the same agenda? Schools and teachers are aware of the changing face of education policy from central government. It washes over them on a regular basis and undoubtedly has an eroding effect. It rarely causes a radical reshape of the landscape. It must seem easier to go through the motions and give more attention to a 'talented' group of musicians who will then go on to take music at Key Stage 4 and post-16. No one will ask any really searching questions.

The purpose of the curriculum

In the February 2007 QCA (Qualifications and Curriculum Authority) consultation on the latest revision to National Curriculum for schools in England reference was made to 'personal, learning and thinking skills' (PLTS). This provided a focus on music education's possible relationship with the wider context of a student's personal development. In particular how students can use music to become:

♦ independent enquirers

♦ creative thinkers

♦ team workers

♦ self-managers

♦ effective participators

♦ reflective learners

With thoughtful planning, a range of PLTS can be embedded in any sequence of work. For example pupils might be asked to prepare a group composition or performance to a given brief, over a period of time. This would involve pupils:

♦ researching a brief (independent enquirers)

♦ planning rehearsals (self managers)

♦ extending and developing musical ideas (creative thinkers)

♦ working collaboratively (team workers)

♦ performing a finished piece (effective participators).[1]

These seem like desirable and sensible areas to develop and are not that radically different from the sort of music education promoted in the 1960s or 1970s. They certainly do not seem to be areas that many music educators would want to disagree with, although some might have more specific priorities.

Curriculum stakeholders

In trying to make sense of curriculum priorities and why they change, it may be helpful to consider the perspective of the various stakeholders concerned. What do they want from the curriculum?

---

1 QCA, *The National Curriculum: The New Secondary Curriculum* (London: HMSO, 2007).

1. Students

Students want to enjoy school and learning and often find it hard to see the relevance of the next stage of education/employment until it is very imminent. The student needs guidance and where curriculum choice is available the student will probably choose enjoyment, even though this may not lead to the best route to future employment and economic well-being.

2. Teachers

The teacher will want students to enjoy the curriculum but there may be a gap between the teacher's interests and those of students. The teacher will have to respond to local and central government changes of direction. S/he will also have to moderate the strong influences of his/her own education/life experiences and teacher training. The teacher will bring a set of strong values that are promoted strongly to students, sometimes in an unintentional way. This is one of the reasons why the climate created by the teacher can be such a strong negative or positive force for learning.

3. Politicians

Politicians have an enormous influence on the curriculum because they dictate government policy and this is what schools are required to follow. Politicians change on a regular basis and as a result so does education policy and ideas about curriculum content. A few teachers demonstrate strong resilience to these changes and are more likely to hang on to the traditions that they have learned at school or through teacher training.

4. Employers

Employers require certain skills and attributes from young people and sometimes feel that education is too remote from the 'real' world of employment. These needs often include:

- literacy—this usually means the ability to write letters with sufficient skills of grammar, spelling, and punctuation
- numeracy—the ability to calculate using addition, subtraction, division, and multiplication
- ICT skills—an increasingly important requirement
- team work—something which music can contribute to very strongly if curriculum planning allows for it

Employers want young people who can read, spell, add up, and look you in the eye. Music education can contribute strongly to the attributes valued by employers but the activities that are delivered in classrooms will need to reflect these skills.

5. Parents

Parents will often have strong views about the curriculum and what should be taught. Often these will be based on their own experiences at school. When there is an element of choice their influence over young people is often very strong. Parents who value music may suggest a strong focus on musical literacy, performance on an instrument, and participation in extra-curricular activities. Other parents may be more negative about music in school and not see it as a relevant subject likely to lead to employment.

6. Further and higher education

Higher education has particular requirements and influence on the skills developed by post-16 students. This is because an increasing number of these students may end up in higher education. The content of A levels (and other courses) is important to the higher education teaching community. Much of the curriculum for the 16–18 age range has tended to be 'academic' in order to suit the needs of traditional higher education providers. This is one of the reasons why the 2007 UK government's 14–19 reforms attempted to develop a broader curriculum that included a range of vocational courses and work-based experiences.

I can remember talking to a parent about her primary-age daughter who was quite unwell but determined to go to school because she was studying the Great Fire of London. The class had made a model of London and were going to set fire to it in order to study how the wind direction would affect the progress of the fire—a key factor in the way that the fire spread so rapidly and caused considerable damage. They were also going to experiment with how much water her class could collect with rudimentary buckets in order to see how this affected the ability of contemporary Londoners to deal with the fire. The girl was determined not to miss out on what the class found out on this day! I think you would find it difficult to find a better example of a group of

* independent enquirers
* creative thinkers
* team workers
* self-managers
* effective participators
* reflective learners

than her class. The curriculum at this primary school worked very well. No overemphasis on preparing for tests here, just a lot of imagination and creativity, which led to strong motivation and high standards.

The different stakeholders find it difficult to agree on the purpose of the curriculum. The content, shape, and direction moves from one agenda to another. Given this dilemma we have to be brave enough to be innovative, take risks, and evaluate the impact of what we do. As government initiatives come and go we will probably have to apply an element of common sense to see what is worth salvaging and what is likely to lead to students being disadvantaged. I recall the primary-school head who on receipt of the National Curriculum in 1988 sent it back with a polite note saying, 'Thank you very much but we already have a really good curriculum and don't need another.' Or the middle-school head who when I was in his office one day went to get something from a filing cabinet. I noticed a file labelled 'Complete crap from the LEA and government'. I realize that it takes considerable bravery, intelligence, and determination to decide on a course of action that you believe in. It may be that the views of the head or class teacher at this school were complete crap as well. In this case government directive would have been preferable. If the experience being offered to the young people is vibrant, exciting, and engages them 50 per cent of the battle will be won. If the school also produces rounded students who are motivated and enjoy learning as well as achieving, they should ignore all local and central philosophy and initiatives. It will be worth it when young people are desperate to get to school in the morning in order find out more about something that they have been working on.

How students learn

An important element in motivating students is understanding how they learn. This is picked up by Diana Pearman in Chapter 6. It is often referred to as 'learning styles' or 'learning to learn'. For example the VARK system[2] assessed how learners process information in order to access learning. The commonly defined ways are:

◆ visual (sight)

◆ auditory (hearing)

◆ reading and

◆ kinaesthetic (other sensations which includes touch and temperature as well as movement).

---

[2] N. D. Fleming, *Teaching and Learning Styles: VARK Strategies* (Honolulu: Community College, 2001).

Much of the development has been channelled through work in subjects such as English or humanities. The theory is that a student might say 'I'm an auditory learner' (meaning that they are comfortable absorbing information which they have heard or discussed); or 'I'm a kinaesthetic learner' (if they prefer to learn through practical classes and hands-on activities, rather than by reading books and listening to lectures). This sort of approach has a lot of validity and encouraging students to become aware of how they learn most effectively is extremely useful. In practice it can be difficult to apply. If for example I am teaching a group of thirty year 9 students for sixty minutes how can I respond to all the individual learning styles of the students in the group? Is this realistic? Probably not, although it is probably more manageable if I am a year 5 teacher and I see my class for the whole day every day of the week.

Most of us use all of our senses to absorb information. The majority of us learn best through doing things (kinaesthetic learning). However, the majority of teaching in schools involves high levels of visual, auditory, and reading activities but relatively little kinaesthetic learning—despite the fact that active learning is the style that most students enjoy and which helps them to learn. A lot of learning in schools is passive. This is true in many music lessons, although the best are very practical (and therefore kinaesthetic). Effective lessons need to be engaging and interesting. Structuring a lesson so that it involves a high degree of kinaesthetic learning can be extremely motivating for students. An open and experimental curriculum is more likely to include kinaesthetic activity than a closed, prescriptive, and information-driven curriculum. Take the following example.

A group of year 10 students move towards their English room. On arrival they are greeted by a semi-darkened room and the sound of Maria Callas performing Bellini's 'Compane teneri amici'. On the whiteboard is projected the image of a woman in period costume, obviously painted in the late eighteenth century. Around the room there are various artefacts: a coat on a tailor's dummy, a picture of a donkey, a paintbrush and some paints, some cherries, and a quill pen. The students are immediately immersed in the atmosphere of the room and invited to wander around looking at the various objects. They feel excitement and emotional engagement with the atmosphere. The teacher recaps on some of their learning to date. Students are appointed to take cards with key definitions around the room and talk to other students about what terms (such as 'iambic pentameter') mean. Two others (designated 'learning monitors') also wander around the room and note examples of how individual students are able to give answers, which show an understanding of the key terms. They give feedback to the rest of the class on their findings. The teacher notices that the class seem to have a less secure understanding of one term so spends a few minutes going over this with the students. She then asks them to look at the artefacts around the room and write questions on post-it notes about these objects. One writes 'Why is there a coat?' 'Is the woman from the royal family?' 'What is the music and what significance does it have?' Students are intrigued by what is happening and want to know more. The teacher reflects on some of these questions and then asks them to look at a copy of the poem 'My Last Duchess' by Robert Browning. As they go through the poem she encourages the people who wrote questions to write information on another post-it saying if they now understand why an object may be significant and why.

This is just the first thirty minutes of an English lesson where the teacher has tried to engage the students in a range of ways. The students are a set three English group (i.e. middle ability in a low-achieving inner-city school). There are a few clear outcomes:

- the students are very interested in the lesson—mainly due to the atmosphere created by the teacher
- they are all engaged and develop a good level of thinking about the topic
- they look upon the poem as something that is to be investigated with interest
- they use a wide range of their emotions to immerse themselves in the learning.

There are questions still to answer about this lesson and where it will take the students.

- How does it relate to the examination specification and will this work enable them to achieve well?
- How does it relate to other activities they will be doing?
- Will it contribute to key skills such as their ability to write well?

The teacher did not try to anticipate the learning style of each student in the room, although she was aware of what they are because she has researched them with the students. What she did was to provide a range of activities that are suitably engaging for students' learning styles. The lesson was not passive and reliant on the teacher talking or the students copying information. The students were asked to engage with their feelings. This approach made more sense than trying to analyse each student's preferred learning style and trying to cater for it on an individual basis. It also meant that a potentially difficult poem was introduced in an effective and engaging way for a group of students who had relatively little previous experience of this genre and in another context may not have found it interesting.

The profile of students in a school

I will consider students for a moment as discrete groups because I think this is a helpful way of making a particular point. I will refer to NSG as a case study example because I knew many of these students well and understood the contexts they brought to the school. However, what I describe also includes references to a wide range of other schools that I have encountered. I will start by considering the profile of a typical year group. NSG had about 1,700 students and about 300 started in year 7.

How many will become professional musicians?

This may seem like a surprising question to ask but it is possible that such students may require some special experiences in order to help them in their future career. I also believe that thinking about the needs of this cross-section of students is important because many music education practices in schools stem from an unwritten assumption that we need to cater most effectively for the students that we regard as 'musical'. What are the needs of this group? If by the term 'professional musician' we mean someone who makes a living as either a soloist, or a regular member of an orchestra, band, or other group, we can probably predict that about one student every generation (i.e. about twenty years) will follow this career. This is a very small number. Especially when you consider that NSG is a Specialist Music College and therefore attracts students from the area who are interested in music (even before it became a Specialist Music College).

The number is so low because music is an extremely competitive field of employment and there are very limited opportunities available to those who might consider performing as a full-time career. It can also be an extremely precarious, low-paid, and unsociable occupation. Out of the few people who earn a living performing music an even smaller number end up in well-paid and secure employment. I am not aware of the proportion of students who become full-time professional musicians having attended one of the Specialist Music Schools mentioned in Chapter 1. Presumably, it is a higher number because the schools use a rigorous selection process, they are geared to this one intended outcome, and students often start on this path at a young age. Attendance at such a school may also open doors to them. If so we might say that the system works—since if you want to be a performer you will need to seriously consider attending one of these Specialist Music Schools (assuming you can gain access) or alternatively take part in one of the Specialist Saturday Schemes run by the various Music Conservatoires. Either way state-funded secondary schools, even Specialist Music Colleges are not likely to supply a high number of performers to the music profession. The logical outcome then is that the curriculum should therefore not revolve around the one-in-a-generation student who might take this career path.

How many might become full-time or part-time music teachers?

Currently, most teachers will require some form of specialist higher education training, although the school workforce of the future will probably require a wider and more flexible range of skills. Current training may include additional post-graduate courses in education, or some form of vocational training in order to gain an equivalent experience or qualification. The future shape of the teaching workforce is likely to change radically with a greater number of support staff employed—partly as a result of demographic changes that will lead to a shortage of teachers from 2010 onwards. What proportion of students will become teachers? In 2004 NSG had three students who elected to take a higher education music qualification. This number was slightly above average. These students may not all choose to go into teaching. Some may, but others might try to gain other employment in the music industry and need to supplement this with teaching. Others will find employment not related to music. This means that out of a school of 1,700, many of whom may have an interest in music and chose the school for its musical reputation, only a very small number may use their musical skills to teach, or perhaps undertake a mixture of teaching and some performing.

How many may play an instrument but do not continue with it once they leave school?

In 2004 about 240 NSG students learned an instrument. Younger students were more likely to play and far fewer played in years 9–13. The numbers learning in years 10, 11, 12, and 13 were quite low. Looking at a typical year group, about six from year 13 might continue with an instrument in higher education (either as a result of studying music) or as a result of participating in extra-curricular groups (even though they were not taking a higher-level music course). A few more may continue to play outside school if they were involved in some form of community music-making such as a brass band, a choir, or other group. Many more will stop playing altogether or perhaps drift into more informal performing opportunities. The purpose of asking these questions is to explore whether or not the curriculum (in its broadest sense) meets the needs of the large majority of young people as well as the needs of specific groups (such as instrumentalists or those who take the subjects as an examination course).

The numbers of students who will go on to be performers or teachers is a very small proportion of the school population, even in a school that has a strong reputation for music. It is therefore essential that the curriculum in a musical school is capable of meeting the needs of this small group of students but also matches the interests and aspirations of the far larger group of students who may experience music only in Key Stage 3. If we don't consider carefully how to address the needs, interests, and wants of the large majority of students we may as well elect to teach music just to a small group of students who opt for it when they start secondary school, or perhaps make a similar sort of choice in a primary school.

What do the larger group of students want and need from the curriculum?

A questionnaire survey carried out with NSG students gave a lot of information about the music that this group of students liked. They wanted to be able to engage with music from 'popular' culture and to have the opportunity to learn an instrument and enjoy participation in music-making. This would probably be using drums, guitar, and keyboard. I think they were typical of many students of their age. However the formal education sector (schools) provided something which was more likely to 'educate' students in western art music, possibly to re-enforce the fact that music is for 'musicians'—leading them to believe that music in school is for a small, select(ed) group. The curriculum in many schools may be more suitable for the minority, who may go on to take music as a higher education course. Music curriculum planning needs to cater more effectively for the needs and interests of the majority of students in order to be more relevant to them.

Planning the curriculum—student pathways

Pathways are the long-term direction taken by students as they move through the curriculum and on into either employment or further/higher education. In secondary schools these might include choices at Key Stage 3: some students may choose a particular focus in year 9 or might choose to do extra class music lessons. Some may choose to take an examination course (such as GCSE) early—for example in year 9. Some schools may choose not to do music in Key Stage 3 except for a small, 'select' group of students. Generally, the Key Stage 3 curriculum will tend to be quite homogenous and all students in a setting will have a similar sort of diet. However, my experience suggests that many students are not motivated by the experiences they receive at this age. They are quite keen to give up music and study other subjects aged 14+.

At the end of year 9 most students will opt for particular courses they believe will be useful for them as they move into the next stage of education and employment. These have tended to be GCSE courses. Music has not been a relatively popular choice. Far more students opt for drama and art. When I have talked to students about this the strong response has been that art and drama are subjects where they feel they will achieve well. A few students feel they will do well at music, most generally do not. The ones who do are almost always those who have extra instrumental lessons. One outcome of this is that the GCSE, which was set up to cater for the needs of a wide ability range, is seen as something that needs to be supplemented by other equivalent (level 2) qualifications. This is sometimes because teachers do not opt into choices available within a course that might be of more interest for some students. Popular music choices are available at GCSE but the teacher may not let students choose these options, because it would mean that s/he has to prepare activities and materials in areas the teacher does not approve of or feel comfortable with. Music technology has started to emerge as a possible alternative option along with 'BTEC' diplomas, creative and media diplomas, and other courses that offer a more popular and contemporary approach. These developments are exciting. A dilemma facing us is how to make sure that they attract equal parity and esteem from students, parents, employers, and further/higher education providers.

A similar picture emerges post-16. Very few students take music as an option. Many schools struggle to recruit the break-even class size of about eleven and students end up taught in very small uneconomic groups, or not able to take music. AS or A level courses are often the only options available, even though these courses are almost certainly only suitable for the students who have been learning an instrument since they started secondary education (or earlier). Alternative courses are available, in increasing numbers. Many offer the chance to follow content that is more popular and contemporary in style and with less emphasis on individual performance in western art music. Despite the availability of these courses few schools offer them because A level is seen as the obvious course to offer. General FE Colleges are more likely to offer these sorts of practical options.

There can be hidden elements to the A level curriculum. At NSG I taught a girl who was an outstanding composer. She was able to plan really imaginative, rich, and complex ideas with fluency. She loved arranging them into interesting textures and forms, using imitation, augmentation, polyphony, and a range of compositional devices that created pieces with a strong sense of structure and style. I have taught composition to a high level for many years and she was one of the most talented students I have encountered. She used a modal style that was reminiscent of Bartók. Being an accomplished string player she had studied and admired his music and was happy to write a string quartet as a free choice composition. I checked the examination specification to make sure that this piece would fit the criteria. I could not find a published mark scheme. Contacting the examination board proved fairly fruitless since after claiming that the mark scheme was on the website, they admitted that it wasn't but 'hoped it would be soon'. Eventually I obtained by e-mail a copy of what they described as the mark scheme:

25–30   Stimulating interesting and imaginative work showing a sensitivity to musical balance and sure handling of form and structure. Musical ideas are imaginatively developed and there is a clear awareness of timbre in the effective selection of voices, instruments and/or synthesised sounds. The texture of the music is appropriate to the materials and the chosen medium. There is clearly strong expression or original ideas and/or confident handling of an accepted style.

19–34   The work is musically interesting and satisfying. It shows an understanding of balance, form and structure and the musical ideas are well developed. The selection and use of voices, instruments and/or synthesised sounds show sensitivity to timbre and texture. There is evidence of originality and/or assimilation of accepted styles.

13–18   The work is structured and organised and there is some development of musical ideas. The choice of voices, instruments or synthesised sounds shows reasonable variety with some control of texture. Imitation of an accepted style is evident but there may be little evidence of development beyond the original.

7–12   Musical ideas are apparent but tend to be simple and repetitive. The notion of structure and form is apparent but lacks clarity. There is an appropriate choice of voices, instruments of synthesised sounds although ensemble is limited in its tonal variety. Some control of texture is evident in the music but its appropriateness may not always be effectively gauged. Imitation of an accepted style may be without originality or sense of progression beyond the example chosen.

0–6   There is evidence of a rudimentary grasp of structure or form and musical ideas are apparent but tend to be undeveloped or unsustained. A rudimentary awareness of timbre and texture is apparent in the selection of voices, instruments or synthesised sounds. Imitation of an accepted style may be seen in the choice of voices, instruments, form or structure.

I actually believe that this is too general to be a mark scheme. However, it seemed to me that the work clearly fitted the 25–30 description. I was interested to follow up another element of the specification. It said that 'one composition must be in a recognisably tonal idiom'. I made sure that the student composed one piece with a pretty standard set of chords—it was an imaginative theme and variations. I decided I wanted some more information about what this phrase 'tonal idiom' meant. To me it meant having a clear tonal centre that a piece returns to for resolution. Bartok pushes the boundaries but has a well-defined tonal centre. His music is not exactly cutting edge now, although I concede that the harmonic language is rich and complex. So I asked what was meant by the term 'tonal centre' and was amazed at the response I eventually received:

This means that one piece must have a recognisable tonal centre. Therefore the composition could be a techniques-based piece in an 18th century style (simple 4-part harmony or 2-part counterpoint); on the other hand a rock composition using contemporary modal harmonies is equally valid. (Response from exam board 2006)

This is an interpretation that I found difficult to live with. It was not made explicit in the specification—it only said 'recognisable tonal centre'. A slightly more promising (but contradictory reply came back):

I hope I can clear up this issue for Mr. Bray. My interpretation as Principal Examiner (bearing in mind that I was not involved in devising the specification nor the mark scheme) is pretty broad. Mr. Bray is right to concentrate on the issue of there being a tonal centre: all the examples he describes would be likely to fit the bill for our purposes (ultimately we need to treat each piece on its musical merits and not focus on labels and how they might be interpreted).
   In practice this 'hoop' is rarely one that candidates trip over—there are not many submissions in any given year that do not include at least one piece that is clearly tonal—classical pastiche (in its broadest sense), blues-based works, and pop ballads cater for most candidates. There are a few instances where a very able candidate—a true composer—works in a harmonic idiom that may stimulate an interesting debate among musical intellectuals as to what is tonal music due to its approach to modality, chromaticism or dissonance, but does so in such an assured manner that it would be a very unimaginative examiner who wanted to penalise a candidate with such impressive skills. (Response from exam board 2006)

This sounded reassuring, because here I was encouraging a 'true composer'. She was awarded a C grade for the composition element of her coursework! It seems she encountered one of these unimaginative examiners who wanted to penalize the candidate for such impressive skills. When this mark was queried and the Chief Examiner's comments were used as evidence the grade was improved without further explanation. This experience had a detrimental effect on the talented student. She lost a lot of confidence and decided that for her A2 work she would write something much more boring that stood a chance of getting a better mark without being queried. What a waste of talent.

The challenge of creating a curriculum that caters for all students

NSG began to attract increasing numbers of students who played an instrument prior to year 7. This became apparent in the second year as a Specialist Music College. Despite this, there were still large numbers who did not play an instrument on arrival. In year 7 there were probably four types of student (these are very broad descriptors).

1. Students who play an instrument already and want to carry on

2. Students who want to start learning an instrument

3. Students who are more interested in a more informal way of learning music—as part of a band or drums/guitar in a less formal way

4. Students who do not want to learn an instrument but are interested in listening to and enjoying music informally.

Traditionally schools have probably been most successful at catering for students in categories 1 and 2. Those in categories 3 and 4 have probably relied on out-of-school activities to meet their needs or have perhaps looked upon music in school as a subject which is at odds with their own love and enjoyment of the music that they listen to. Groups 3 and 4 probably constitute the very large majority of the students in a school. In truth we have probably not catered well for the 'wants' of these students because the curriculum has been focused more on the students (and their parents) in groups 1 and 2. This is where the 'hidden curriculum' becomes powerful because these issues are not stated overtly or planned for. It is just how things are and beyond the scope of this chapter to explore why.

It may now be helpful to ask ourselves what sort of experience we can offer groups 3 and 4 (the majority) in order to meet their needs and aspirations? A key to answering this question may be to plan for the students as discrete groups. After all this is what often happens at the moment, but we tend to cater for groups 1 and 2 (knowingly or not). We can start to map out the 'pathway' that a student may be able to take through the curriculum, ensuring that we cater, where possible, for groups 3 and 4. This approach is likely to give rise to a high level of satisfaction amongst a wide range of students and stands the chance of providing good opportunities for them to progress. We will need to consider some competing priorities:

1. How we join up the extra-curricular, curricular, and the hidden curriculum experiences in a positive way in order to make them accessible and appealing to a wide range of students

2. How we ensure that we produce a curriculum that offers students the chance to try things out, reject ideas, and re-engage if they want to

3. How we offer good curriculum pathways that enable a wide range of students to engage with music at any stage of their development

4. How we understand the needs of employers, parents, and those other important stakeholders so that the experiences of students lead them to

develop skills which are useful and relevant for the society in which they will work and play in the future.

Such an approach will almost certainly lead to a more complex and difficult task for teachers and managers. This is where the hidden curriculum can once again be a powerful force. Schools are often organized around principles that suit teachers. Challenging custom and practice can be difficult. Sometimes staff will talk about the need to cater for all students but their actions will reveal that their actual values and beliefs mitigate against this—though they often don't realize it. If we were to consider the intake of a school and possible pathways the students could take we might come up with the following:

Year 7 consists of the following main groups of students:

(a) Non-instrumentalists—main interest is contemporary music (they would like to play a contemporary instrument)

(b) Non-instrumentalists—main interest is classical (they would like to play a traditional instrument)

(c) Those who already play instruments—main interest is contemporary music

(d) Those who already play instruments—main interests is classical.

This is a crude definition. However, each of these groups arrives with different interests and experiences. A personalized approach to the curriculum will need to respond to these. As well as a core curriculum element a musical school will consider the students' needs and interests. The provision offered might be as follows:

Group (a): use gigajam (an online tutoring course in keyboards, guitar, and drums) and encourage students to attend rock and pop school.

Group (b): group instrumental lessons with extra on-line support.

Group (c): small-group tuition (below grade 5). Students signposted to rock school.

Group (d): small-group tuition below grade 5 and individual if more advanced. Students to participate in one or more extra-curricular activities.

After year 7 students elect to join one of two curriculum pathways:

1. Contemporary route

These students follow a curriculum in years 8 and 9 that uses technology and other resources to give them a good grounding in contemporary popular music. They are also offered small-group tuition and individual tuition (depending on needs/standard) on guitar, drums, or keyboard. Students are encouraged to attend after-school activities/Easter and Summer Schools to supplement this. These students are able to elect for a Key Stage 4 course in contemporary music and them move on to take Music Technology AS/A2 or BTEC practical music/arts courses.

2. Traditional route

These students are offered a curriculum experience that includes elements of contemporary music but also covers more traditional musical styles and genres. They are offered small-group tuition below grade 5 and individual tuition for those above. Students are also able to access a good range of extra-curricular activities and are encouraged to attend appropriate enrichment activities.

'Rock and pop' is used here as a somewhat inadequate descriptor. It attempts to categorize those students who arrive at the school with an interest related to 'popular' music and whose musical interests are often not catered for in formal settings such as schools. The music needs to be lively and students need to develop the individual performance skills that enable them to feel that they are 'musicians' and can therefore carry into Key Stage 4 and post-16 education. Most schools appear to cater for the traditional route and do not make sufficient coherent provision for the remaining students. This group will be the large majority. It gives us a clue as to why school music seems to miss so many of our students.

I talked to some teachers about using this mapping model within their school. Their reaction was 'we do not want to categorize students'. This is perfectly understandable. However, I found it ironic because this is what they, and the majority, of teachers, did all the time—but in a covert way! Their planning, language, and actions all supported the needs of the students in groups (a) and (b) above. They strongly categorized students already but could not see this. None of this was done consciously but it is a very powerful example of how the hidden curriculum works.

This curriculum is not suggested as a model to be adopted by every school. Each is different and the profile of its students will be unique. However, the approach forces us to consider the needs of all students and may result in different and possibly radical conclusions about how we organize the curriculum. Perhaps GCSE is the not the best option for the majority of students? I know there are arguments that say GCSE should be for any student, regardless of whether they have instrumental lessons. I understand the argument. I just don't feel that this is the reality of what happens in many schools. It would help if many music teachers were not so dogmatic about using musical notation, since most of the world's music doesn't. Adults teaching music need to be more adventurous and imaginative in how they approach lessons, resources, and expand their general horizons.

A change of philosophy may start to meet the needs and aspirations of a wide range of learners and help to move music into the mainstream of the curriculum (instead of something for a few 'gifted' pupils). However, this sort of approach will be a huge organizational and cultural challenge and perhaps few schools currently have the understanding or resolve necessary to achieve it. A philosophy that promotes the idea that music in school caters for all students will probably only happen gradually and through sustained efforts at local and national level. This is because it takes a huge effort to change the hearts and minds of a generation or two of teachers and without them, the change can not happen. Ironically this sort of egalitarian approach was promoted strongly by music educators in the late 1960s and early 1970s. Very few teachers in today's schools have had any experiences outside being taught the National Curriculum or of teaching it themselves.

To engage with most young people we need to understand what they are listening to. We also need to give them the opportunity to play an instrument. They may not want to take it up, but they should make that choice themselves rather than someone looking at them and deciding for them. We can then start to influence them and stretch their horizons. In fact we can educate them. We won't achieve this by pretending that they are not there and constructing our curriculum around the needs of the ones who may take music as an option at Key Stage 4. All of this sounds a bit negative and critical. It is meant to be honest and realistic. I understand fully that I am suggesting quite radical approaches. I also know as a practitioner that what I am advocating is inconvenient, hard work, and sometimes seems unrewarding. I feel that the musical climate of 2007 is probably ready for change, more ready than it has been for a long time and that contemporary initiatives and developments all champion a more inclusive approach.

Planning the curriculum—long-term content planning

Long-term planning gives the broad direction of the curriculum. Many teachers plan this level and then use activities from published resources. The topics define the way that the curriculum enables the student to build the experiences needed for the next stage of education. For example at Key Stage 3 a school might decided to construct a curriculum around these topics:

Year 7

- Elements of Music
- Rhythm and Texture

- Instruments of the Orchestra
- Medieval and Renaissance Music
- Caribbean Music
- Programme Music

Year 8
- Baroque, Classical, and Romantic Music
- Contrast and Repetition
- Rock and Roll
- Waltz
- The Scale of Things
- Rhythm and Texture
- Music for Special Events

Year 9
- Twentieth-Century Music
- Song-Writing
- Musical Forms
- Music and Media

These provide broad 'themes' that will be covered each half-term. This level of planning does not describe the detail of the activities that will take place and how they will ensure students develop the necessary skills, knowledge, and understanding of music as well as a positive attitude to their learning. The long-term planning above poses some particular questions:

1. Will this lead to sufficient engagement with contemporary musical styles in order to engage a wide range of students?

2. Will it provide **all** students with the skills they require to access the Key Stage 4 curriculum?

3. How can you possibly spend a half-term looking at instruments of the orchestra in a meaningful way in year 7?

4. My conversations and research with students tells me that they want to have the opportunity to learn an instrument and that they want to engage in activities that are lively and kinaesthetic. How will the teacher achieve this through looking at 'Medieval and Renaissance Music'.

I could go on. One of the interesting issues here is that sometimes a curriculum outline like this can be brilliantly taught and can manage to motivate and inspire students completely. This is usually because of the positive climate created by the teacher, the relationship s/he has with the students, and a sense of mutual respect. A curriculum that looks deficient in outline may end up being motivating and inspiring. Sadly, these teachers are few and far between. It also means that I cannot write down a sure-fire recipe for long-term planning that will meet everyone's needs. Even if I could, there would be teachers who managed to turn it into something more negative for a large group of students.

A useful, but often underused, stimulus for long-term planning is a clear focus on the point that the teacher wishes all students to have reached by the end of a year or Key Stage. The principle revolves around deciding where we want to be and then planning what is required to get there. Planning how to achieve this can be a very effective starting point. A more common but often less successful technique involves putting together a series of topics and units (sometimes based on published materials or resources). These activities may look reasonable on paper but may not add up to the necessary skills and understanding for accessing the next stage of education. They may also not lead to the development of skills and understanding in a structured and coherent way even though there will be a lot of activity taking place in lessons. For example, many students may arrive at the end of year 9 ill-equipped to take a music GCSE course unless they have had extra instrumental lessons. This need not be the case. If the teacher had planned the Key Stage 3 curriculum so that all students can access either a GCSE course (or other Level 2 course) at the end of year 9 planning will be inclusive. However, in many cases the curriculum may be affected by hidden assumptions. Some teachers will believe that a large majority of students will not be capable of continuing with music at Key Stage 4. They may not openly realize or admit to this. If they are not committed to developing everyone they will not approach the Key Stage 3 curriculum from the standpoint that all students can succeed. These views will therefore be overtly and covertly communicated to students. Some of the medium-term and short-term planning issues are dealt with by Sharon Green in Chapter 5.

Lesson climate

In June 2000 Hay McBer carried out some research for the government on what made teachers effective. They found that three factors within a teacher's control affected pupil progress in a positive way:

* teaching skills—involving all students, using differentiation effectively, using variety of questioning techniques to probe knowledge and understanding

- professional characteristics—self-image, values, approach to situations, and motivation
- climate—the perceptions by students of what it feels like to be in a particular classroom and how these influence the students' motivation.

I think that this research was quite significant and tells us a lot that could be applied to music education. It certainly addresses the issues of the hidden curriculum because the professional characteristics and climate in music education are often two areas that need considerable further development. One of the interesting features of the research was the conclusion that teacher effectiveness could not be predicted by analysis of gender, ethnicity, age, or school context. In other words anyone can be an effective teacher if they have, or develop, the right characteristics. This is exciting. I can think of a good example. I remember a violin teacher I observed who was nearing the end of her career and had a slightly formidable demeanour. These two factors led me to assume that she had a particular and rather narrow approach. To some extent she did. She was quite formal with the students. I observed her teach a group of mixed age (and mixed standard) violinists. There were seven in the group. The teacher told me that there was not really room for such a large group but they were all keen and she didn't want anyone to miss out. At this point I realized that I had misjudged her through applying my own prejudices before I had seen her teach. The standard of the group was fantastic given their age and experience. She addressed their individual needs in the lesson, managed the group very effectively, and clearly had very high and inclusive expectations. It was truly personalized and inspiring. I felt humbled by the experience. The Music Service missed out on the opportunity to learn a lot from this teacher and develop the methods of some of their so called expert teachers—who were assigned to more advanced students (and were actually just the best performers).

Making the curriculum relevant

I have already posed a key challenge for the curriculum: How can the school make it relevant for all students and ensure that it is of sufficiently high quality? Will Taylor is an excellent teacher who worked at Stantonbury Arts College and Northampton Academy. One of Will's strengths is that he has achieved an ethos that is very inclusive. I asked him about his views on the matter:

In September 1999 I began my first head of music post at one of the country's first specialist arts colleges. It was a fabulous opportunity for me to develop both musical and leadership skills with the support and encouragement of a head teacher with real vision and passion for the arts, and a team of determined and experienced teachers.

The school had taken the brave and innovative decision to turn conventional thinking on its head by scrapping the traditional year 9 options model and replacing it with a system that resulted in high numbers taking arts GCSEs with nearly 25% of students taking GCSE music.

The first year of this regime almost overwhelmed me. I found myself trying to sell the subject I loved to a large percentage of students who would not have opted to take GCSE music, did not play an instrument, did not sing and had no intention of doing either. All this, whilst being set stringent A*–C performance targets on which the success of the specialism would be judged. My lessons were characterised by anger, conflict, resentment and disillusionment, not to mention the betrayal felt by the small numbers who did wish to participate in music.

It was at this point that I really began to appreciate what had made my own music education so inspiring. As a student at my comprehensive 'musical' school, I had an identity as a musician. I felt part of something special—an exclusive club which everyone was invited to join. I was forced to accelerate my own learning by sitting next to older students with greater experience, playing music at the edge of my ability. Rehearsals were a balancing act between keeping up with the tempo and listening for clues from my neighbour. These older students became role-models and by the time I was in their year group, I was nurturing younger students too. This helped me gain respect from my music teachers who treated me as a partner in the learning experience. The fact that all my musical learning could be packaged and presented to an appreciative audience on a regular basis was the best feeling in the world. I found myself composing for school ensembles in an effort to tailor our music to the needs of specific ensembles and performance occasions. The biggest motivator for me was us.

There was no such sense of us in my GCSE classroom and I could see no obvious path towards such a goal. Suddenly, the need for an extremely engaging key stage 3 curriculum became paramount. In fact, my whole perception of music at KS3 changed overnight. My colleagues and I had no choice but to become very innovative.

The problem with innovation is that well over half of what you try doesn't work. But when the students in front of you have only one chance to gain the grade they are capable of, such risks aren't necessarily wise. (I often feel frustrated that more educational policy makers in schools and beyond don't appreciate this.) However, in the situation I found myself, such innovative risks were essential. In a sense, my team and I had very little to lose.

As each attempt to crack the nut developed, my whole perception of my role as music educator changed. I realised that I didn't want to teach my students about music, but I wanted them to become musicians. I tried to treat every student like a musician and teach them how musicians behave and react. I tried very hard to run all lessons like rehearsals with every student playing a vital ensemble role regardless of the complexity of their part. So instead of just aiming to teach students how to perform a solo in front of the class, I began to teach the class how to support a soloist, give generous applause and detailed constructive feedback. Instead of just aiming to teach the class a piece of ensemble music, I taught them how musicians deal with recurring errors, and how they adapt to the difficulties of a key player without stopping.

The impact of this simple but significant change of approach for me was life-changing. Watching a group of 'me's become an 'us' has been the most satisfying thing about my teaching experience.

Needless to say, this approach has seen significant improvements in attainment, but there's more to it than that. Sure, what students learn is essential, how students learn is vital, but why they learn currently seems to receive little attention. It seems to me that young people are most motivated when they have a role and a goal which is bigger than just them. From this perspective, difficult issues such as classroom singing evaporate. Right across the world in every culture, singing is a statement of group identity and purpose. Whole school impact anyone?

The Music National Curriculum tells us that music changes the way people think, feel and act, but sometimes I think that perhaps we hope this will be a positive by-product of music education rather than its core purpose. We live in a culture where music has been largely owned by individuals perceived to have talent rather than communities who have identity. (I wonder if the advent of MySpace and YouTube might already be changing this trend?) In any case, skills learnt in the process of becoming a musician could make a huge contribution to the lives of today's young people who will emerge to a society increasingly based on large numbers of people working in unison to meet the needs of individuals. (When I was at school, there were just 4 TV channels and no internet or mobile phones. It's easy to forget how much things have changed.)

My definition of a musical school is one where music is the conduit by which the community expresses its identity as a learning institution where each and every member shares the responsibility for the learning of others. In a musical school, learners would be constantly seeking ways of reaching a wider audience. This would be the purpose—not the fortunate by-product.

I've never been anything other than a long way away from this ideal, but it's definitely the vision that gets me out of bed on a Monday morning. In the current educational climate, I would be very surprised if many head teachers would buy-in to this perspective as it doesn't appear to directly relate to raising achievement. However, I would argue that the roots of even the strongest learner focused curriculum can't flourish in anything other than rich cultural soil. In fact, the more sophisticated and bespoke our curriculum becomes in the future, the more vital the learner's sense of responsibility will be.

Somewhere in our collective consciousness, we've always known that music should remain a compulsory aspect of the school curriculum.

Perhaps now is the time to show everybody why.[3]

Will proves that it is possible to create a state of mind that is inclusive and determined to engage a wide range of students in a positive way. He managed to find the right climate that suited not only him but the students he taught. I have encountered several other people like him and I believe that it is this approach that is the key. It is one of the reasons I cannot give a magic curriculum formula which will engage students. The teacher's state of mind is the thing that makes most difference to the experience of the majority. The enthusiasm and positive approach (or climate) is the element that shines through.

---

[3] Will Taylor, original article written for this book, 2007.

This can be done formally or informally. It doesn't really matter. Once s/he develops this approach the teacher creates a climate where students from a range of backgrounds feel valued. Students quickly pick up hidden messages. Curriculum structures and planning help, they fine-tune things but the teacher has to believe that all the students can be musicians. Once s/he has reached this state of mind there is a good chance of creating a curriculum fit for a musical school.

Chapter 5

Improving motivation for music at Key Stage 3

Sharon Green

In this chapter Sharon Green, Learning Adviser for Music with the Learning Achievement and School Improvement Division of Northamptonshire County Council, describes some of the work that she has done to develop greater engagement and motivation with students. Much of this work has been carried out with great success in schools facing challenging circumstances.

> One of the biggest obstacles to progress has been the conventional, limited and relatively fixed image of 'The Musician'. For many of us that image has become a goal in itself and we have seen our task in schools primarily in terms of producing more musicians (with capital Ms!); an outlook appropriate enough for a specialist music college, perhaps, but unsatisfactory for normal schooling where the curriculum must be constructed with all pupils in mind.
>
> John Paynter[1]

John Paynter's words still ring true nearly thirty years later. He was, of course, referring to the type of Specialist Music College dealt with at the start of Chapter 1—an auditioned, western art performance-focused residential school. As we have seen, the term Specialist Music College does have the potential to include a wider range of schools since the advent of the English government's Specialist School scheme. However, Paynter's words have relevance and a certain amount of poignancy because in many schools we are still struggling to construct a music curriculum that is sufficiently relevant and engaging for 'all pupils', especially at Key Stage 3.

---

[1] J. Paynter, *Music in the Secondary School Curriculum*, Schools Council (London: HMSO, 1982).

In Chapter 4 David Bray describes a primary-aged child determined not to miss school because her class were going to set fire to their model of London; and a year 10 English lesson where the pupils were completely immersed in their learning because of the atmosphere created by the imaginative teaching. What strikes and saddens me immediately from reading this chapter is that he did not use examples from inspiring music lessons. Why is this? Is there something different about the way that we have traditionally approached learning and teaching in music that makes it less inspiring than other subjects? Is music a difficult subject to teach in an interesting way or is it because we are still trying to teach the 'musicians' and neglecting the imaginations of the vast majority of our students?

It wasn't until I was faced with teaching music in an inner-city school as a Newly Qualified Teacher (NQT) that I realized how narrow and largely irrelevant my own musical experience was. At school and college I was an apparently successful musician with a 'capital M' (to use Paynter's terminology). I went through a traditional and formal music education that involved

- learning an instrument to a high standard
- learning theory
- doing harmony exercises
- practising aural tests
- learning about the history of music within a western classical style.

Unfortunately, however, I had little understanding of how to motivate or meet the enormous range of needs, experiences, interests, and capabilities that faced me with each group that burst through the door of an inner-city Leicester school. In an interview a few years later I was asked to talk about how I differentiated in music lessons. I gave the standard answer by task or by outcome and elaborated on this a bit. What I hadn't properly considered was that differentiation is about more than task and outcome. It is about valuing all learners and motivating students so that they want to learn. It is also about recognizing that everyone has learning needs, finding out what these are, and developing strategies for addressing them. It requires

- a real commitment to the concept that music is for all
- an examination of the different ways that people learn to be musical
- a reassessment of what it is to be a successful musician.

I remember a conversation with a PE teacher who measured his own success not in terms of how many students became professional footballers, rugby stars, and PE teachers but by the number of students who were motivated to do some kind of sport as an adult. This might be anything from aerobics to coaching a football team. If one of our success criteria is to equip all of our students to take part in music as an adult we first need to acknowledge that there are many different ways that people do this—as audiences, critics, consumers, performers, composers, technicians, etc. We also need to value these different routes equally and construct a curriculum that caters for them all. Constructing a flexible curriculum that responds to the needs of individual learners is one of the key principles set out by the DCSF personalized learning initiative. The Report of the Teaching and Learning in 2020 Review Group define personalized learning:

Put simply, personalised learning and teaching means taking a highly structured and responsive approach to each child's and young person's learning, in order that all are able to progress, achieve and participate. It means strengthening the link between learning and teaching by engaging pupils—and their parents—as partners in learning.[2]

David Miliband (2004) described personalized learning as:

High expectations of every child, given practical form by high quality teaching based on a sound knowledge and understanding of each child's needs. It is not individualised learning where pupils sit alone. Nor is it pupils left to their own devices—which too often reinforces low aspirations. It means shaping teaching around the way different youngsters learn; it means taking care to nurture the unique talents of every pupil.[3]

In order to shape the music curriculum 'around the way different youngsters learn' we need to recognize and celebrate the different strategies that people use to learn, the different rates at which they learn and the idea that what we consider worth learning might not coincide with those of our students. Perhaps the most important thing to remember is that all learners need to feel valued and will learn most successfully if they are encouraged to achieve. A checklist for achieving a positive learning environment might include the following:

- celebrate what students can do
- resist telling what they can not do (directly or indirectly)
- use a balance of praise and challenge
- leave students feeling positive
- recognize that some learners are motivated when they are challenged and have the desire to prove that they can achieve
- find the time to ask students about themselves and how they learn.

---

[2] DfES, *2020 Vision Report of the Teaching and Learning in 2020 Review Group* (London: HMSO, 2006).

[3] David Miliband, *A National Conversation about Personalised Learning*, DfES (London: HMSO, 2004).

Really good teachers do this instinctively. Most of us have to work at these skills and the traditional focus that we have had on the 'Musician' means that this has not been a strong area of music education. We therefore have to recognize that there are many different ways to learn and that these are not hierarchical. You are not a better musician, for example, if you can read notation. We all know brilliant musicians who cannot read music. If our ultimate aim is to enable every individual to participate in music as an adult—not to simply pass instrumental exams or GCSE music—then we must make sure our lessons are relevant and engaging.

Responding to individual learning needs

Personalizing learning in any subject is complex and some teachers may argue that it is even more difficult in a music lesson because of the reasons discussed above. Let's consider some specific examples of how a teacher might respond to the needs of individual learners (Sophie and Israel) in a typical year 7 class. The music teacher has quite a lot of information about Sophie and Israel as individual learners. This information is outlined below:

> **Sophie** has grade 4 piano. She has private individual tuition with her father, who used to play in a dance band. She has never passed the sight-reading part of her piano exams. She finds rhythm quite difficult and doesn't really understand time signatures. She wants to study music.
>
> **Israel** is an able but disruptive pupil. He finds it difficult to concentrate in lessons. He is able to pick out tunes by ear and plays these on the keyboard using two hands and backing rhythms. His behaviour hampers the progress of others.

The year 7 class are working on a whole-class ensemble piece in a blues style. In order to respond to Sophie and Israel's learning needs the teacher plans to: give Sophie a notated piano part to perform that will stretch her piano skills and help her to improve her sight-reading, and give Israel a big drum to play hoping that will humour him. She tells him that if he disrupts the lesson she will give him a woodblock to play or that he will be sent out.

The teacher has made some attempt to cater for Sophie's needs but her strategy is partly based on the idea that in order to be a successful musician it is important to be able to read traditional notation. Instead of assuming that Sophie needs to practise her piano-playing and sight-reading (more of the same skills that she does in her individual lesson), she could help her by challenging her to think and make her own decisions, to learn by ear, from memory, and to improvise within the context of blues. In fact Sophie's needs are far more complex than initially seems the case. She does not understand notated rhythms. She has been taught that a dotted note is a bit faster than the note before it—she doesn't know what this means. She has been taught from a book and has been told off for wasting practice time improvising or 'messing about'. Sophie needs to try out some different ways of learning, she needs to try learning by ear. She also needs to develop some confidence—she thinks that she has no sense of rhythm because she doesn't understand how to make the notation work.

Israel needs to understand the relationship between music that he listens to at home and music at school. He needs to learn about chords. He needs tasks that are challenging and relevant to him broken down into small steps that he can achieve. He needs to perform to the class and to feel special (because he has succeeded). He needs clear instructions, routines, praise, and encouragement. By giving him a big drum the teacher is seen by the rest of the class as pandering to him, rewarding his previous poor behaviour. What does the teacher's comment reveal to the class about the value of a woodblock?

The example above provides us with a lot of information about two individual students but raises some questions. How can we possibly understand the needs of each young person in a class of thirty? How can we cater for individuals and ensure that they make sufficient progress?

Putting planning for individual needs into practice

The next example illustrates how a teacher might cater for individual needs when teaching a class. I will describe the planning of a year 7 music lesson and an evaluation of what happens. This evaluation is based on things that the teacher has noticed about individual students in a class. However, these observations are not written down by the teacher. The teacher sees many different classes during a week and hasn't therefore got the time to write down the detail. Nevertheless the teacher has made these observations informally and uses them as a basis for planning the next stages of the learning (an example of assessment for learning one of the components of personalized learning).

In this example a year 7 class are doing a unit of work exploring the context of samba music. In the first lesson of the unit they will learn an ensemble piece using Brazilian instruments. The objectives for this lesson are that the students should:

- know some musical vocabulary e.g. syncopation, groove, call and response, cue, break, and understand how these features are used in the context of samba music
- be able to perform samba rhythm patterns by ear and from memory following aural and visual cues accurately

◆ be able to perform with a sense of ensemble maintaining steady patterns independently of others.

Achievements

By the end of the lesson the class have managed to play the main 'groove' together and have learned one 'break' and some of a call and response opening section. Most students are able to maintain a steady rhythm pattern.

In this lesson the students have been encouraged to talk about their learning. The teacher asks questions and encourages individuals to talk about what they have found challenging. She asks them to think about how they learn new rhythms and shares with them her own strategies—she models her own learning and explains that one of her strategies is to learn by watching, copying, and standing by somebody who already knows the rhythm. She asks the students to talk about their own strategies by posing questions such as:

◆ How did you learn the rhythms?

◆ What helped your learning?

◆ What did you find most difficult and why?

◆ What do you think that you need to do next?

The information gathered from discussion and observation helps her to plan the next stage. She noted that Mitul, Adam, Mary, and Darshna were struggling with their rhythms. She plans strategies to support these students such as:

◆ using the rhythms that they are struggling with as a warm-up activity with the whole class. Adding movement to the rhythms and simple words that reflect the rhythms such as 'I would like a holiday'

◆ playing the rhythms on a large instrument such as a drum, exaggerating the movement so that the students can watch the rhythm. The teacher will do this with all of the rhythms so that she does not draw attention to any individual learner

◆ placing the students who are struggling next to those who are more confident

◆ discussing with the students the different strategies that they use to learn rhythms such as watching, copying, listening, reading notation(s).

The teacher has also identified students who need extra challenge: Jack, Pritesh, and Jessica were able to play the rhythms confidently. The teacher decides that these students may need extra challenge and she will try some of the following strategies:

- challenging them to learn new pieces by listening to a recording, learning the rhythms by ear, and teaching them to the rest of the class
- giving them a more complicated part which includes changing rhythms
- asking them to make up their own short patterns and teach them to the others
- leading the ensemble.

Joe, Ellethea, Vishal, Sophie, and Michael receive extra instrumental lessons. The teacher doesn't assume that because these students learn instruments they are not going to be challenged by this activity, since it may require different but equally important musical skills. She decides that the next stage of planning for this group's learning might include:

- thinking about whether they should have the same experience as everyone else
- discussing this with them. Do they find the work interesting, easy, challenging, appropriate? If not how might it be changed?
- catering for different learning styles playing by ear, from memory, from notations
- discussing strategies for challenging these students with their instrumental teachers
- creating some melodic parts for their instruments or asking the students to do this themselves
- introducing some notes or chords for them to improvise around using their own instrument
- treating these students as individuals, they all have their own learning needs.

The teacher in this example catered quickly and effectively for the needs of the individuals within the class by

- devising clear objective-led lesson planning
- ensuring that the lesson was practical, challenging, and engaging
- making judgements about the individual needs and progress of students through observation, discussion, and reflection upon their learning
- challenging individual learners through skilful and well-planned questioning.

Questioning skills

Questioning is one of the key ways to increase the challenge of lessons and to check the progress of individual learners. In 1956 Benjamin Bloom carried out research on questioning by analysing thousands that were asked by teachers. He categorized these according to the level of thinking required from the lowest level (the simple recall of information or knowledge) up to the highest order of questioning (that he defined as evaluation). Bloom suggested that by sequencing questions a teacher can develop students' thinking skills, deepen their understanding, and promote more effective learning.

The example shown in Table 3 has been adapted from the DfES (2004) *Pedagogy and Practice: Teaching and Learning materials,* Unit 7: 'Questioning'[4] and Sharon Green with Gary Spruce, *Making it happen in the classroom,* training material prepared for the Open University and Trinity Guildhall Continuing Professional Development Programme for Primary Music Practitioners.[5]

Bloom's taxonomy can be used to help plan key questions in music lessons and to ensure that all learners are sufficiently challenged and motivated. Effective musicians will need to be able to make their own musical decisions when composing and performing and realize that there is no such thing as a right or wrong way. We can help them to develop these skills by asking them higher-level questions such as:

- What is an effective performance/composition?
- How can I make the performance/composition more expressive?
- What would happen if . . .?
- How many different ways can I . . .?
- Which is the most effective of these and why?

Students need to be taught to listen to, appraise, and evaluate music. They need to understand that music exists beyond the written notes on a page, that interpretations can be applied, and that it is acceptable to experiment with ideas. This can be done in a variety of ways. For example, if a teacher is introducing a new performance task such as learning a tango piece he can

- play two different performances of the same piece and encourage the students to compare and contrast them

---

[4] DfES, *Pedagogy and Practice: Teaching and Learning in Secondary Schools,* Unit 7: 'Questioning' (London: HMSO, 2004).

[5] Sharon Green with Gary Spruce, *Making it Happen in the Classroom,* training material prepared for the Open University and Trinity Guildhall Continuing Professional Development Programme for Primary Music Practitioners (Maidenhead: Open University with Trinity Guildhall, 2007).

Table 3 Developing questioning skills

Cognitive objective (hierarchical)	What students need to do	Possible musical questions/tasks
Knowledge (lowest level)	◆ define ◆ recall ◆ describe ◆ label ◆ identify ◆ match	How many beats is a semibreve worth? How many symphonies did Beethoven write? What is a tabla? Match the words and definitions.
Comprehension	◆ explain ◆ translate ◆ illustrate ◆ summarize ◆ extend	Explain why you think this piece is in binary form. Show me how to play this chord.
Application	◆ apply to new context ◆ demonstrate ◆ predict ◆ employ ◆ solve ◆ use	What do you think will happen if I change this section from major to minor? What would happen if the tempo changed?
Analysis	◆ analyse ◆ infer ◆ relate ◆ support ◆ break down ◆ differentiate ◆ explore	Why does the tempo change in this section? What is the effect of this?
Synthesis	◆ design ◆ create ◆ compose ◆ reorganize ◆ combine	What other ways could you end this piece? How could you reorganize the structure of this piece to create a different effect?
Evaluation (highest level)	◆ assess ◆ evaluate ◆ appraise ◆ defend ◆ justify	Compare two interpretations of the piece 'Killing me Softly'. Give some musical reasons about which you prefer and why.

- ◆ challenge the students to think about what they have learned through the listening task and how it will affect their own performances
- ◆ take a section of the piece and use it as the basis of a composition task by focusing on a musical feature such as dotted rhythms or the use of minor chords
- ◆ compare it with other dance music from a range of styles and cultures

- ask the students to suggest ways to practise and rehearse the piece
- record the performance and ask them to evaluate it and suggest ways to improve the performance/sense of ensemble, etc.

The teacher might use Bloom's taxonomy to help her plan some specific questions such as:

- What do you notice about the structure of the piece?
- Are there phrases that are repeated? What is the effect of this?
- Does the melody move in steps/leaps? What effect does this have on the mood of the piece?
- What is an appropriate tempo for this piece? Why? What would be the effect of changing the tempo?
- What effect does the expressive use of dynamics have on the mood and character of the piece?
- What if we removed the dotted rhythms?
- What if we changed the minor chords to major chords?
- What would be the effect if the piece was played on different instruments? In a different register?

Music lessons that are challenging and engaging, where questioning is well planned and students are taught new skills are likely to motivate the majority of learners. Another key factor in this is judging the pace needed to maintain interest and stimulation. Some students will need small, achievable tasks (with positive feedback) whilst others will need to be challenged with well-planned higher-level questions and learning opportunities.

Structuring music lessons to maintain pace and improve musical understanding—starter activities

Short achievable tasks or 'bite-size' chunks (such as a four-part lesson) can be a successful way to manage behaviour and improve the motivation of KS3 students. Some students find it difficult to have too many unstructured, open-ended, and unchallenging activities. The DfES National Secondary Strategy promotes strongly the 'episodic' lesson. This amounts to more than just writing the learning objectives on the board, carrying out two different tasks, and following up with a plenary. Like most initiatives the strategy can be reduced to a formula by less effective teachers who will not analyse sufficiently its effectiveness and appropriateness for their students.

In this section we will consider the potential for starter activities to engage and motivate learners but also some of the pitfalls. The DfES (2002) defines starters as 'purposeful, whole-class, interactive teaching which involves all students. They should be designed to immediately engage the students. They should be stimulating, thought-provoking, and designed to develop thinking and learning.'[6]

Here are two fairly typical examples of starter activities for year 7 classes. In each of these examples the students have one 60-minute lesson of music a week.

Example 1

The class were learning about melody writing. They had listened to and performed some melodies consisting of steps and leaps. In this lesson they were asked to start composing their own 16-bar melodies.

Starter (10 minutes)

As the students entered the room they were given envelopes containing a set of laminated cards. Each envelope had a musical stave, a treble clef, and a set of semibreves with letter names inside. The students were asked to work in pairs and to place the notes onto the correct lines and spaces of the stave. If they finished this activity they were asked to open their manuscript books, practise drawing the treble clef and plot some words onto the staves e.g. cabbage, face, baggage.

We might analyse the strengths and weaknesses of this starter activity in the following way:

Strengths

◆ the teacher was well organized and made an attempt to design a starter which engaged students immediately they walked through the door.

◆ the teacher had tried to cater for kinaesthetic learners by providing a set of cards.

Weaknesses

◆ The teacher fell into the trap of devising a starter that gave the students an activity (plotting notes on a stave) based on knowledge and required little thinking.

◆ Many students had finished the card sort activity before everybody was seated. They passively plotted notes on the stave. The starter did not sufficiently challenge or engage these students.

---

[6] DfES, *National Strategy Training Materials for Foundation Subjects* (London: HMSO, 2002).

- There was no 'musical' learning taking place during this starter activity. Students were not involved in the musical activities of playing, singing, listening, appraising, composing, improvising, using instruments, making sounds.
- The task was not differentiated in any way. Students who had instrumental lessons made no progress in their musical learning.

Example 2

Starter (10 minutes)

This class were learning about the conventions of Impressionism in music. The students were put into pairs and given a mini-task to do using their own instruments or keyboards. They were given six minutes to complete the task. A few students were asked to read out their task to the class and then perform their work.

Strengths

- the students were immediately engaged in musical activity which challenged them to think and to make musical decisions
- the students responded well to the strictly applied timing—they knew that they had exactly 6 minutes and no time to waste
- the tasks were differentiated—the teacher had devised tasks that stretched and challenged all students appropriately
- the students' response to the tasks allowed the teacher to assess the progress that students were making
- the activity was set up to ensure that all students took part
- the students were encouraged to use their own instruments.

Weaknesses

- this activity might be time-consuming to set up and could take over the lesson if not managed properly

In both of these examples the teachers tried to plan activities that engaged the students. Some were more successful than others. Perhaps the key thing to bear in mind when planning starter activities in music is that they are engaging and thought-provoking and 'focus on an appropriately demanding pace in thinking and learning rather than on the business of activity'.[7] A starter where students do a series of activities that have right or wrong answers such as sorting a set of cards (letter names) onto the correct lines or spaces of a stave

---

[7] Ibid.

may keep the students busy for five minutes but are not sufficiently musical, thought-provoking, or challenging.

Effective musical starters might include some of the following

1. Lively and engaging rhythm activities developing aural skills, musical memory, responding to visual and aural cues

2. Singing and vocal warm-ups

3. Mini composition tasks linked to a unit of work e.g.

   'You have 5 minutes to compose a short piece that explores the difference between pentatonic and chromatic scales'

   'You have 5 minutes to create a piece that uses chords Am and G and demonstrate the difference between block and broken chords'

4. Which is the odd-one-out and why? E.g.

   | Piano | Djembe | Dholak |

5. Mix and match some descriptive writing to pieces of music.

The exact format of a successful lesson is elusive because good teachers adapt what they do, to the needs of their students. Most good teachers do, however, develop a basic format that works for them and which can be adapted for the individual needs of particular groups and individuals.

The four-part lesson

I worked with an excellent teacher in Derbyshire who managed to organize his lessons at KS3 and KS4 with the same four-part format. The example below is based on a lesson with Year 7 students

Example 1

Section 1: Starter

The room was set up with five large tables. As the students entered the room they were given an envelope containing a starter activity. In groups they were asked to listen to the song 'Eternal Flame' and to place the cards from their envelope (containing graphic notation of the melody) into the correct order. They were very engaged and challenged by this activity.

Section 2: Listening activity

The students were then given the learning objectives and taught the five key words for the lesson:

◆ solo

◆ a capella

- unison
- imitation
- call and response

These key words were explained and demonstrated by the teacher. He then did a listening activity. The students listened to music from a range of styles and cultures and identified which of the five key words were being demonstrated.

Section 3: Performance task

The students moved the tables out of the way and arranged their chairs in rows facing the piano. The teacher did some vocal warm-ups with the students focusing on diction and breathing.

The students sang the song 'Eternal Flame' and spent a few minutes answering questions about how to improve their singing and about what they noticed about the structure of the song. The teacher then asked them to suggest ways in which they could use their five key words and apply them to the performance of the song. They tried these out, e.g. 'imitation'. A student suggested that half of the class sing line 1 of the song quietly and the other half of the class copy them.

Section 4: Plenary

The lesson ended with a recap of the new vocabulary. The teacher gave out a laminated card to each student with either a word or definition on it from the five key words. He asked a student at random to read from their card. The rest of the students had to find the word or definition which matched.

The teacher concluded the lesson by reviewing the learning focusing on the learning outcomes. He asked the students to reflect on 'what have I learned today?'

Outcomes of this approach

The students were clear about what they were learning and why. They understood how features such as call and response and imitation are used in music from a range of styles and cultures and were able to suggest ways to use these features in their own work. They were also highly motivated and engaged by the task.

The climate created by the teacher was a key factor in this lesson. Another teacher might follow exactly the same set of activities and not achieve the same level of success. The teacher:

- welcomed the students to the lesson
- gave lots of positive feedback

- knew the students well and offered an appropriate level of challenge and support
- demonstrated by his actions that he respected the students and that he expected them to respect him and each other
- believed that they could all achieve highly
- had chosen materials that would appeal to a wide range of learners.

These features contribute to the hidden elements of the curriculum which are a very powerful force in determining the achievement, motivation, and attitude of the students. The teacher was also extremely effective at using higher-order questioning and developing students' thinking skills.

Creativity and critical thinking

Effective thinking skills can help students to be more creative, flexible, and committed learners.

The teaching of thinking skills should enable students to leave compulsory education well equipped and motivated to continue learning. This does not conflict with the more direct teaching of basic skills.[8]

In music lessons we often think of composing and performing as creative activities but forget to apply creative thinking strategies to our listening tasks. A listening activity designed to develop thinking skills and improve musical vocabulary can be challenging and motivating for all learners. In the example below the students were learning about film music and the teacher used the Batman theme from the 1989 film. The teacher posed questions such as: 'How does this piece of music create the mood of a camera drifting through the gloomy alleyways of the city of Gotham?'

The teacher divided the class into groups of about six students and gave each group a set of twenty statements like the ones shown in the diagram.

The music was composed by Danny Elfman in 1989 for the film Batman	The music starts with a single line, the texture builds up gradually creating a creeping effect
The opening is based on a five-note motif that is heard throughout the film played in different ways	The music starts slowly and quietly

---

[8] DfES, *Secondary National Strategy, Module 11: Principles for Teaching Thinking* (London: HMSO, 2002).

Glockenspiels (metallic sounding instruments) are used to create a spooky effect	A repeating pattern of notes moving down in pitch (descending) on the glockenspiel creates tension
The music was composed to accompany the Batman film	There are sustained (long held) chords

The students listened to the music and then placed the cards on a grid designed to focus their decision-making. They were asked to agree where each statement should be placed in response to the teacher's question.

Irrelevant

Fairly important

Important

Some of the cards used language that the students were not familiar with. The activity encouraged them to discuss and find out the meanings of new vocabulary within this context. Once the groups had completed the task they were asked to write their own sentence to answer the question—drawing upon their discussions. The students were encouraged to understand that there were no right or wrong answers and that the purpose of the activity was to improve appraisal and thinking skills, musical understanding, and the use of musical vocabulary.

I worked with another local teacher to try to improve the motivation of KS3 students under very different circumstances. The school was in an OFSTED category (Special Measures). There was very low achievement on entry and a history of poor behaviour/low student self-esteem.

The teacher wanted to use contemporary culture and devise a series of lesson that were well structured, challenging, and involved short tasks where students could achieve success and move on quickly. She wanted to do this in order to try to improve the attitudes and motivation of several groups of disaffected students. Poor behaviour was a real problem and students were unmotivated by music lessons that they felt were boring and irrelevant to them. We decided to trial a unit of work with a year 7 class mid-way through the spring term. One of our key objectives was to get the students to give feedback about their learning and levels of motivation.

Lesson 1

Objectives: What students should know/understand/be able to do by the end of the lesson.

All students will be able to:

◆ know some musical vocabulary e.g. ostinato/riff

◆ perform the opening section of the James Bond theme melody (by ear or from notation).

Most will be able to:

◆ perform the melody and ostinato pattern with a partner with an appropriate sense of rhythm

◆ plan appropriate fingering

◆ understand and use some musical vocabulary e.g. ostinato, melody, accompaniment.

Some will have made more progress and will be able to:

◆ perform the melody and ostinato pattern using two hands on the keyboard with accurate sense of rhythm and style

- learn and perform the next phrase by ear
- use more sophisticated vocabulary to analyse the piece of music e.g. syncopated, chromatic.

The sixty-minute lesson was broken into sections or episodes

Section 1: starter activity

A short mix and match listening activity based on ostinati in music from a range of styles and cultures.

Section 2

Students listened to the opening of the James Bond theme and were asked to describe the melody—they were taught key vocabulary such as ostinato, riff, syncopation. The teacher gave the students the starting note E and ten minutes to work out the opening by ear on keyboards.

The class were asked to stop playing after five minutes and were asked to describe what and how they were learning.

- What are you finding difficult?
- What learning strategies work for you, for example, by listening or by watching and copying someone else?
- How are you practising?
- How many people are only using one or two fingers to play the melody?
- How can we plan appropriate fingering?
- What are your top three tips that might help somebody else to learn this piece?

They were also asked to listen to a couple of people perform and to give feedback and set targets: for example, plan appropriate fingering.

Section 3

They listened to the theme again and were asked questions about the accompaniment such as 'What do you notice about the bass part'? The teacher used a powerpoint slide to display the notes E and B and asked, 'Can anybody hear what is happening to the B?—it is rising to C, C# and back to C) The teacher demonstrated this on a keyboard and set a new task (ten minutes) to learn the accompaniment

Section 4

The teacher demonstrated how the two parts fit together and asked the students to do this individually or with a partner.

Section 5: Plenary: Self-assessment task and target-setting activity

Outcomes of lesson 1

In this lesson the students were well motivated and stayed on task. They liked the piece of music and were motivated by their success. The lesson was broken into bite-size chunks and the targets were clear. By the end of the lesson they had all made progress and some went away making comments like 'that was cool—can we do it again next week?'

The student's self-assessments showed they were generally able to identify what they could do but very few had planned an appropriate target. This section was either left blank or had a comment like

'I need to concentrate harder'

'I need a better beat'

'I talk too much'

'I can't do it by ear'

'I need to remember my pencil and pens'

The teacher decided that she wanted their individual target-setting to be sharper and more related to musical outcomes so she started the next lesson with a target-setting activity. We devised a card sort using statements similar to the ones above but also included some more focused musical targets. These statements were photocopied onto different coloured card, cut up, and put into envelopes

I need to make sure my piece has a good beat	I need to concentrate better
My target is to listen more	I need to plan appropriate fingering
In order to improve my performance I need to practise carefully	I talk too much
I want to learn to play all of the notes in the piece	I need to remember a pen and pencil
I need to learn the right hand first and then the left hand	I can't do it by ear
I can only learn if I have the notes	I need to improve my listening skills so that I can play by ear

At the start of the next lesson the students were asked to work in groups of four and to sort the cards into columns of musical targets and non-musical targets. We discussed with the students what 'SMART' targets look like in music and asked the students to rewrite their target from the previous week.

They responded really well to this task, their target-setting improved, and they were increasingly able to take more responsibility for their own learning.

The teacher went on to teach the class about block, broken, and 'oom pah' chord patterns. They were asked to listen to the beginning of some pieces from a range of styles and cultures that used block, broken, and oom pah chord patterns e.g. 'Lose Yourself' by Eminem, the 'Moonlight' Sonata by Beethoven, 'Beautiful' by Christina Aguilera, 'Politik' by Coldplay, and then to learn a short phrase using broken or block chords from one of the songs. These activities were effective at engaging the students and made them much more positive about music lessons.

The examples below describe other activities that the teacher tried with the same group of de-motivated students later in the term. She decided that after a number of closed and structured tasks the students were ready to try some more open-ended activities. She tried a listening task similar to the Batman activity described earlier but using the piece of music 'Praise You' by Fatboy Slim. The students were given a selection of twenty cards with statements like the ones below:

The piece was composed in 1998	Most of the song is based around the opening 2-bar piano loop
The piano loop is based on 3 chords F, C and G.	The use of the piano and the crackly scratched record effect give the song a 'retro' feel
Fatboy Slim's real name is Norman Cook	The time signature of 'Praise You' is 4/4

The class was divided into groups of about four to six students and the cards divided equally among the group. The students were given key questions and asked to listen to an extract from 'Praise You' by Fatboy Slim.

- What features of the music give this piece a 'retro' feel?
- What are the key features of dance music that are used in this music?
- Describe the musical features that make this piece effective.

The students were asked to place the cards in turn on the table. Cards placed at the centre of the table were the most important answers to the question, ones placed around the outside of the table were irrelevant/don't answer the question. The task was complete when everyone agreed where to place each card. After a discussion each student was asked to write a sentence answering the question.

The student's response to this task surprised the teacher. She spent time before the lesson organizing the class into small groups so that the students with more challenging behaviour and poor concentration were supported by more motivated students. This strategy worked well and the students responded to the challenge in a mature and responsible way. They enjoyed the activity and their sentence writing used musical vocabulary well.

She used a similar strategy as a practical starter task. The teacher devised a set of mini-tasks based on chords, like the ones below. The students were divided into pairs and given a task that matched their stage of learning. They were given just ten minutes to complete the task.

Make up a very short piece that shows the difference between major and minor chords. You have 7 minutes to complete the task.	Make up a very short piece that shows the difference between broken and block chords. You have 7 minutes to complete the task.
Make up a very short piece that uses oom pah chords and block chords. You have 7 minutes to complete the task.	Make up a very short piece with an alberti bass. You have 7 minutes to complete the task.
Make up a very short piece that uses only the chords of E minor and G. You have 7 minutes to complete the task.	Make up a very short piece that demonstrates the difference between unison and harmony. You have 7 minutes to complete the task.
Using single fingered chords on a keyboard make up a very short piece that uses the chords Am and G. You have 7 minutes to complete the task.	Make up a very short piece using only the chord of D minor. You have 7 minutes to complete the task.

The students said that they enjoyed the mini composition tasks because they were expected to work quickly, the tasks were challenging but 'fun', and it 'made them think about the things they had learned'. However, the more extended composition tasks were generally the most difficult to manage with more challenging students. These students were well motivated by the very structured four-part lesson with plenty of short and achievable activities, familiar routines, and musical examples that they liked. They were much less focused when asked to create their own pieces unless they had access to sequencing software on computers.

In order to address these issues the teacher tried to maintain the four-part structure of the lessons so that students had a maximum of fifteen minutes on a composition task. She also started to devise some 'composition scaffolds' for students who were easily distracted or lacked the confidence to get started. They were given one card at a time with some instructions. Once they had completed the short task on the card they would receive a reward such as a sticker or point towards a merit and a new composition card. The first few cards contained closed tasks involving little scope for creativity. As the students built up confidence the composition tasks became more open ended.

Examples of composition scaffolds

Card 1

Use chords	A minor (notes A, C, E) and G major (notes G, B, D)
Play	A minor as a block chord 4 times G major as a block chord 4 times

Card 2

Use chords	A minor (notes A, C, E) and G major (notes G, B, D)
Play	A minor as a broken chord 4 times (A, C, E, C) G major as a broken chord 4 times (G, B, D, B)

The teacher's evaluation of the effectiveness of the musical learning in this project was very sharp. One of her conclusions was that the composition scaffolds supported the students with behaviour problems well but that the tasks were too closed for the more able students. One of her targets was to introduce some higher-level questioning and thinking challenges such as:

◆ What if you changed the major chords to minor and vice versa—what would the effect be on the mood of your piece?

◆ Try changing the type of accompaniment from block to broken chords—what is the effect of this change?

◆ What would be the effect of changing the tempo?

◆ Create a lullaby from the chord sequence that you have chosen. How could you change the mood of the lullaby to create tension as if something sinister was about to happen in a movie?

A key feature of this teacher's work that led to an improvement in motivation and challenge was her desire to try out different teaching strategies and to talk to the students about their musical interests and learning. She sought and valued their feedback. She used one particular class as the focus for this experiment and she involved the class in the process. They responded well and their behaviour improved. One of the things that this particular group of students had asked for at the beginning of this project was to learn some more 'up to date' music. The teacher made this a priority and kept asking for feedback from the students about the choice of music.

Choosing music that appeals to students

Using music that students are familiar with from the media and popular culture is an obvious way to engage the majority of young people. However, 'pop' music is still sometimes frowned upon as inferior and not 'real' music by teachers many of whom (like myself as an NQT) relate to more traditional and potentially highly regarded musical pathways. There is an apparent hierarchy in music that views western art music as a higher and more worthy form of musical achievement than popular culture. Chapter 1 of this book addresses several issues that flow from this and how schools sometimes welcome a particularly narrow musical focus because it can be used to promote a higher-status view of a school. Does a similar hierarchy exist in other subjects? English and Drama teachers seem to use popular culture and media very effectively in lessons, even in well-regarded schools. They use it as a way to motivate and engage students, to bring material of a range of styles to life, and to teach the skills that are needed for young people to make decisions as consumers, audiences, and members of an ever-changing society.

Peter Dunbar-Hall considers one of the reasons why popular music is a difficult area for music teachers:

Popular music, despite its existence on syllabuses in various forms, is still a problem area for many teachers. This is due to a number of factors: both the study of popular music styles and methods for teaching them are missing from many tertiary courses; the mainly art music backgrounds of many music teachers act against an understanding of popular music; there is a shortage of critical material in this area to which music teachers can refer; and an accepted model for teaching popular music has not yet been developed.[9]

We clearly need to address this problem. Choosing music that the students like will have a positive impact on their learning. For example, teaching them

---

[9] P. Dunbar-Hall, 'Designing a Teaching Model for Popular Music', in Gary Spruce (ed.), *Teaching Music* (Maidenhead: Open University Press, 2000), 217.

to play a carefully chosen bass riff from a piece of music that is relevant in their lives will usually engage and motivate even the most difficult of students. Their initial reaction might be that the piece you have chosen is 'crap' but in my experience this is usually because they are scared of failing. As soon as they realize that they can play it, the activity becomes more acceptable and the sense of achievement is obvious. The popular style helps them to engage because it seems relevant and acceptable.

The Musical Futures Project sponsored by the Paul Hamlyn Foundation features a project based on the informal learning model devised by Professor Lucy Green from the Institute of Education, University of London. In this project teachers are encouraged to reflect on how pop musicians learn and to act as facilitators enabling students to 'learn alongside friends, through independent, self-directed learning'. The project claims to offer ways to 'bridge the gap between students' musical lives and interests outside the classroom and the experiences of music in school'. Projects such as this one might begin to break down the barriers and make pop music a more acceptable medium for meeting the needs of the majority of young people.

Conclusion

It seems to me, however, that the most important factor of all in setting out to improve motivation is to develop a mind set that is inclusive and which doesn't just cater for the minority of motivated musicians, but values and transmits positive feedback to all students—the type of approach that Will Taylor advocates so eloquently in his views on the curriculum in Chapter 4. Students understand very quickly when someone has already written them off as a trouble-maker or a non-musician (even though this is not articulated). The hidden curriculum operates through more subtle signals. The Specialist Schools and Academies Trust vision of a Music College, 2003, underlined the importance of valuing all students. It stated that music colleges will 'encourage their students to develop a lifelong passion for, and appreciation of, music not only as composers and performers but also as audiences, technicians and critics'.[10]

In order to achieve this vision at KS3 we need to:

- teach all students to become independent musical learners
- use resources that are relevant to their needs interests and prior experiences
- improve pace and challenge in music lessons

---

[10] DfES, Specialist Schools and Academies Trust, *The Music Specialism: Application Criteria and Guidance for Specialist Music College Status* (London: HMSO, 2003).

- ensure that all students have the opportunity to be creative, search for solutions, and develop their thinking skills whether performing, composing, or listening to music
- ask for feedback from the students and listen to and respond to their comments.

These things will help students to be more interested and motivated in all year groups. They are certainly features that are exhibited by really effective teachers. These teachers do, however, have one other characteristic that is absolutely crucial. They are interested in the learning needs of all students. In fact they are often just interested in students, regardless of their backgrounds or prior experience. For these teachers the focus is not just on the musicians (supplemented by a time-occupying series of tokenistic activities for the remaining majority). The climate they create in their classroom says 'I am interested in all the students in this school and I will not make assumptions about your abilities, musical styles you are interested in, or what your potential is'. This approach often ensures that the musical activities are relevant, that students enjoy them, and feel that they can make progress. The students who are fortunate enough to encounter this approach respond to it very well. In truth, however, many music teachers find it difficult to break through the barrier of their own experiences, prejudices, and assumptions about musicians (and by implication non-musicians) in schools. A musical school will understand these issues and have strategies to address them successfully.

Chapter 6

Music across the curriculum

Diana Pearman

In this chapter Diana Pearman, Deputy Head Teacher, Northampton School for Girls Specialist Music College, describes the work that she led to create a culture of music across the curriculum. The work was based on an approach promoted by a commercial organization that had developed work on learning styles and how music could be used to accelerate and contribute to learning. This project was embraced strongly by the school and used to complement similar work on learning styles that had been developed over several years. Diana was a very powerful force behind creating the momentum to make it happen right across the school. The approach provides an interesting example of how a particular approach to music across the curriculum can be used and the fact that a whole school project can have an effect if there is the right amount of energy behind it.

> Music is the manifestation of the human spirit, similar to language. Its greatest practitioners have conveyed to mankind things not possible to say in any other language. If we do not want these things to remain dead treasures, we must do our utmost to make the greatest possible number of people understand their idiom.
>
> Kodály

Where did we start our journey?

We became a school that focused on teaching and learning as its top priority, with the appointment of the current Head, in January 1998. Both she and I had come from schools outside Northamptonshire and were astonished at the

---

Contributors: Elizabeth Bonner, Head of RE; Martin Barratt, Head of Geography; Jackie Broadaway, Advanced Skills Teacher; Ita Casey, English and Film Studies; Alison Curran, English Teacher; Margaret Finch, Head of Art; Jane MacDonald, Gifted and Talented Coordinator.

underachievement of the students we were teaching. For me they were very similar girls to the ones I had previously taught who were gaining 78 per cent grade C and above at GCSE (some 50 per cent above the NSG results). Alongside our shared view about underachievement was the research she had pursued for her MBA qualification, based on using the Cognitive Abilities Test scores to raise teachers' expectations. The only limit to what students can achieve is what the teachers think they can do. When the Head introduced her theories, she showed the graphs that demonstrated how students in her previous school had achieved not only their target grade but way beyond those grades. Subsequently there were howls from the staff at the 'unrealistic' National Curriculum target levels and GCSE grades set for each NSG student (which in our case were one above the NFER Cognitive Abilities expectations, because we only have girls in our school!).

My MA research had been to investigate ways in which teachers worked together to improve teaching and learning in schools where achievement was either consistently high or had been dramatically raised in a short time. There appeared to be a number of models of working which were successful. This led in the early days to us working with a project known as the Raising Standards Project (RSP). A key figure emerged in the form of Ian Gilbert, whose influence over subsequent events has been monumental. I established a 'Learning Action' group, a successful model of teachers working together. There were a number of willing volunteer teachers and Ian came to work with them, sometimes as individuals and other times in small subject groups. His mission was to incorporate a range of multiple intelligence approaches into schemes of work in as many subjects as I could find volunteers. As a model for staff development it was very powerful. The teachers who actively engaged with it knew what they needed to do and were then able to put it into practice and more significantly develop it on their own. The signal for success for me was when teachers felt they had outgrown his advice and it was no longer needed. This was not always a shared perspective as many continued to seek help and advice from him and then felt frustrated that it was more of the same ideas. These same teachers were experienced practitioners, still looking for the 'Holy Grail' and not realizing how good they were and that perhaps a different source of inspiration was required for them, so that they might feel renewed.

Two other influences began to shape the reality of what 'music across the curriculum' meant for us. Nina Jackson was a practising music teacher in a school in Wales and researching for her doctorate on how music could be used as a tool for learning in classrooms. The second inspiration came from further afield, New Zealand this time, in the form of Barbara Prashnig and a course in Manchester called The Magic of Music.

However, the story needs further clarification at this point in order for the history of our experience to be understood. The members of the Learning Action group were given the opportunity to share their expertise with the whole staff on a training day way back in 2002 and, subsequently, using multiple intelligence approaches in every lesson and subject became a whole-school priority. We devised a learning plan which had the various intelligences printed as a border to remind us all, as we prepared each lesson, that we should be looking for ways to include activities to support this approach. On one of the training days we developed our vision for the new school based on the use of Howard Gardner's theory of the multiple intelligences. All of the teachers were allocated to a linguistic, naturalistic, visual, mathematical, intrapersonal, interpersonal, or musical group and worked together to develop their vision for our new Music College. They then presented their ideas using their 'intelligence' style to do so. It was the group that used music which captured and engaged everyone's attention!

The influence of Howard Gardner's multiple intelligence theory

We remain firmly wedded to the idea that engaging all learners in at least a significant part of each lesson can and does raise achievement. Howard Gardner in his book *The Unschooled Mind* argues that 'the broad spectrum of students . . . would be better served if disciplines could be presented in a number of ways and learning could be assessed through a variety of means'.[1] If I remember correctly Paul Black, in his work *Inside the black box,* was advocating a variety of assessment techniques some eleven years ago![2] Subsequently we have incorporated Gardner's ideas into revision techniques, memory strategies, and the principle has been overlain by the three-part lesson and assessment for learning, which have added to our rigour and pedagogy.

The one aspect that we had not really developed up to this point was the musical intelligence and how this might help us to raise achievement across the school. It was this that provided us with the whole-school priority for the Music College—music across the curriculum.

---

[1] Howard Gardner, *The Unschooled Mind* (New York: Basic Books, 1991).

[2] Paul Black and Dylan Wiliam, *Inside the black box: raising standards through classroom assessment* (Kings College, London University, 1998).

Why did we choose to become a Specialist Music College?

So back to 'Why Music?'. This was our situation back in 2003 when we decided to try to become a Music College. Our Director of Music, working entirely on her own, although ably supported by a team of peripatetic teachers, had established a local reputation for our extra-curricular music.

Under her direction, students who learned to play musical instruments were able to train in ensembles and orchestras run by the peripatetic teachers, and performed in termly concerts. She also worked with a local businessman and our Director of Drama to produce various shows that included primary-age children, our students, and adult members of the community, often professional actors themselves. So although Drama was a strong department it made sense for us to focus on music, partly because the opportunity arose while we were making our decision; that is, it coincided with the Specialist Schools Trust announcement that Music was a newly created specialism.

It is worth emphasizing here that our choice of music as the specialist subject was rooted in two strong influences, one being the strength of aspects of the department and the other the importance of the use of Howard Gardner's theories, and our desire to develop the musical intelligence.

Music 'has a miraculous effect on learning too—children have been shown to do better in class, to concentrate and behave more calmly. And that's when they're only listening to music. When they start playing, it opens up a world of possibilities.'[3]

Our fundamental belief in the inclusion of all students in all aspects of the curriculum fed another of our targets: to increase the range and number of students learning to play a musical instrument. There has always been a belief that students who learn to play a musical instrument develop good listening skills, motivation, and focus. However, one of the other learning outcomes was that these students also achieved highly at school. The suggested link between these two aspects was that these students largely came from families where there was plenty of money to pay for the lessons and that the nature of the home and level of support were probably more relevant factors (rather than learning to play a musical instrument per se) and that this led to their offspring's high achievement. However, a significant research study in Canada found that all students, from a range of socio-economic backgrounds, achieve well at school if they learn to play a musical instrument and, more recently, this has been further substantiated by a similar study in American

[3] Amanda Holloway, 'Seven Musical Ages of Man', *Classic fm Magazine* (February 2006).

schools. Professor Susan Hallam from the Institute of Education at the University of London adds further evidence from her research: 'Learning to play an instrument has demonstrable effects on intelligence and, when children play music together, teaches them about cooperation and working together'.[4]

Is music the 'master intelligence'? (Gardner)—music as a tool for learning

It seemed to us that increasing the access to a student's musical intelligence would add to our students' classroom experience and when used as an effective tool for learning would then increase students' listening ability and raise achievement. However, as with all whole-school initiatives, engaging teachers' hearts and minds is where we needed to begin. As the Music College was launched in September 2004 it became the cohesive force for bringing the new secondary school together. It was a new and exciting prospect for everyone. On one of the training days before term started Julie, the Music Director, and I introduced the staff to some of the ideas we had learned at the 'Magic of Music' conference.

In the afternoon we listened to, and were inspired by, Nina Jackson and the use of music in a variety of classrooms operating in her school. She gave us access to the CDs that she had compiled for her research and so began the great classroom experiments.

Educational innovation is frequently dependent on systems that work, and without them good ideas rarely see the light of day. So the use of the CDs, players, and lockable cupboards (to keep them safe) that made these ideas a reality were organized by two key appointments within the Music College. The first was our administrator and the second a technician. Both of these appointments were crucial to the early success of the Music College, and as a small part of their work they certainly enabled the 'music across the curriculum' initiative by organizing and setting up CD players and CDs for the 104 teachers on our staff. As well as providing CDs, Greg, the technician, maintained our 'state of the art' music technology room, which was a prime funding activity as soon as we gained the status, as much of our other capital spend was caught up in the politics of new build and PFI.

The potential of music to improve students' learning and motivation in the secondary school is a claim made by researchers and investigated by Nina Jackson. Her findings suggests that music has the potential to motivate students, and improve concentration and study skills—thus aiding learning.

The research Nina led in her school resulted in the compilation of a series

---

[4] Susan Hallam, *Music Psychology in Education* (University of London, January 2006).

of CDs, and by following her recommendations we were able to create a school of positive learning. Methods such as accelerated learning empowered pupils to access information with the aid of music, thus producing an enhanced learning environment. The CDs we used are based on grouping pieces of music together that have different beats and timings; pieces for

- getting the mind ready for learning and remembering and for problem-solving
- releasing the stress in the classroom and for students to relax or calm as they enter the lesson
- energizing and stimulating brain activity before learning a new concept
- reflection, during the review part of the lesson
- a signal to change activity in a lesson.

Our vision to have music in every classroom was intended to become a strategy to provide access to every student's learning style at some point in the lesson. It was to be seen as another tool for learning, just as every teaching room might have access to computers, books, whiteboards, and other resources, to enhance the learning of our students. Music engages the emotions: for example music that is loud and fast increases metabolism, whilst slow and quiet music calms us down. It can be used to heal and self-help the individual and will assist us in our support of youngsters who are disturbed by events in their past and current lives.

'Sound waves make brain waves'

We believe that music plays with our state of mind; it creates brain waves and influences the frequency of these waves. The human brain can be considered to have two parts to it and education has traditionally focused on the left brain as a filing system to store large numbers of facts. The right side of the brain is engaged through our emotions and is often not used effectively in classrooms. Ironically it is the right side of the brain where the long-term memory is found. Music can be used as the carrier signal to provide the bridge between the left and right brain, thereby significantly increasing students' memory and retention. The outcome is to make students more successful learners.

Particular types of music need to be used for different activities. Certain music can prime the mind ready to receive complex information, such as mathematical theorems, while relaxing music can set the scene and calm the students ready for positive learning, particularly in subjects that need to engage the emotions. If the lesson is particularly long and there is a dip in students' concentration, then music can be played to stimulate and energize and will refocus the students' minds on their learning. Relevant pieces of music can set the scene—for example, playing the *Stars Wars* theme could be used as an introduction to a Discovering Space lesson in Science—while at the end of a lesson music can help students focus on what has been learned and help them with the successful storage of the information.

The opportunities are limitless, the benefits only restricted by our selection of the pieces of music we play. Put simply in the words of Nina Jackson:

- listening to music in lessons helps students' concentration and study skills
- listening to music in lessons makes students feel happy, relaxed and ready for work
- listening to music in lessons helps students achieve more.[5]

Starting the good practice

By 2004 the staff had a clear understanding of why we wanted to introduce the use of music in their classrooms and felt it was equally important that the students knew why we were introducing this approach and that they heard a consistent message. So in a series of assemblies during early October the students had explained to them the rationale for this work and hopefully at the very minimum they remembered the newspaper balls winging their way across the theatre to represent the sound waves. This was intended to show how the sound waves, triggered by music, connect the two parts of the brain, our analytical and creative parts, and enable us to make learning more effective. And the teachers were reminded too!

The rationale was based on a simplified version of how the brain works. The brain is made up of a hundred billion neurons. Each neuron can have between 1 and 10,000 connections to other neurons. This means the different patterns of connections possible in a single brain is approximately 40,000,000,000,000,000. Music seems to have the ability to create extra links between neurons—almost like extra motorways between brain cells. Imagine a series of links being created in the brain by the process of engaging with music. These links would be made by music's unique ability to give access to both the right and left hemispheres of the brain. Described differently, music is the carrier signal for dual brain thinking and the interstate highway to the memory system. Music also has an ability to connect these two parts and assist the learning process. This connection was symbolized in assembly by the newspaper balls being tossed from left to right

---

5 Nina Jackson, 'Music and the mind' in Ian Gilbert (ed.), *The Big Book of Independent Thinking* (Carmarthen: Crown House Publishing, 2006), 32.

and back across the theatre. The importance of this connection is that the left brain tends to deal with more analytical and word-driven tasks (language and logic), predominantly the type of education seen in our schools for many years, whereas right brain favours more creativity and spatial ability (perception and abstract, intuitive leaps). Music fires the neural activity and makes brain waves which can connect us to our right brain and here we can find a much better long-term memory system where the more effective use of this storage system can lead potentially to more effective learning, better examination results and higher point scores on the league tables . . .

It was important that we developed a way of measuring what if any difference in practice was occurring in classrooms. So I compiled a learning styles checklist that included a range and variety of activities likely to be happening in our classrooms (which also reflected the use of multiple intelligence strategies) and asked for six volunteer students from each tutor group to keep this inventory for a week. In every lesson they attended they were asked to tick the box where they had been involved in one of the learning styles. These were returned and collated and this became the benchmark so that we could compare what was to happen in the future. The whole learning styles inventory grid is not collated here, but those sections relevant to music have been abstracted in Table 4.

Progress was slow in the first year. Our teachers were grappling with the demands of teaching years 7 and 8 for the first time and many were travelling between two sites several times a week. Those who did experiment became very concerned that 'they were not doing it right', as though there was a magic formula for us all to work to. It seemed that we were all lacking in confidence and so another invitation was issued to Nina Jackson to run a further training day. This time it was felt the emphasis should be on the fact that she had been conducting research and had discovered many benefits from the use of music

Table 4 Checklist of learning styles, years 9–13 and 7–8, with special reference to music, showing number of times each style was used in a lesson

Types of music	2004	2005		2006	
	Years 9–13	Years 9–13	Years 7–8	Years 9–13	Years 7–8
Use of music to memorize	5	12	9	17	42
Music for calming	10	52	52	17	97
Music to energize	21	47	21	12	60
Music connected to subject	21	42	18	39	62
Music as background	40	42	36	23	117
Surveys returned	**56**	**63**	**17**	—	—

that we could learn from and apply in our situation. Our aim was to try to implement a whole-school approach and across all subjects. The research model used by Nina had clearly been very successful and had recruited willing volunteers who must have felt well supported by the information they provided for her and the feedback thereby gained. Her theme for the day was 'Making learning powerful with Music and the Mind' and our staff evaluation was very positive.

As part of this teacher training day subject teams worked together to decide their aspects of development for 'music across the curriculum' in their subject. Selected priorities are listed here and commented upon later.

Focus areas for using music in lessons

Each subject group decided on the areas that they wanted to focus on for using music in lessons:

English

To improve the reading habits of year 9 students and thereby increase their levels in the Key Stage 3 tests.

Art

To introduce themed music linked to the taught curriculum.
To use music as a mid-lesson reward in order to refocus student concentration.

Geography

To experiment with the 'Mozart' effect to aid content recall.

History

To use music as a lesson starter and for plenaries.

RE

To use music for reflection and to support the content.
To use music as a lesson starter, for example, Christian music and other chants.

Research and development during the second year

The second year of the Music College saw some really exciting examples of teachers experimenting with music in their classrooms. A number of ground rules were decided upon in the early days:

◆ the teachers, not the students, decided the type of music to be used in their classroom

- students were not allowed to listen to their MP3 players throughout any lesson
- music was not to be used as background 'musak', so that it just became 'wallpaper'.

In my work as a history teacher of mostly GCSE classes, I have used a range of music for different purposes. As an introduction to the lesson as students enter the classroom I like to have a piece of music playing that is linked to the content, so, for example, when we are studying Roman medicine the theme from *Gladiator* is playing; when it is the Homesteaders, as part of the American West, then it is *Oklahoma*; or Ghost Dance music when studying the final destruction of the Native American way of life. Students respond very positively as it is an up-beat introduction to the lesson. During the lesson, when an activity requires concentration, I have experimented with a variety of pieces. One example (first heard in Cesar Madrigues cave) uses chime bells and has a very slow beat, and this was played while students were working on individual tasks. At the end of lessons when the learning is being reviewed I have used many examples of music for personal reflection and realization.

Music in Personal, Social, and Health Education

Jackie, our advanced skills teacher, used music in a Personal, Social, and Health Education lesson to show the students how it can affect their mood and how it can help them to memorize information more effectively. She writes:

I have used music in the classroom in many ways; one in particular was in PSHE. I wanted my students to understand how and why music could help their learning, and how they responded to music in their lives.

As the students entered the room I judged their moods. If I felt they needed soothing I played 'Intermezzo' or if they were sluggish, 'I'm a Believer'. I then used the traffic lights system for them to let me know how effective they thought the pieces were at changing/supporting their state, ready for learning.

I then asked them to complete the Harvey's response to music intelligences to 'Dream Chunnate'. The timing gave a musical support to the length of time I wanted the activity to take.

We shared their findings in groups, with friends to identify interesting points about their friendships, who they liked working with, who they worked best with, or not. Did their preferences reflect their learning styles? We brainstormed how they responded to music in their lives and shared our thoughts. As a class we looked at an overhead transparency of the brain and what functions were left- and right-side governed and discussed what they thought were the effects of music on their learning.

We then experimented with learning a set of facts to music—also linking them to a memory technique, 'one bun two shoe . . .'. Whilst they learned the facts I played

'Captain Scarlett's Theme' (1 min., 51 secs) to support the learning of facts. The track also became the music 'trigger'. They then wrote down as many of the facts as they could using the music to aid their memory. We repeated the process with ten facts of their own choice, for example some chose elements from the Periodic table. They set themselves really boring facts (in their opinions) that they had trouble remembering using the song '21 seconds' as the trigger this time. They felt that the technique and the music helped.

We reviewed the learning to 'Cappriccio for Chinese Flute' by thinking over and reviewing the lessons in their heads. The next week the lesson started with a graph of how much they thought they should remember of the previous lesson. We then did a quick individual test, I played the first 'trigger' piece of music and asked them to write down the facts. Then the second 'trigger' piece and repeated the task. For both sets of information 90 per cent could recall all twenty of the facts, the other 10 per cent between 80 and 89 per cent; an effective piece of learning.

Music in English lessons

Three further English teachers describe their experiments with music in their lessons, to enhance year 9 students' concentration in silent reading at the beginning of a lesson, as a technique to add meaning to a poem, and as a stimulus for creative writing.

The focus for the English team, agreed on the training day, was to use music to improve year 9 reading habits. Here Alison, one of the team, describes her evaluation of the work:

Like any other teacher in the English Department I use music regularly in my lessons to set up a theme or infer a context, to stimulate images, to develop concepts, plots, or characters and also to extend language and skills. As a department we agreed at the beginning of this academic year to use music to set the mood for a Private Reading Focus for all year 9s, the rationale being that if students are encouraged to read and share their reading, their language skills, and ultimately their Key Stage 3 reading levels, should improve. In the past our reading levels have been weaker than writing scores.

I begin every year 9 English lesson with 5–10 minutes of private reading. As students come into the classroom calm music is playing and they know to come in silently, take their seats and get out the materials they need for the lesson as well as their reading books. I evaluated this approach using a student questionnaire at Easter. Without exception, in all three groups I teach, students were positive about both the use of music and private reading.

Some typical comments were:

'The music helps me concentrate and helps me get ready for learning' (Martha)

'The music is calming and great for setting the scene for reading' (Zoe)

'Certain songs made me remember the bits from my book' (Lauren)

'The music makes me concentrate and gets me hooked on the book' (Emma)

'Starting English lessons with private reading and music has a great effect on the rest of the lesson. I feel ready and alert afterwards' (Charlotte)

'The music helped me read more of my book. Thank you' (Stacey)

'The music made me feel focused' (Serena)

'The music made me relax and feel more confident of reading' (Holly)

'The music has helped me get into a routine' (Becky)

Jane describes a lesson where she uses song lyrics to emphasize the interplay of language and music:

For this lesson I use the Simon and Garfunkel song 'The Sound of Silence' in order to demonstrate the way lyric writers make use of many of the devices commonly found in poetry, particularly those associated with sound, and how these combine with the music to reinforce the meaning. We listen to the song a couple of times, trying to listen carefully to the words. We listen a third time reading the words at the same time.

Looking at the lyrics, we discuss the techniques used. There are examples of oxymorons, personification, metaphors, similes, alliteration, and imagery patterns in the verses, and by studying these we try to explore the writer's meaning. We also look closely at the use of rhyming couplets and the effect of disrupting this with the chorus/refrain line. Once we've grappled with the meaning of the lyrics, we listen again to the song and think about the way the music enhances the meaning by such things as adding emotion, atmosphere, emphasis, and tone. The students begin to see how a song creates meaning by utilizing both language and music, working in careful interplay.

The example above is just a snapshot of the work developed by the English department. The whole year group at NSG take English Literature GCSE, taught in a mixed-ability situation, and they have to study a huge number of poems. The team have used music and the lyrics to give association to the poetry studied and thereby made it more accessible and memorable for the students. The impact upon GCSE results has been significant.

The mnemonic power of music is still evident in modern culture. Many of us remember the words of songs and poems more accurately than we can remember prose. The notion that music facilitates memory has been objectively confirmed by the study of 'mentally retarded' children who can recall more material after it is given to them in a song than after it is read to them as a story.[6]

The poems have been linked with different pieces of music to help the students respond to the poetry in a variety of ways. The English team try to avoid too much classical music as they feel this tends to turn students off, though some examples are included. The students are fantastic at matching the songs and poems, a useful homework/revision exercise (see Table 5).

---

[6] P. R. Farnsworth, *The Social Psychology of Music* (Iowa: Iowa State University Press, 1969), quoted in Nina Jackson, 'Music and the Mind' in Ian Gilbert (ed.), *The Big Book of Independent Thinking* (Carmarthen: Crown House Publishing, 2006), 33.

Table 5 Linking poems to particular styles of music

Poem	Style of music
Limbo	Sitting in Limbo—The Best of Jimmy Cliff
Nothing's Changed	South African National Anthem any Ladysmith Mumbazo
Island man	Kokomo—Beach Boys
Blessing	Sanctus—Libera Wade in the Water—Eva Cassidy
Two Scavengers in a truck	Take It Easy—Eagles
Night of the Scorpion	Amyad Ali Khan—track 9 American Dream—Jakatta
Vultures	Schindler's List
What were they like	Tayal Folk Song
from Search from my tongue	Brimful of Asha—Cornershop
from Unrelated incidents	Throw the R away—The Proclaimers
Half-caste	Ebony and Ivory—Stevie Wonder Melting Pot—Blue Mink
Love after love	What Becomes of the Broken hearted—Jimmy Ruffin
Not my business	Hurricane—Bob Dylan
Presents from my aunts	anything from Bollywood any Bhangra
Hurricane hits England	Stormy Weather—classic Singing in the Rain—Gene Kelly
Storm on the Island	Riders on the Storm—The Doors
Death of a Naturalist	Frog Chorus—Paul McCartney
Digging	The JCB Song—Nislopi
Mid-Term Break	Funeral March Abide with Me On Earth as it is in Heaven—from *The Mission*
Follower	Father and Son—Cat Stevens The JCB Song—Nislopi
At a Potato Digging	Feed the World—Band Aid
Catrin	No Charge—Tammy Wynett My Momma Said—Abba
Baby-sitting	Little Children—Billy J Kramer
The Field Mouse	The Voyage—Christie Moore
On the Train	Good People—Jack Johnson
Cold Knap Lake	Search for the Hero Inside Yourself—M People Memories—Barbara Streisand

On My First Sonne	Tears in Heaven—Eric Clapton
The Song of the Old Mother	No Charge—Tammy Wynette
The Affliction of Margaret	Missing—Everything but the Girl
Titchbourne's Elegy	Theme music from *The Green Mile*
The Man he Killed	Brothers in Arms—Dire Straits In the Army Now—Status Quo War—Edwin Star
Patrolling Barnegat	Massive Attack—Several of these would suit
Sonnet 130	Summer Time
The Laboratory	Toxic—Britney Spears
The Village Schoolmaster	Another Brick in the Wall—Pink Floyd To Sir with Love—Lulu
The Eagle	Eagle—Abba from Thank you for the Music
Inversnaid	Wind Chimes
Sonnet	Four Seasons—Vivaldi

Ita describes her use of music for learning:

One example in which I found the use of music to be a significant enhancer to learning was when introducing a narrative writing unit to Key Stage 4 English students. The overall objective being to produce a piece of original writing coursework for Writing to Imagine, Explore, Entertain (EN3). The music introduction to this unit was a success and I have used a variation of this with several GCSE classes.

I chose to use particular music in a proactive way to fire the students' imagination and to stimulate ideas about any imagery present within the chosen songs. Students understood that the chosen music had a specific outcome and this would prepare them for later activities. Students would later be expected to analyse the use of imagery, presentation of characters, and use of sound within extracts from a variety of film genres. These would act as stimulus for individual story writing.

Music is a relevant and effective introduction to such a unit as it requires careful attention and the development of listening skills. Each piece of music should be accompanied by a choice of activities; therefore students participating would need to be fully engaged with the music. Suggested activities which I find most useful and suitable for personalized learning include mind mapping of imagined events and key words, storyboarding of the imagined events, free drawing, and writing lists of the imagery that comes to mind while listening to the music.

Resources required for such a lesson included an MP3 or CD player and several music CDs that set a particular scene or tell a story. I found Michael Jackson's 'Thriller' to be highly effective and was delighted with the range in responses from students. One example in which I found the use of music to be a significant enhancer to learning was when introducing a narrative writing unit to Key Stage 4 English students, the overall objective being to produce a piece of original writing coursework for Writing to Imagine, Explore, Entertain (EN3). The music introduction to this unit was a success and I have used a variation of this with several GCSE classes.

Table 6 Northampton School for Girls, Key Stage 3 results in reading, 2005–2006

Reading level	2005 (%)	2006 (%)
7	6	25
6	27	38
5	46	27
4	13	6

The fact there is a landmark music video to accompany the song was beneficial and fortunately the students had not seen this before. When they had assessed how the music inspired creative devices such as tension and character analysis within their minds, students watched the video and discussed how the director had chosen to present this imagery. Overall, students were enthusiastic and engaged with learning, discovering the links that run across written, audio, and visual media.

In the second year and after another training day with Nina the subject teams identified their own development targets within their departments. The most outstanding results come from the English team. They had chosen KS3 reading levels as their target and music was used to support the students' individual reading at the beginning of the lesson (see the previously described evaluation by one of the teachers). The results of this strategy are significant and need no further comment:

- in 2005, 6 per cent of students gained a level 7; in 2006 it was 25 per cent
- 27 per cent gained a level 6 and in 2006 it was 38 per cent
- 46 per cent gained level 5 and in 2006 it was 27 per cent
- 13 per cent remained at level 4 and only 6 per cent in 2006

In year 9, 94 per cent were reading at or above level 5 and over the two years there was a 30 per cent increase in the higher levels 5 and 6 (see Table 6).

In 2005 twenty students were either absent or registered N on the reading test. In 2006 only nine students were N or absent. This may be speculation that students now felt more confident about the reading test. What is a fact is that there were more students in 2005 who achieved less well in the reading test than they did on the other parts of the English tests and far fewer in 2006.

Music in Geography

Martin, our Head of Geography, developed an exciting introduction to the study of the European Union (A level topic) that effectively engages students in what might otherwise be considered a rather dry topic.

'Antheming the new European Union'

He writes:

I have a specialism in the political Geography of the European Union, having recently completed a Doctorate in the subject at Durham University. I was thus delighted to find the option appearing in the OCR A level geography course to teach 'Geographical Aspects of the European Union'. Taking this option provides students with an extraordinary insight into the range offered by the subject of Geography. It is the synoptic module, so is intended to bring together all the aspects of physical and human geography studied to date. It goes some way to breaking down the artificial, but too often fiercely guarded, distinction between the sub-disciplines in Geography. It also provides students with a level of knowledge about the EU way beyond that of their peers and even their parents. It is actually the least popular option module on this course, therefore offering rarity value for our students, the majority of whom will go onto study at university level.

All that said, engaging students with the politics of the EU at sixth-form level when they have had very little grounding throughout their earlier studies provides something of a challenge to say the least. This is where one of the many advantages of working in a Specialist Music College comes into play. All our students find it easier to engage with complex ideas through the appropriate use of music, and the following section recounts how music was used in a particular lesson to introduce the very complex issues of national identity, Euro-scepticism, and the need for the new Europe to create a shared sense of belonging—something akin to Anderson's vision of the 'imagined community'.

Students were presented with a series of overhead transparencies which set out the debate around the value of the official European Anthem (set out below). Launched in its revised format in 2000 it has been roundly criticized for presenting Europeans with a vision of the EU that is almost entirely abstract and aspirational. Many commentators suggest this to be symptomatic of the whole policy of involving the peoples of Europe: 'keep telling them how good an idea it is and they will agree in the end.' The students were told that their overall task was to write and perform a 'new anthem, for the new European Union'.

And here are the words, which we all sang to a backing track downloaded from the Europa Website:

The European Anthem Translated into English

Europe is united now
United it may remain;
Our unity in diversity
May contribute to world peace.

May there forever reign in Europe
Faith and justice
And freedom for its people
In a bigger motherland.

Citizens, Europe shall flourish,
A great task calls on you.
Golden stars in the sky
Are the symbols that shall unite us

By way of final preparation for the task of constructing a 'more' effective anthem, students were shown video footage of two national anthems from recent football matches in the World Cup. By studying the different themes presented in both the USA and the British anthem, students were encouraged to appreciate the value of celebrating freedom, and monarchical power respectively. The USA anthem is deferential to a flag, the British anthem deferential to the Queen. The influence of both can clearly be seen in the anthems produced by students (reproduced below).

Students then formed into teams of eight to produce an anthem. Each group first conducted a mind-shower of ideas and great emphasis was placed on all students making an input. The next phase was to organize ideas into coherent themes, and finally to put them to the music. After a number of practice runs the video recorder was switched on and all students performed each anthem (i.e. they all sang each other's). Group work is the only way to approach a task such as this. The bouncing of ideas off each other was a wonderfully creative process and, with pointers and guidance from myself, each was actually able to explain the rationale for the inclusion of their selected phrases and comments.

When evaluating the success of this process, one must separate the fun from the learning. Yes the task was certainly fun, but much more significantly, the learning was intense. At the end of the session, students reported that they had 'felt' a connection with the Union and the process of creating a sense of belonging. They had considered the potential contradictions between national and ethnic identities and how they are effectively scaled up when operating at the supra-national scale of the Union.

Finally, I was able to impress upon students that no matter how heavy the course becomes when discussing the detail of regional policies and decision-taking within the Union, the starting point for understanding remains at the level of the citizenry, of which they are now fully paid up members.

ANTHEM 1

Italy makes the best Lasagne
England's trifle's the best pud
Ikea comes from the land of Sweden
Indeed the meatballs taste quite good

We are the greatest peeled banana
Beaches, mountains are the views
Where else is there this diversity?
And a scene of different shoes

Oh what a joy, what a joy, what a joy
To see the unity in our eyes
Us Europeans will stand together
Let us eat from the same pie

Note: This anthem goes from the banal to the profound in three verses. Starting with popular engagement issues, such as food and furniture, makes people aware that they are part of the Union even though they might not have thought of it in that way. Building to a climax focused on unity and solidarity. The 'peeled banana' reference is to the shape of the so-called hot banana of the EU's economic core. The shoes reference derives from the student's home town of Northampton being famous for shoe manufacturing!

ANTHEM 2

> Europe is flying the flag
> United by the Euro
> Range of land from high to low
> Optimistic for the future
> People will have freedom and peace
> Equal opportunities
> All the countries trade their food
> Nothing will divide us
> Unity and diversity
> Nice flag with a load of gold stars
> Ireland, Great Britain, France and Germany
> Oh what a great Union,
> Norway wants to join us too!

Note: This anthem is more profound throughout; very focused on the high ideals of the Union. Notice the added complexity of the acrostic nature of the lyrics!

Music and art

The Art department decided on a time-scale trial of eight weeks for their use of music. They found that the themed links to lesson plans worked well with year 10. Students listened to minimalist music as part of their Minimalism project and it helped them to focus on meaning and concept of visual characteristics of the art form. Students responded well even though they thought it was 'weird'. After the initial introduction they concentrated and listened well, which supported that series of lessons. In year 9 surrealist music has been used to aid concentration and the development of ideas for teaching Surrealism. Year 8 was the main target for the mid-lesson experiment. Some groups responded well, while others did not respond as well, often due to particular students whose needs were difficult to meet. One of the teachers allowed the students to choose, as a reward, a mid-lesson track and a senior colleague observed that this was done with obvious enjoyment by the students. The advanced level students are currently compiling music to fit with Fibonacci and the theme 'Structures'. Fibonacci also fits with proportions of musical instruments and not just with their sound.

Music in Religious Education

A newly appointed Head of Religious Education has inspired her team and ensured that there is a musical element in the scheme of work for each year group. She describes some of the examples here:

As a department we use a lot of music in Religious Education. It can be very positive to use music thematically to introduce a new concept or simply to confirm learnt information. We use music for reflection on a regular basis, which includes Buddhist Chant music when examining its use as a form of meditation. We are lucky enough to have access to a huge range of religious music from different cultural backgrounds. These add further depth to our lessons and allow the students to explore their own spirituality at the same time.

Our year 7 and 8 lessons about Christian ways of life have all begun with a simple starter activity. Students have been asked to sit down and listen to a different piece of Christian music each week. This has worked really well on many levels; the students no longer think about Christian music as an episode of 'Songs of Praise'. They were asked to give the music a rating 1–5 as to whether it is something that they would listen to again and list places where the music might actually be played. Not only did it change their perception of Christian music but also it made sure that all of our lessons started calmly and with a clear focus on the students' learning.

In year 9 we have used music to reflect and guide the students' thoughts on the difficult topic area of life after death. I have used Enya's 'Now we are Free' from the film *Gladiator* when examining what the afterlife may look like. The students were asked to listen to the piece of music with their eyes closed. When it had finished they then discussed their responses to the music.

◆ How did it make them feel?
◆ What images did they see?
◆ What colours did they see?
◆ What would the piece of music be if it were not music? (For example what kind of building, flower, or animal would it be?)

I have also used music thematically with year 9, using tracks like 'The Circle of Life' to introduce complex ideas such as reincarnation.

In year 10 we use Buddhist Chant music to calm students on entry to the classroom and prepare their minds for study. Buddhism is a complex unit and students must be in the right frame of mind or the lessons are pointless. Buddhism is all about peace and shared understanding; reaching enlightenment is challenging and helped by meditation. The chant music is something they have never come across before and it therefore makes a great impact on the students.

Thematically, I use the U2 song 'Pride' when teaching students about prejudice and discrimination. It has a specific verse that deals with the untimely death of Martin Luther King and gives a religious reference to Jesus' betrayal. This always promotes a lot of discussion and is a song that every year 10 student can identify with on some level.

In year 11 we study a unit called 'Religious responses to the Media'. Within this unit we have a whole lesson dedicated to music. The students listen to a selection of religious and secular music that relates to religious issues. A good example is Joan Osborne's 'One of Us' or Robbie Williams's 'Jesus in a Camper Van'.

In our post-16 lessons music is mainly used to allow the students time to reflect on philosophy studied. It gives a short time to think in a focused manner. It is also a useful tool when teaching about revelation because it can highlight the main issues with witness reliability. A class of thirty students can listen to the same thing but all recall different sections of the music or key lyrics as being more important. Some students even use short bursts of music on which to hang their learning and help them revise at a later date.

Music seems to be a great leveller in RE; it is no longer about who is religious or spiritual or even about what they like or dislike musically, but what they gain from the musical experience on that particular day. We have had great fun using music in RE and will continue to do so, but more importantly it has helped our students to improve their own learning experience.

Some (interim) concluding thoughts

We are mere beginners in this journey to create a school where music operates across the curriculum, but I do feel we have the potential to become a musical school. In the first chapter of this book David describes the features that might be found in such a school. One of them is about innovative teaching and learning, and many exciting examples appear in this chapter illustrating just a small sample of what is happening in our classrooms. For the last ten years the focus has been on teaching and learning, and a consideration of current issues and developments has been part of every staff training day. Alongside this work we have a core of traditional high-quality teaching and a set of basic classroom expectations, adhered to by all teachers, together with a clear agenda that is about

- respect for learning
- respect for others
- respect for themselves.

David also suggests that new ideas can be helpful in reshaping thinking and in many ways this is what happened in the first year of the Music College. The majority of the 'music across the curriculum' experiments were undertaken by the group of enthusiastic teachers with whom I had already worked. They had been the teachers who had been used to trying out different learning strategies in their classrooms and were more comfortable with experimenting with new ideas. Some had joined the more newly formed (2005) learning action group and were incorporating music into their action research. Examples of their interesting work have already been described.

One of the consequences I did fear, in this attempt to encourage our musical school, is that music (with words) would blare out from most classrooms and consequently very little of it would be enabling students to learn more effectively.

This was always a danger with the approach adopted by the 'music across the curriculum' whole-school priority that had been written into our bid. To the credit of our teachers they have not done so. This could have been the 'easy' option to have 'satisfied management requirements'. These professionals have all tried in their own individual way to respond to the initiative in a way that has been presented by the philosophy shared with us by Nina Jackson. Many have found it a significant challenge always looking for the 'right' way to do things rather than trying it out and finding what works for their classroom and our students. A further study has shown that there are appropriate times for music in the learning process just as there are appropriate times for silence.

It can be very threatening to be experimental and as teachers we tend to take the safe option. Perhaps, the extent of the challenge we have set for our teachers is summed up by Howard Gardner when he said many scientists believe that 'if we can explain music, we may find the key to all human thought'.[7]

Students' perceptions

One surprising outcome appeared on the year 7 reports. Each of the students wrote a personal statement about their first year in the school and their many achievements. At the end of 2006 their comments were significantly different, as they included an expectation that they should be 'doing something musical'. Even those students who were not learning to play a musical instrument went on to describe their enjoyment of music in class, attendance at concerts, and resident musicians' workshops. Perhaps the key lies here: these are the youngsters who will be part of our transition to a musical school as they progress through the years.

The future

The school will move into our new buildings. Every classroom has a data connection, so each teacher will be able to plug in their laptop and, through the projector, provide lessons that include DVD footage and musical tracks, allowing them to more easily provide the type of use of music that will be the most effective tool for learning. It will be yet another weapon in our armoury to engage and inspire young people and, most importantly, enable them to learn effectively.

---

[7] Howard Gardner, *Frames of Mind* (New York: Basic Books, 1983).

Chapter 7

Extra-curricular music and instrumental teaching

Use the talents you possess, for the woods would be very silent if no birds sang except the best.

Henry Van Dyke

The purpose of this chapter is to set out the ways that extra-curricular ensemble activities and instrumental music lessons can contribute to the curriculum experience of students in a musical school. One of the key issues that I will explore is the way that these areas can be set up so that as many students as possible feel they are able to engage with them. In Chapter 4 I set out the proposition that the class music curriculum may not always meet the needs and interests of a wide range of learners. I approached this by considering the needs of different groups of learners within schools. I will apply the same process to the provision of extra-curricular activities.

The very 'experienced' musicians

I have used the term 'experienced' to define a particular group who are often thought of as talented. I am sure they are, but my view would be that they are probably no more talented than a large group of other students who may not have had the opportunity to learn an instrument, or the parental support to develop this set of skills. I do not use the term talented because it implies that there is a set of students who are born with different attributes from their peers. I will develop the reasons why I take this view later in this chapter. For now, I am assuming that this group of 'experienced' students probably represents a very small proportion of the school population—perhaps 1 per cent. For many schools it will be much lower than this and for a few it may be higher. The Specialist Music Schools designated under the government National Music and Dance scheme will have a considerably higher proportion. For the moment I will describe these students as having achieved instrumental examination results of grade 5 or above. Grade 5 will probably have been gained by about year 9 and is a relatively modest measure of success. These students need activities that will cater for their skills and enthusiasm in order to motivate them and ensure that they feel engaged. Most schools do so because this gives a positive message about their ethos. The needs of the students are overt, the parents of this group will often have strong views, and there is kudos to be gained from nurturing them. This is also the group of students who music teachers will often get most personal satisfaction from working with and success in meeting their needs can lead to a promoted post.

The school could choose to signpost these students to suitable activities that take place out of school in order to develop their interests. This approach has some advantages. It would mean that time and resources are not over-committed to this group at the expense of others in the school. However, if there are strong out-of-school opportunities where students can mix with similar students, the school may come to be seen as low status and peripheral for this group of students. For example, at NSG the most able students were encouraged by the Music Service to have lessons at the central Music Centre (because they could access better, more specialist teachers). The fact that county-organized groups met weekly meant that students invested considerable amounts of their time attending rehearsals and performing in concerts outside school. This was within a context where these students could mix with like-minded musicians and feel no negative peer-pressure about music-making. These students enjoyed the extra opportunities and would often see school activities as being relatively unimportant. Although they might participate in groups, they might not engage fully or with great enthusiasm, perhaps feeling that they should come along to the last rehearsal before a concert. The centrally organized ensembles met their needs well but actually had a negative impact on the school's organized ensembles. Some local areas will not have local youth groups that meet on a weekly basis. Many meet only during holiday sessions. A school can either try to set up groups that are so good that these students will want to participate or decide not to compete and put its energies elsewhere.

Very few choose the latter route—since the relatively high standard of performance of these students adds to their cultural capital and ethos. Schools can engage these students positively through a range of activities. For example:

- as a soloist with a school ensemble
- as a sectional coach for a school ensemble
- directing a school ensemble
- composing music for a school group or event

- giving the student opportunities to develop a range of other skills that s/he may need in the future as a performer or teacher—marketing, concert management, choosing repertoire, etc.

Students with reasonable fluency in playing an instrument

This group of students is probably about 6–10 per cent of the average school population. Each school will have a different profile. A definition of reasonable fluency will depend on an individual school's circumstances. I am referring here to the main group of students in a school who play an instrument, not the very small group who may be very accomplished. For some schools it may be students who have a reasonable level of proficiency (grade 2 equivalent, for example) up to students who have a quite high level of proficiency (perhaps up to grade 5 equivalent). This is a largish group with quite a wide spread of experience. For some schools the achievement of this group may be more modest and there may be a smaller number. This group are able to play with reasonable accuracy and would often be welcome members of a school ensemble. In some schools they may need to reach a certain standard before having access to opportunities. Their level of skill is not so high that they are likely to be exceptional for their local area and starting to identify with groups outside the school, unless they already play in another ensemble such as a community brass band or wind band. They may see a school group as something which enables them to play regularly and they may be happy with the status of the group. The needs of these students are relatively easily met through the provision of a suitable range of school-based extra-curricular activities.

Most students who learn instruments will probably mostly have their needs met. There may be exceptions. Beginner students, up to grade 1, for example, may not have the opportunity for ensemble playing. This group of students may be helped by being tutored by the most able in the school. Certain instruments may be under-represented. Guitars, drums, and keyboard are all very popular. The needs of this group are often not met well by schools. They are difficult to organize because large-group activities are problematic and the style of music they utilize is often not considered as being high status by senior managers.

Vocal groups such as choirs

The term 'instrumental' is used to include vocal activities because the voice is an instrument. In order to avoid clumsy syntax I have considered the two as synonymous. However at this point I will briefly consider singing separately.

Singing is a popular activity amongst many young children. In early years settings it is a very natural and expected form of play and communication. Even at this stage some misconceptions exist. They usually focus round the fact that some children can't sing, are 'growlers', or that boys sing lower than girls and probably don't enjoy singing anyway. Singing starts to become a feminized activity from the age of about 3. The hidden views of carers and parents start to suggest that boys are not naturally good at singing or that it is not a common thing for them to do. Many people, affected by their own experiences, will often make a joke about how bad their singing is or make thoughtless comments about the singing of others. In a good setting this is not a barrier and children will enter reception very happy to participate in singing regardless of their background or gender. In the infant years singing is still often a popular and natural activity when approached in a positive way. However, boys are gradually put off singing by their experiences and the messages they pick up from school and home. In years 3–6 boys often suffer due to a lack of encouragement and sensitive teaching. By the time they reach year 7 very few boys want to sing, unless they can see themselves as part of an individual talent show or 'fame academy'.

Singing is often not a very popular activity for older boys and girls especially as a communal activity—such as a choir. Primary-age children will often sing with a great deal of enthusiasm and will happily participate in groups called 'choirs'. Many more girls will participate than boys. At secondary school singing is harder to develop. There are exceptions:

The College has two critically acclaimed choirs which all students are invited to join. Recent choral highlights include Vivaldi's Gloria, Haydn's Nelson Mass, Handel's Messiah, Mozart's Requiem and Poulenc's Gloria. The choirs have also had works specially written for them by eminent composers. (Countesthorpe Community College website 2006)

These exceptions usually focus around a particular teacher who has a strong enthusiasm for singing. In fact most successful and well-known school ensembles are influenced by the particular interest and passion of an individual teacher. It seems not to matter whether this is for bagpipes, ocarinas, or brass bands. Students respond well to strong role models and enthusiasm.

Singing and participation in choirs seems to have a slightly different currency to playing an instrument. Some of the singers may not have instrumental lessons and represent a different cross-section of the school population, particularly if the style of the music sung in the choir is contemporary and popular. Some may have singing lessons—in which case the school will probably expect some form of participation in a group such as a choir. A school may audition students for a choir. Some schools manage to put on singing activities for everyone to participate in. This sort of open-access activity can become very popular and have a very strong ethos. A school choir can therefore have quite a distinctive character (which will depend on the approach of the person leading it):

- it may include almost the same students as instrumental groups
- have quite a few students who only participate in this activity because they do not have lessons on an instrument and this is one way they can still participate in music-making
- be a blend of the two groups

Sensitive tutoring of choirs for young people is essential. A recent programme on television called *The Choir* featured a tutor working with a group of students to form a school choir. One of the aims of this group was to take part in the Choir Olympics in China. The programme showed the tutor choosing music that seemed to be unsuitable for the students' abilities and tastes and rejecting several who had given a high level of commitment, because only a certain number were allowed to go to the competition. The tutor knew this before he started and the segregation of the 'can go to China', 'can't go to China' students appeared especially thoughtless. The tutor seemed to do little to help the students improve the quality of their singing through the rehearsal techniques he used. Despite this many of the students responded positively to the evident enthusiasm of the tutor. This is not unusual. I can recall a teacher who regularly played out his own ambitions and enthusiasms through his school choir. They sang totally unsuitable repertoire that he had always wanted to conduct. A performance of the Allegri Miserere haunts me. The choir sang the whole, very long piece in an unsuitable venue with a young girl struggling to manage a treble solo that was well above her range. The only saving grace was that each section descended by at least a semitone so that the solo eventually became manageable. The experience was miserable for most listeners but the enthusiasm of the tutor was infectious and continued to motivate many of the students. I can recall another, exceptional choir flourishing in a very run-down area of Kettering. The choir would rehearse most mornings before school. One of the girls told me that in the choir she felt special. Outside the choir she declared that she was 'nothing at all'. This student had found something that really motivated and inspired her within a social area that generally lacked aspiration and self-esteem.

Secondary-school students may actually be quite keen on singing but feel uncomfortable with the term 'choir'. They may have aspirations to be a singer—particularly as an individual performer. The popularity of television shows that seek out aspirational performers from the general public and put them through a series of audition stages where a panel of experts vote for them demonstrates that there is a huge appetite amongst people of all ages to be a solo singer. This is a different concept to being in a choir. A different sort of approach is needed. It may need to be more informal, less focused on 'classical' styles of music and may require the teacher to be less concerned with the unanimous tone and blend that a choir sound requires. It may also require a high degree of patience, since the results may not initially sound that appealing to a critical audience. Secondary-age students will often participate very enthusiastically in shows, since the type of music associated with these productions seems to meet their interests and offers them an environment where they feel comfortable. Given the right approach to styles and genres, singing can be a hugely enjoyable and accessible activity for students. Currently it seems to be underdeveloped and this is something I think a musical school ought to be able to tackle effectively.

Getting a balance of extra-curricular activities that meet the needs of all students

The very experienced and reasonably experienced students are relatively easy to cater for. A constraint may be the amount of teacher time available to run the number of groups that the school would like to offer. For example, the groups which NSG ran in 2004 are shown in Table 7.

Table 7 Different musical groups run by Northampton School for Girls in 2004

High-status groups	Opportunities for students with some experience	Open-access
Wind orchestra*	Junior strings*	Steel pans (× 3)*
Choir (auditioned)†	Guitar groups (× 2)*	junior choir†
String group*	Rock groups*	
Jazz group*	Junior wind band†	
Percussion ensemble*	Flute choir†	

† Groups run by teaching staff from the school

* Groups run by 'outside' hourly paid staff

The model had some advantages:

◆ students got access to a good range of activities within school time (or after school)

◆ the time commitment given by school teaching staff was small because of the relatively large number of hourly paid extra staff. This enabled the full-time staff to concentrate on the curriculum

There were also some potential disadvantages:

- the open-access activities for other groups of students were relatively limited—possibly emphasizing that music was an activity for students with prior experience or special skills

- the large number of visiting tutors taking groups meant that students did not have the same strong loyalty to ensembles that they often seem to feel with groups run by a class music teacher.

In 2005/6 the range of groups at NSG was expanded further. Extra groups were established—these included an extra jazz ensemble, a small vocal ensemble, a junior percussion group, and a contemporary music ensemble. These groups, together with the groups mentioned above, gave a good range of opportunities—mostly enabling those who already learned instruments to participate.

The addition of a junk orchestra, led by post-16 students, gave an opportunity for those with no previous experience to become involved. The group proved to be extremely popular, especially with the younger students and managed to create an open-access ethos. The group did not use notation, emphasized inclusion and a sense of enjoyment and involvement. The participation of post-16 students (who did not have prior musical expertise) was a real strength. The group often seemed to be viewed by staff as being of lower status than existing instrumental groups. Where there was competition for rehearsal space or time the junk orchestra had the lowest priority. This was a crucial issue, since engaging a wider group of students is difficult to achieve and demands a high level of cooperation from everyone. The hidden curriculum message can be very strong here.

Music therapy in a mainstream school

NSG planned to start offering music therapy to students with emotional difficulties. I engaged a qualified music therapist. Music therapy assumes that the ability to appreciate and respond to music is something that all humans possess. It usually remains unimpaired by handicap, injury, or illness and is not dependent on music training. For those who cannot use words adequately, for whatever reason, music therapy offers a safe and secure space for the release of feelings. Music therapists work with adults and children of all ages. Those who can benefit from music therapy include:

- people with learning, physical, and sensory disabilities, including multiple disabilities and neurological conditions
- people with mental illness or emotional disturbances
- people with speech and language impairment
- people with disabilities within the continuum of autism
- elderly people

Music therapy is not designed to:

- teach students to play instruments
- have a therapist entertaining the student and playing music all the time
- be a miracle cure which will work for all students

Music therapy develops a therapeutic relationship between the student and a therapist. Within this relationship, interactive improvised music is used to work on individual objectives. The therapist does not teach the student to sing or play an instrument. Students are encouraged to use accessible percussion instruments and their own voices to explore sound and to create a musical language of their own. By responding musically, the therapist is able to support and encourage this process.

The music played covers a wide range of styles in order to complement the individual needs of each client. Much of the music is improvised, thus enhancing the individual nature of each relationship. Through whatever form the therapy takes, the therapist aims to facilitate positive changes in behaviour and emotional well-being. S/he also aims to help develop an increased sense of self-awareness, and thereby enhance quality of life. The process may take place in individual or group therapy sessions. Music is essentially a social activity involving communication, listening, and sharing. These skills may be developed within the musical relationship with the therapist and, in group therapy, with other members. As a result students may develop a greater awareness of themselves in relation to others. This can include developing greater confidence in their own ability to make relationships and to find positive ways of making their needs known. It can greatly enhance their self-esteem.

Students were referred to the therapist via the school's existing pastoral systems and many found it a valuable and worthwhile experience. The confidentiality of the relationship between the student and the therapist means that examples of these transactions cannot be given here.

Instrumental tuition

In September 2004 approximately 240 NSG students received instrumental tuition provided by visiting teachers supplied by the Local Authority Music Service. This was almost 15 per cent of the school population. There are no official statistics on the number of pupils learning instruments in English secondary schools. However, a generally accepted norm is between 5 and 10 per cent—so NSG was providing lessons for an above average number of students. However, the profile of students learning instruments nationally is much more weighted towards girls than boys. The reasons for this are often to do with the fact that girls are more enthusiastic participators in music activities at secondary school and that where selection processes are applied girls seem to fare better. Therefore, the figure of 15 per cent, whilst above average, is probably not greatly different to similar girls-only schools.

Most lessons were taught individually for between twenty minutes and half an hour. Prior to September new students had joined the school in year 9. In September 2004 the school had taken students into year 7 for the first time as part of a reorganization of education within Northampton. The unwritten policy and practice had been that students who previously played an instrument at middle school generally carried on when they arrived at NSG. It was unusual for students coming into year 9 to start tuition for the first time. A similar sort of approach had been applied to the September 2004 intake, even though this included years 7, 8, and 9. This pattern of provision did not fully match the school's general aims of being inclusive and offering maximum opportunities to students. It also did not match the aims of government priorities to increase access (as promoted through the Wider Opportunities Programme and Music Manifesto).

This situation presented two particular challenges for the school. How could access to lessons be increased, whilst still maintaining quality and keeping within a reasonable budget? If changes were introduced how could the staff be made to feel comfortable and sign up to the philosophy? In September 2004 students paid an annual contribution of about £15 per year. Any form of charging is a key responsibility for governors but a lack of connection between instrumental tuition and other charging policies within a school is relatively common, although surprising. Instrumental tuition often seems to be treated differently. However, where a school is applying any sort of a charge this should really be accommodated within the governor's overall policy on charging. This should include information on what can be charged for and what remission arrangements, if any, the governors wish to apply.

The profile of students learning instruments

The profile of students learning instruments at NSG had not really been analysed prior to 2004. This is relatively common in schools, even though a school may be spending reasonably large sums of money supporting this sort of provision. I undertook an analysis of the profile in March 2005. The results are shown in Table 8.

The balance of instruments was fairly good, with many string players and a good range of double-reed instruments. However, like most schools, lower-pitched instruments such as bassoons, cellos, basses, and tubas were in short supply. The numbers learning brass instruments was also small. None

Table 8 Analysis of the profile of the 240 NSG students learning an instrument in 2005

Instrument played	Numbers of students learning
Woodwind instruments (with flute and clarinet being by far the most popular)	82
String instruments	48
Piano or keyboard	33
Brass	31
Voice	20
Guitar	13
Percussion	13

were learning tabla, sitar, djembe, ukulele, bagpipes, or harmonium, although there might well have been the demand for these instruments. A high proportion of the brass players were relative beginners. There was a strong instrument-playing culture in feeder schools, particularly for wood-wind and strings. Some form of stereotyping was clearly taking place. This type of instrument gender bias is relatively common around the UK. It was one of the reasons why I chose the trumpet player Alison Balsom to be the guest performer at NSG's Music Celebration Day in March 2006.

The numbers learning instruments in years 7 and 8 (new to the school that year) were relatively high—representing about half of the students, even though this was just two year groups out of seven. This suggests that the profile of the school intake was starting to change, with a higher proportion of students arriving already playing an instrument. Trying to balance the range of instruments played in a school is a difficult and thankless task. Students want to choose what to play and this may result in significant numbers playing 'popular' instruments such as flutes and clarinets. Providing students with extra-curricular playing opportunities where there are large numbers playing a narrow range of instruments is difficult. It can be done, but requires a high degree of organization, research, and extra work. Students need to be guided sensibly because their opportunities for playing outside school and into adult life may be hampered by choosing instruments that are very popular. The flute, for example, is a commonly played instrument. As adults the students may want to play in an orchestra. Amateur orchestras are not very common and they only require two or possibly three flutes. A proficient cellist, however, will nearly always be able to find a welcome.

Further analysis showed that the proportion of students who were studying for instrumental exams (or who were of an equivalent standard) was surprisingly low, especially given the fact that students received individual lessons of between twenty minutes and half an hour. Higher grades (i.e. grade 3 equivalent or above were surprisingly low) (see Fig. 2).

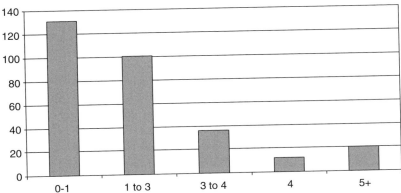

Fig. 2 Analysis of those learning instruments in September 2004 by instrumental grade (or equivalent)

The school did not have sufficient information to review the ethnicity, social circumstances, or other factors that would give a clear picture of whether the students were representative of the general school population.

There seemed to be five main challenges for the school:

1. To develop a policy and practice that was clear and consistent so that all students and parents knew what it was. This would also require that the governors take a view about this policy and they should ensure that it matched with their other policies on charging (assuming that they wanted to charge).

2. The need to increase the quantity of students learning an instrument, assuming that there was the desire amongst students to take lessons if available.

3. The need to ensure that instrumental teaching was given a high enough priority by students so that they attended lessons, practised, and therefore made reasonable progress (a factor in the lack of progress was the fact that several were not attending lessons on a regular enough basis).

4. Getting a good balance of instruments that challenged stereotypes (such as brass instruments not being for girls), introducing a wider range of instruments, and enabling the school to develop ensembles that would offer the girls rich opportunities.

5. These aims would need to be achieved within a budget that was sustainable and within a philosophy that senior leaders and other school staff could feel comfortable with.

Instrumental tuition policy

I wrote a draft policy which was then discussed by the governors. They were very keen to ensure that instrumental tuition was not too costly for the students. This fitted in very much with their belief that curriculum and extra enrichment activities should not be inaccessible due to financial need. However, they did not yet appreciate some of the other factors surrounding access and equality to instrumental lessons.

The school spent £60,000 from its budget in order to keep the cost low for the students. This meant that the numbers able to learn was capped, since larger numbers would result in either a prohibitive cost to the school or the need to increase the charge to students. The governors were not keen to increase charges because they felt that this might make finance a barrier. However, the policy of keeping the cost down, an important philosophical principle for the school, also meant that the numbers able to learn was fixed. Therefore the policy inadvertently contributed to a relative lack of access for some students—especially the ones who did not learn before they came to the school. It is relatively common for schools to mix the two priorities of access and cost. Much of this stems from the period before Local Financial Management in Schools when Local Authorities provided tuition to schools and paid for the cost centrally. This period was characterized by free music instrument tuition in most Local Authorities and is often looked upon as a golden age when there was greater access. In fact the tuition was limited by the amount of teaching time available so students were chosen for their 'suitability' to learn an instrument, even though the cost was free at point of use. Some schools received more tuition than others if it was felt that they would make good use of it. This means that this golden age was only golden if you happened to be in a school that had this provision and you were a student who passed whatever suitability test was applied. If you did you probably got free tuition. If you were in a school that did not receive tuition, your teeth were the wrong shape, fingers too short, or whatever other criteria were applied, you did not qualify. As schools started to receive the funding to buy in tuition they often focused on the issue of keeping the cost as low as possible but failed to spot the fact that there were generations of children who would have liked to have played an instrument but had not been given the opportunity to do so. It is important to keep the two principles of cost and access as complementary but separate concepts.

There was also a trend for more and more students to arrive at NSG in year 7 having already learned an instrument. This was clear from the profile of students learning by year group and the trend increased in 2005 and 2006. The specialist status of the school, not surprisingly, appeared to attract more students who already learned an instrument. A model plotting this trend showed that if the same policy were applied (supporting those who already learned at a low cost) the school would need to spend at least £200,000 from its own budget by 2007. The provision in 2004 was relatively inefficient because the overwhelming majority of students were taught individually, even though there are many schools across the country that embrace group teaching—especially for younger students. This was compounded by the fact that attendance at lessons was quite erratic. We therefore needed to decide which approach they wished to take:

- continue to support those students who already learned an instrument when they arrived at NSG and keep the cost as low as possible, whilst accepting that the Specialist College status may result in this cost rising to a quite considerable degree
- find a model that matched the governor's aims of access and inclusion whilst remaining affordable.

A way of developing this agenda about payment, access, and entitlement was to ask the governors to approve a policy. This is something that all schools should do.

Some key elements needed to be prioritized.

- The policy should encourage wide participation, equality, and access for as many students who wanted to learn—this was a shift from the present position because currently some might want to learn but not have the opportunity if they had not already started an instrument.
- Charging would be necessary in order to offset some of the cost. Evidence from other schools around the UK suggests that where a charge is made parents (and therefore students) value the provision more and are more likely to attend on a regular basis.
- Free places would be offered in line with the governor's other charging policies—for example those students on income support or other defined benefits.
- The school might introduce specific themes within the policy that would be regularly reviewed—in this case the school wanted to encourage brass players and girls who played lower-pitched instruments such as cellos, bassoons, trombones, and tubas, so they might get the first year of tuition free. Once the number of brass players had increased the policy would be reviewed and adjusted. However, the principles of access and inclusion would remain in any policy because they reflect the core values of the school.

What should be contained in an instrumental tuition policy?

A school policy on offering instrumental tuition might address the following points:

1. A brief policy statement on how pupils gain access to instrumental lessons.

2. If the number of pupils who wish to learn is the same, or less than the spaces available, all pupils should automatically be allocated a place. There ought to be no need for any test of 'suitability'.

3. If the number of applicants exceeds the number of spaces available, clear information needs to be prepared about procedures for allocating spaces. This process should be fair, open, and even-handed. It is helpful if any policy is contained in the departmental policy or handbook. Reference should be made to the school's equal opportunities policy.

4. If it is a condition of receiving tuition that pupils participate in ensembles this should be made clear at the outset.

5. If there are alternative means of obtaining tuition this information should be available (e.g. local private teacher, local music centre), particularly when the number of pupils wanting to learn exceeds the places available.

6. Tuition available should reflect the culture, traditions, and interests of the pupils as well as the school (e.g. including access to popular music as well as 'classical').

7. Equal opportunities and charging are not the same thing. Equal opportunities applies to the full range of ways that pupils access tuition and includes things such as selection and availability of tuition. Charging may include an element of equal opportunities but if a charging policy is consistent (i.e. applied to all pupils fairly) and allows pupils who are at an agreed level of benefit, equality of opportunity will have been provided.

8. Most standard tests of musical ability give an indication of prior experience and attainment rather than potential (e.g. the Bentley test). Several tests such as singing back a phrase or recognizing which of two notes is higher have no known link to likely future success in playing an instrument. There is, however, a direct correlation between future 'success' and the amount of time a pupil spends practising. If a school can help a pupil to develop good practice routines they will almost certainly be contributing to likely success and enjoyment. For example: a school can encourage the use of practice diaries and help to ensure good communication between pupil, parent, and teacher(s).

9. The work of the instrumental teacher should be seen as complementary to that of the class teacher. Pupils should be encouraged to use the skills they develop with their specialist instrumental/vocal teacher in class lessons. Pupils who receive instrumental lessons should not be viewed as having higher status than those who have received class music lessons only.

Charging

At the time that this policy was put together a charge could be made for individual and group lessons (up to four pupils).

The most recent advice from the government on charging was contained in DFEE circular 2/98:

1. It allowed schools to charge for an activity such as individual instrumental tuition. Individual tuition has been defined in this context as a group of up to four.
2. Precluded schools from charging more than the cost of providing such a service or of charging above the cost of an activity in order to subsidize other pupils.
3. Precluded schools from charging for vocal tuition or for a part of National Curriculum or examination courses.

Music Services and schools often responded more to custom and practice or, in some cases, market pressures. In 2007 the guidance was adjusted and allowed charges to be made for any size of group provided that the provision was not part of the National Curriculum or a particular Wider Opportunities project to encourage participation.

Charging for lessons has some particular implications. The following options are possible:

◆ Schools may wish to charge the full cost of providing the service to pupils. A contract can be issued to parents who will commit themselves to paying for a specified number of lessons and who will need to give an agreed period of notice if this arrangement is to be terminated. In some cases the parents will be paying an outside agency directly for a service and the contract will be with this agency.

◆ Schools may wish to charge the full cost of providing tuition but offer free, or subsidized, tuition to pupils who qualify for a specified level of benefits (e.g. free school meals). The school will probably wish to issue a contract for pupils paying the full cost of lessons and a signed agreement for those who receive free or subsidized tuition.

◆ Schools may wish to provide free tuition to all pupils who wish to learn. It will probably be helpful to provide parents with a written agreement on what expectations the school has as a result of providing this tuition.

The school will be responsible for ensuring that the teacher is a fit and proper person to carry out this duty. This will include an appropriate CRB check. The responsibility for monitoring the quality of tuition rests with a school where it purchases a service.

This instrumental teaching policy set out to offer maximum opportunities for all students joining the school. A covering letter was sent to all to parents, and an extract from the letter is shown below.

Provision of instrumental/vocal lessons 2005–2006

The lessons will be organized in groups of two or three students. Lessons on NSG East site (years 7 and 8) will be taught in groups of three and lessons on NSG West site (years 9–13) will be taught in groups of two. The difference in group size is determined by the differing sizes of the teaching spaces available on the two sites.

The cost for receiving tuition is £75 per year. This can be paid as an annual amount in advance, or as a termly payment of £25. Lessons are taught in twenty-minute sessions and timetabled so that students will not miss the same lesson each week. Thirty-three lessons are taught in each year. A reasonable amount of practice will be required during the week in order to maximize the benefits of these lessons. Regular practice every day is much more beneficial than longer, intermittent bursts. Advice on how to practise effectively is available from the relevant instrumental/vocal teacher.

The actual cost of providing tuition is far higher than the charges applied. The school subsidizes the cost of tuition by approximately three-quarters of the cost. However, if you are unable to pay the costs outlined the governors have agreed that families who receive income support or job seeker's allowance will have their fees waived. Please complete the relevant part of the application form. Post-16 students are entitled to free tuition as are students taking up 'endangered' instruments such as bassoon, tuba, trombone, cello, and double bass. These instruments are worth considering because as fewer students play them the players are always sure of a warm welcome in ensembles and groups.

If a student does not attend a lesson no refund will be given. If a teacher misses a lesson the time will be made up subsequently. If you request lessons for September and do not continue with them you will still be liable for the annual cost of £75. This is because the school enters into an annual contract with the service provider and can not change this during the year.

Students will be responsible for providing their own music, strings, resin, and other consumables. Parents and guardians are advised that they should make sure that their home insurance covers instruments whilst at home. All students will be provided with an instrument. It should be maintained in reasonable condition during the year. The school also operates the Assisted Purchase scheme which enables students who want to purchase instruments to do so free of VAT. For further details please contact the Director of Music.

Students who receive instrumental vocal tuition are expected to take part in up to two extra-curricular activities during a week. A full copy of the policy on instrumental tuition is available on request. I hope that you are able to enjoy the benefits of learning an instrument during this year.

The policy represented some changes in practice. In particular there was an attempt made to maximize opportunities for younger pupils by making provision open to all. This meant that tuition for younger pupils was provided in groups in order to facilitate as many as possible having the opportunity whilst making the costs and accommodation requirements manageable. This sort of provision had the additional advantage that group instrumental teaching is widely regarded as being more successful than individual tuition.

Putting the policy into practice

In June 2005 all year 7 students were asked to request lessons so that provision could be planned for September 2005. At this stage it was not clear what the response would be. The numbers actually asking for lessons was much larger than anticipated and showed that when given the opportunity many young people want to play an instrument. This experience is not unique. The English government's Wider Opportunities Programme, which had been running over the previous two or three years, had clearly demonstrated that

- young people would like the opportunity to learn an instrument and really enjoy it once they have started
- large-group or even whole-class tuition can be very motivating for these students (more so than individual tuition).

There are also sometimes barriers which stop them from being able to take up this opportunity. These mostly revolve around the views of teachers and other adults that music is for a small group of talented students and that group teaching must be inferior to individual tuition.

I put the numbers wanting to take lessons into a spreadsheet, which enabled me to apply a formula for group or individual tuition. This was then linked to a further calculation which showed the likely cost in teacher time, financial cost, and the total budget required once free places had been allocated and income from charging had been received. This meant the model could be adjusted in order to see what the impact was of (a) charging a different rate (b) changing the group size (c) numbers of hours required or accommodation requirements. An able student could help with this task.

In the new model the school was able to offer:

- tuition to 625 students (up from 240)
- individual tuition for more advanced students
- group tuition for students at a beginner level

It also meant that I had a clear view of the likely impact of this provision. For example, the total cost to the school would be £80,000. The total cost of provision would be £130,000. The model still allowed the school to support particular groups. These were post-16 students, those on agreed levels of benefit, and girls learning instruments such as brass and lower-pitch instruments (for one year in the first instance). The split of tuition over the two school sites in shown in Figs. 3 and 4.

There were two key barriers to progress.

1. Accommodation was limited so the school had to be careful that open access was manageable and in 2006 one extra practice room had to be built (achieved through a simple partition wall being added to a redundant space).

2. Instrumental teachers generally viewed group tuition (teaching in groups of two or three) as being an inferior model and were resistant to change.

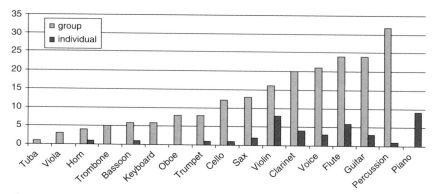

Fig. 3 Instrumental tuition on West site 2006/7 (years 9–13)

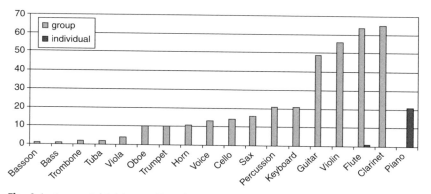

Fig. 4 Instrumental tuition on East site 2006/7 (years 7 and 8)

Group instrumental teaching

Group teaching is used as a term to describe teaching students in a group of two, three, or exceptionally four. In the NSG policy it stated up to six, which I felt would be suitable for a group of beginners but in fact was never used. Groups of three were the largest size scheduled. This matched the aims of the English government's Wider Opportunities Programme and enabled students to have a chance to start an instrument at a modest cost. In each case the students would be learning the same instrument, although there are other models of group teaching which involve whole-class tuition and mixed instruments taught within the same group. All of these have been very successful.

I can see that it is possible to see group teaching as an inferior, cut-down version of individual teaching, particularly where it results in students being given short individual sessions, whilst the remainder of the group wait for their turn (which is not really group teaching at all). This approach uses an individual tuition model within the context of a group setting. However, real group teaching actually offers many rich opportunities, provided the teacher has the skills to develop them. In particular, the social aspect of group teaching provides opportunities for the students to evaluate the work of others, develop a sense of ensemble and of performance. Research into this issue has shown that group teaching often has an overall positive effect on the progress of the students learning in this way, although it does require the teacher to be flexible, adaptable, and well organized.

In spite of group-taught students having received less time . . . their level of achievement in fluency of notation was disproportionately high. Perhaps teachers made fewer repetitive statements in group settings and saved instructional time. This, coupled with the possibility of learning from others may account for the alacrity with which the group-taught students acquired notational skills.[1]

The 'Suzuki method' advocates the social aspects of learning an instrument in a group as a preference to individual tuition. Even on an instrument like the piano:

Carefully led group sessions can develop pupils' confidence, giving them opportunities to get to know each other and to work together. Even if children find the practising tough, they usually love their group lessons. Their enthusiasm is infectious—parents and children alike are greatly motivated by working together and socialising together.[2]

---

[1] K. Thompson, 'An Analysis of Group Instrumental Teaching', *British Journal of Music Education* 1/2 (January 1984), 153–71.

[2] Jenny Macmillan, 'Ideas for Group Teaching', *Ability* (Summer 2006), 11–13

The English government's Wider Opportunities programme gives some good examples of how this group approach might work:

Wider Opportunities grew out of the Government's pledge that 'over time, every primary school child that wants to, should have the opportunity of learning a musical instrument'.[3]

Youth Music and the Department for Education and Skills (DfES) initiated a programme with thirteen Music Services to illustrate different models of how this might be done. OFSTED (Office for Standards in Education) reported on twelve of the models (six DfES-funded and six Youth Music-funded) and Youth Music carried out an evaluation on the seven pilots it supported.[4] We know that this sort of action research tends to create positive, 'halo' feedback. However, the enthusiasm was impressive:

All children are musical—at last we have found a way to enable all children in class to explore, develop and realise their potential through a programme which not only enables them to learn to play an instrument, but also develops the whole musician. (Rita Burt, Head, Barking and Dagenham Community Music Service)[5]

Large group teaching is the answer to wider opportunities. (Julie Spencer, Deputy Head, Haringey Music and Performing Arts Service)[6]

The Wider Opportunities Programme has enabled us to move a little closer to the two questions 'What do we mean by instrumental teaching?' and 'Can we all have the opportunity?', the answers to which I believe will define the place and professional practice of our Music Service and all Music Services this century. (Maureen Hanke, Head, Norfolk Music Service)[7]

The Wider Opportunities Programme explored the model of large group or whole-class instrumental teaching offered to young children in order to fulfil the aim of ensuring that every child had the opportunity to lean an instrument. OFSTED also carried out an evaluation of the pilot projects and concluded that many aspects were a great success.

Models of provision in the Wider Opportunities pilot were many and varied but there were a number of key features which were common to all. For example, to create maximum access, programmes in the Wider Opportunities pilots were generally delivered to whole classes during the school day. Often, instrumental learning served as the

---

[3] David Blunkett, Department for Education and Skills, *Schools White Paper* (London: HMSO, September 2001), 12.

[4] OFSTED, *Creating Chances for Making Music: the story of the Wider Opportunities Programme*, Youth Music (London: HMSO, 2004).

[5] Ibid.

[6] Ibid.

[7] Ibid.

delivery mechanism for the whole of the National Curriculum for music. Lessons were team taught by a combination of freelance and community musicians, Music Service tutors, classroom teachers and teaching assistants. All teaching staff worked together to plan and deliver musical experiences across the year. In this way, the classroom teacher was able to learn invaluable instrumental skills from the visiting musicians, while the musicians developed an in-depth understanding of the school context, classroom management and the wider music curriculum. The end result was a fully integrated learning experience for the child.[8]

Programmes in all Wider Opportunities schools consisted of three elements, which were offered simultaneously or one after another, depending on the school and Music Service involved.

1. Taster activities: experiences designed to engage, educate, and inspire so that children can make an informed choice about which instruments they might like to take up.

2. Foundation activities: 'general musicianship' experiences designed to help children learn more about pitch and rhythm, and about how to translate sound into symbol and symbol into sound.

3. Tuition: finally, there was the opportunity to go on and learn a musical instrument, generally in a whole-class setting. This included ensemble playing, composition, and performance, and specialist tuition in both small and in larger groups.

An issue that comes from the Wider Opportunities Programme is whether or not this experience is built upon once the students reach secondary school, or in the next year of their primary-school experience. A secondary teacher reflecting on this was sceptical:

no noticeable difference in my place, apart from students saying that they played the violin for 2 months 3 years ago. It doesn't seem to have been particularly useful. Maybe I'm just tired and jaded on a Friday though! (music teacher on internet forum 2007)

What a missed opportunity this seems, and the jaded music teacher seems to have decided already whether or not to make it work. The hidden curriculum is fully at work and there clearly seems no point in creating excitement and opportunity in primary schools if it is not followed up in the local secondary school. It probably appears easier and more straightforward to teach a small group of highly motivated students in individual lessons than developing a

---

[8] OFSTED, *Tuning in: Wider Opportunities in Specialist Instrumental Tuition for Pupils in Key Stage 2* (London: HMSO, 2004).

model where access is open to all those who are interested. An outcome can be that teachers add extra hurdles for accessing tuition. These hurdles filter students so that the teacher is able to work with those who seem keen, easy to teach, and able to pass some suitability test that is administered. There are few other areas of education that would permit this approach! Group teaching raised some important issues for NSG and caused some focused discussion. The majority of instrumental teachers and some of the class teachers preferred to preserve the status quo. Why was this? I think it was based around custom and practice and a reluctance to consider new ways of approaching things.

Alternative ways of teaching instruments

In order to increase access to instrumental tuition a school might consider offering alternatives to tuition provided by a visiting tutor. For example, through providing students with:

- online learning resources via a self-taught methodology
- online tutoring with an adult helper to monitor the progress of students
- an online specialist supplemented by a visiting specialist
- all of the above with the addition of extra activities designed to support learning.

At NSG this is what I did through the promotion of the 'gigajam' project. Gigajam is a commercial product. It did have some specific advantages (some of these are covered in Chapter 9). These were:

1. The materials were written in a comprehensive way to cover guitar, bass guitar, keyboard, and drums (and my research with students suggested there was demand to learn these instruments that was not currently fulfilled).
2. They are integrated—so once students have completed sessions in a mixed group they can get together to perform pieces using different instruments (because the materials have been designed to be complementary).
3. The materials included the capability for students to assess their own work and monitor progress.

In the first year of running the programme about sixty students accessed the project during after-school sessions. These were taken by the music ICT technician, who was also a keen amateur musician. This provided students at NSG and in the local community with a good opportunity to learn an instrument that suited their tastes. Drums and guitar were particularly popular.

In the second year the programme was expanded considerably with very popular after-school sessions involving about 100 students a week. A good proportion of these were not accessing tuition in any other way. A charge was made, which ensured that the students valued the programme, but arrangements were made to support students who needed help (in line with the policy for general instrumental tuition). This project was then integrated with opportunities for the same students also to develop other skills such as songwriting or setting up a band within a 'rock school'. I also researched the wide range of CD ROMs available for learning to play an instrument. They offer a lot of scope for schools trying to extend the range of their provision and make learning an instrument accessible.

Testing for musical ability or aptitude

I have written elsewhere about the ways that tests of musical ability and aptitude have been used to filter out students from having the opportunity to learn a musical instrument. There has been a reasonable amount of research in this area and I therefore do not propose to rehearse all the reasons why teachers do this or the validity of the methods used. For further information in a readable format I recommend a look at Janet Mills, *Music in the School*.[9] I believe the methods used are often questionable but do suit many teachers. They tests tend to fall into three main categories:

◆ a test of musical aptitude which involves singing a phrase back, clapping a rhythm or some other form of response to a question. The content of these tests is often idiosyncratic and based on scant research or understanding. The test often measures prior musical experience rather than potential.

◆ a test of 'attitude'. These are even more idiosyncratic. They involve the teacher doing things like putting deliberate hurdles in the way of students such as asking them to return at the same time next week in order to see who forgets to turn up.

◆ a test of physical suitability. A student will be assessed to see if they have the right shaped hand, long enough arm, uniformity of teeth, or other physical characteristic the teacher deems to be a prerequisite for learning a particular instrument. This notion often assumes the principle that the child needs these 'perfect' characteristics in order to make a success of playing the

---

[9] Janet Mills, *Music in the School* (Oxford: Oxford University Press, 2005).

instrument. I know many professional musicians who clearly don't fit these characteristics and the idea that these judgements should override the child's wish to play an instrument appears to me to be out of step with modern views about equality of opportunity and open to legal challenge. This sort of approach would not be tolerated in almost any other sphere of educational activity.

People often express their amazement to me when I point out that these things happen. They do, on a regular basis all over the country. Sometimes the practice is overt. Occasionally it is covert and probably not conscious.

Music staff are always happy to give advice about the best instruments to choose if lessons have not been taken previously. All new pupils take a test in aural aptitude when they first join the College, and if a pupil is identified as having musical ability, it will be recommended to his/her parents that he/she consider learning a musical instrument, or take singing lessons. (Ampleforth College website 2007)

The instrumental teacher can test your child's readiness for lessons testing senses of pitch and rhythm and can also advise which instrument your child is most suited to. (Stockton on Tees Borough Council website 2007)

Here are some of the things you should consider when assessing potential music students at a consultation lesson:
     Physique—How big are the student's hands? what his or her physical stamina like? Is he or she going to come across any physical difficulties with regular practice on the instrument?
     Personality—Does the student appear to possess a personality that will be compatible with your style of teaching? Do they have determination & enthusiasm?
     Musical Ability—Basic aural tests will show you any existing musical abilities. Try asking the student to sing back a note in tune, or to tell the different between a rising or falling interval. Rhythm tests: Repeat a rhythm that you play, clap or sing, or get them to clap and maintain a steady pulse'. (Classical Music UK website 2007)

Specialist Music Schools (under the national music and dance scheme) always audition students on entry. Some state-funded 'comprehensive' schools use music as an entry criterion as well:

i. 10 per cent of School places will be offered on the basis of musical aptitude.
     ii. Aptitude' is understood, as described in Paragraph 5.5 of the Statutory Admission Code: 'aptitude is identified as [a child's] being able to benefit from teaching in a specific subject, or [demonstrating] a particular capacity to succeed in that subject.'
     iii. Aptitude will be assessed entirely on the basis of Key Stage 2 Music.
     iv. Applicants for music places will be tested in two elements of National Curriculum Music: listening, performing.
     v. Within the time constraints, it is not possible to assess fairly children's aptitude for the third element of National Curriculum Music, composing, since there is no way of guaranteeing that any work presented is actually the candidate's own. Composing is not therefore a part of the selection process.

vi. Children's musical backgrounds vary considerably and throughout the testing process, staff will be looking for aptitude not accomplishment. A child with a keen sense of pitch and rhythm, good physical coordination and the ability to perform even the simplest piece well, will score more highly than a Grade 3 trumpeter with a weak sense of pitch and rhythm' (Mill Hill County High School, 2007)

On the face of it this sounds like a balanced approach but how the policy is applied in practice will be significant. Other schools are quite unequivocal:

In the Nonsuch admission arrangements, the phrase 'other educational grounds' can refer to outstanding musical ability. If your daughter is an outstanding musician, i.e. she has passed Grade 4 in an instrument, please enclose a copy of her Grade 4 certificate and her application will be considered under this criterion. (Nonsuch High School, 2007)

Some schools are more open in their approach—even though they offer private education often thought of as exclusive:

Even if you think your child has very little musical ability you may be surprised to discover he or she has hidden talents. Visiting teachers are available to offer a wide range of orchestral instruments, guitar and piano and prepare pupils for graded examinations of the Royal Schools of Music. The school can provide for almost any musical requirement your child may have. (Moorland School, 2007)

Most private schools do not test for musical 'ability' because if the parents want tuition and are willing to pay for it the school will be happy to make the necessary arrangements.

We seem to struggle with the idea that musical talent is something tangible, that it can be measured, and that it is something that you either have or lack. This approach seems to be very damaging and a key barrier to creating a musical school. It leads to schools and societies that are made up of a few adults and children who feel they are musical and many more who feel that they are not. Compare this to the enthusiasm that young people have for music outside school, the way they want to listen to music, and the fact that many will learn an instrument if someone gives them the opportunity. If around 10 per cent learn an instrument in school it means that 90 per cent become non-musicians. I believe that a musical school can't exist like this. There are more enlightened views around:

There are many myths and fallacies which surround the identification of gifted and talented students in music. The most common of these is that musicality is led by musical achievement through examination success. Even the ability to play an instrument at all often solicits the comment that a child is 'musical'. Some suggest that highly developed listening skills and better hearing are an indication of musical talent. These may very well be indicators in those of special ability but it is important to remember that all children have musical potential and there may be latent talent and abilities in many children who do not have access to instrumental teaching and who may lack the supportive home environment in which their parents, or carers, make music themselves. Indicators of talent in music may be more clearly identified by a child's intense motivation or commitment, temperament and through aspects of personality, which ultimately are reflected through individuality in their art. Certain talents in music, such as exceptional ability in performance, are much more readily identified in students who have already received instrumental tuition. Latent ability in performance, or abilities as a composer or improviser can be more challenging to identify. In addition, even those identified and recognised as talented instrumentalists tend to be confined to particular styles of music such as western classical which can exclude some pupils who wish to explore other styles of music such as jazz idioms. (Creative generation website, 2007)

In *How Musical is Man?*, the anthropologist John Blacking wrote of his stay with a South African tribe called the Venda.[10] The most unique feature of the Venda was that all its members are regarded as musical. They all played musical instruments, sang, danced, composed music, and wrote lyrics and poetry. Music marked virtually all features of Venda culture. The seasons, holy days, the start of each month, the hours of the day, and rites of passage are all marked by music, song, and dance. There are songs associated with different jobs, songs associated with places or people, songs about animals, foods, emotions, greetings, and departures. There were highly skilled and professional musicians in the Venda society but from childhood all Venda were expected to develop a deep knowledge of music and a sophisticated set of musical skills. It's also a culture where women are considered the best drummers. In a conversation with some Venda men, Blacking tells them that he comes from a culture (western culture) where most people don't play musical instruments, and where only a few are considered talented enough to become accomplished or professional musicians. The Venda are astonished, and one man asks, a bit sarcastically, 'Are not your people human beings?' 'Of course, they're human beings,' replies Blacking. 'Well then,' the Venda man says, 'To be human, is to be musical.' This is the approach of a musical school.

[10] John Blacking, *How Musical is Man?* (Washington: University of Washington Press, 1974).

Chapter 8

Using ICT and e-learning to develop musical skills and create positive attitudes

Everywhere that technology impacts on our lives the pace of change is rapid. The question that vexed our parents, and their parents 'what can I do?' has been largely replaced by the understanding that in fact almost anything is possible, The question for the next Millennium is 'what should I do?' For example in agriculture 'Can I produce more food?' is replaced by 'are these crops appropriate?', in architecture 'how high can I build?' has been replaced by 'what is appropriate to be built?', in medicine 'who can I cure?' by 'who should we cure?', and so on. The debate continues in broadcasting, mobility, sport, science, communications, politics . . . everywhere, including of course, in learning.

Extract from Ultralab's bid to take over the
Millennium Dome site from spring 2001

The purpose of this chapter is to explore some of the ways modern technology can be used to improve learning in music. This includes the use of music software as well as general presentation and communication software. ICT can also be used as a way of facilitating change, since it often requires new approaches from teachers and learners. I will explore some general issues that flow from the development of technology generally as well as looking at some specific aspects of the implementation of music technology in schools.

The education landscape we inhabit is changing rapidly. Change has always been a feature of education and sometimes makes it hard for teachers to respond. It can be exciting and liberating. It can also seem threatening and generate resistance. Everything we know about change tells us that it will keep accelerating and at an ever-increasing rate. One of the key drivers is technology and its effect on the workplace, leisure, and society. Education is not immune to the onset of technological advance. We all instinctively know this, but to illustrate the point speak to anyone in their seventies or eighties about what life was like when they went to school. The majority of people from that generation grew up without access to motor cars, telephones, televisions, and central heating. They have witnessed all of these things being introduced and will probably say that many aspects of the world they recognized as children have disappeared completely. Their experience of education was also radically different from what it is today. The rate of change will not slow down. Think how only thirty years ago music keyboards were uncommon in classrooms or how the computer I am using to write this chapter has vastly more power than all the computers combined that NASA used to send a man to the moon in 1969. In fact several appliances in my kitchen have more power than that early NASA system.

We can catch glimpses of the ways that technology may start to change our lives. For example:

◆ mobile technology will become faster, more powerful, and more integrated —so mobile phones will also become a diary, watch, video camera, and web-browser

◆ entertainment systems will become more integrated—televisions, stereos, and computers will become one system

◆ connection speeds and band width will enable us to communicate effortlessly with people around the world making the virtual world more real and vivid

◆ more and more systems will become wireless or automated

◆ software will be developed that has the capability to design and modify itself

◆ technology will gradually utilize other control systems to make the virtual world nearer to the sensations of the 'real' world. Using temperature, sound, and smell, for example, in order to engage a wide range of our senses and create extra ambience

◆ 'nano' technology will alter the ways that we approach many medical interventions.

I am not claiming to be an ICT expert and I am certainly not capable of second guessing the exact direction that technologies will take us in. A significant number of these technologies have probably yet to be invented. We only need to consider how something like the internet or e-mail has developed in a very short space of time to gain an insight into the ways that new developments take our lives in unforeseen directions. I do know that young people will grow up accepting whatever is around them and that gradually over time, as they get older, the world will seem to become stranger and different from the one they grew up in. To them the present is the norm. It has not changed. This means that older refugees from a past era, who are in charge of learning, have constantly to evaluate what is new, when it can be useful, and also be mindful of when we should preserve activities with important values and roots. Playing instruments in a group or singing together, for example, are universal and ancient activities. They fulfil a social purpose and need. These types of activities need to be preserved (because of their social and psychological benefits). Other activities might be reshaped and redefined virtually. Not every new technology may be beneficial and one of our jobs is to be aware of the benefits and disadvantages they bring. We also need to understand that technologies affect social development, cohesion, and identity since they will cause society and structures to develop and change over time. We can glimpse this now through internet sites such as 'MySpace' and 'YouTube' which have changed the ways that people communicate and interact with each other. They will almost certainly end up being replaced over time with newer, more fashionable areas of interest. However, these sites have certain important characteristics which have very quickly become mainstream for young people:

- they enable young people (and old people as well) to communicate freely over vast distances in ways not possible ten years ago
- the experiences they offer frequently use multi-media, with music being a central defining feature within each person's space
- they develop a language and culture of their own, in much the same way that texting on mobile phones uses a style that abbreviates and misses out vowels—this contributes to the development of a new sub-culture that gradually becomes the norm.

The impact of technology on learning in schools

Many of our education practices are relics from a previous, industrial age when the teacher was the holder of knowledge that s/he would release to students in an orderly and planned way. This possession of information led to a high level of control and power for the teacher. Knowledge is increasingly democratized through the use of the internet. Students are able to access information at a pace and level that suits them and this changes fundamentally the role of the teacher and the learner, creating both challenges and opportunities.

As learning harnesses new technologies effectively, the potential advantages are numerous and profound:

- learning is independent of time and location
- the pace of learning suits an individual rather than a group or a teacher
- learning can happen remotely

- learners can interact with others and with a tutor even though they are not located in the same place
- learning does not need to be constrained by classroom availability or the teacher's timetable.

These opportunities for learners may create challenges for teachers.

- teaching styles will need to be constantly revised and evaluated as learning changes
- teachers may feel less skilled in using new technologies than students and therefore want to restrict the way the technology develops so they can feel in control
- teachers will have to make good-quality decisions about when technology is useful or not in order to ensure it is a tool for learning and not an end in itself. They will also need to ensure that students develop this skill as well.
- as the teaching workforce ages teachers may be in short supply and a children's workforce that includes teaching assistants, higher-level teaching assistants, and informally trained community musicians will be increasingly required. These workforce changes require good-quality planning in order to maximize the potential for learners.

As information and knowledge becomes freely available via a medium such as the internet, society changes. For example, a few years ago a patient would go to a doctor and say 'I feel ill'. The doctor would ask some questions in order to try to find out a bit more. Now a patient is much more likely to say 'I feel ill. I have looked it up on the internet and I think I know what is wrong. I have also looked up the possible treatments and the one most recommended is . . .'. The relationship between patient and doctor has shifted as a result. We are also aware that resources such as the internet pose specific challenges. Because information is freely available and therefore democratic, lots of people can contribute to it. 'Wikepedia' is an online community encyclopedia that proves we can make a collective global resource that meets the needs of a wide range of people. We can all contribute to this pool of knowledge. A lot of 'expert' information is also published on the internet but it is difficult to know just how robust it really is. Electronic information is 'soft'. It can be changed and manipulated in subtle ways. It could be adjusted and then republished, or sent in an e-mail as if it were original. Keeping track of these changes is difficult so the validity of information becomes harder to pin down. A book is written on a printed page and it will be obvious if someone has changed it in some way. Information on the internet is not moderated. How do we know that something is true? The answer is we do not. In the past generally accepted truths were written in books by acknowledged 'experts' in their field. This gave a view about a subject or topic that became accepted as the orthodox view. It also meant this knowledge was restricted to those who had access to the information and who had the necessary skills to be able to interpret it. The internet can be used to promote views and communities of extremism can be created across large distances. All of this means that knowledge is now more widely available but much more fluid than in the past. These factors have particular implications for education and the ways that students access and interpret information. They have a huge potential impact on schools and schooling since many of the organizational structures that we have are an outcome of a previous set of technologies. What implications does this have for music education? To answer this question in part I will refer to Northampton School for Girls.

Creating an infrastructure for the use of new technologies in music education

In June 2004 NSG had limited access to music ICT facilities. There was one computer with some sequencing and notation-based software and a portable recording desk. There was an understanding that achieving Specialist College status offered the opportunity to develop considerably. There were differing views about the best way forward. By October 2004 the school had developed an extremely effective system for using aspects of ICT to teach music, although it still had many areas that needed further refinement. Several schools visited NSG to look at what was available. The resourcing for ICT within music had improved considerably during a very short space of time. I will explore some of the ways this was achieved.

The general rule in setting up computers is that the higher the specification the better. This means a fast processor, maximum amount of memory (RAM), and a large hard disk to store information on. This desirable specification does depend on the set-up used at the school. It applies mostly to computers that are run individually with no access to a network. In this case large hard disk storage space is crucial. The information on this disk(s) will need to be backed up on a regular basis in case of component failure—which could result in a considerable number of students and teachers losing resources and saved work. These computers will also need a regular amount of maintenance to keep the software running effectively and reliably. The more computers, the more maintenance required and a good ICT technician is invaluable. If a computer is run as part of a network the processor speed and the RAM will be important factors—the higher specification the better for most systems. The size of the hard disk will be less important because files will be saved on the server that runs the network. The information on the server will be backed up on a regular basis making it unlikely that information will be lost.

Another option that a school might choose is a 'thin-client' system. This relies on software being delivered from a central point. The computer terminal sends key stroke, mouse clicks, and other information to 'middleware'. The middleware sends screen updates to computer screen but the data that is 'manipulated' stays centrally and it is only a representation that is seen. Thin-client has some specific advantages. It means that the terminals used by the students can be very low specification (so old computers will be perfectly suitable). This makes the terminals very cheap and sometimes free. It also makes maintenance work very easy because it is all done centrally and means that all terminals are consistent—so that if a student logs on anywhere in the school s/he will have access to exactly the same software configuration. Whilst this system has many advantages it can pose problems when running some types of music software so some expert and independent advice is needed.

Models for setting up computer systems

Option 1: a bank of laptop computers that are set up when required (Table 9).
Option 2: desktop computers (Table 10).
Option 3: Tablet PCs (Table 11).

The current choice is bewildering and will grow and become more complex with the advent of new technologies. Teachers often rely on informal advice for support:

Table 9 Advantages and disadvantages of laptop computers

Advantages	Disadvantages
◆ The laptops do not require much desk space.	1. Laptops are easy to move around and this means that they can get stolen more easily.
◆ The space is available for other uses when the laptops are not being used.	2. If a component of the laptop malfunctions the whole computer may need to be replaced.
◆ They can be even more flexible when used in a 'wireless' environment.	3. The quality of the sound card is not good enough for most applications (although you can purchase a separate sound card to be connected via a USB cable or plugged into the PCI socket).
	4. The laptop will need to be configured in such a way that it can be connected to the school network (for internet access etc.).

Table 10 Advantages and disadvantages of desktop computers

Advantages	Disadvantages
◆ The connection with the school network is 'always on' and does not require setting up each time the computer boots up. ◆ Because connections are left in place there is less likely to be problems through wrong leads connected or damage which can occur through constantly unplugging and reconnecting equipment. ◆ The machines are fairly robust and if one component goes wrong it can be replaced quite cheaply.	The permanent layout of the computers means that the room may not be used in a flexible way for other activities.

Table 11 Advantages and disadvantages of tablet PCs

Advantages	Disadvantages
Similar to laptops but they are even more portable and flexible.	Similar to laptops and may be more expensive as well.

Does anyone have any experience of using Tablet PC's for music technology. There is a debate raging at school about how to equip the new music facilities, the ICT manager is saying desktop machines, the advisor is advocating notebooks and the head is pushing tablet machines. I am totally confused and required to make a decision in the next two weeks! Any advice, experience (good or bad) would be welcome. (posted in a music internet forum 2007)

The choice of set-up will depend on factors such as

◆ the space(s) available

◆ the other computers used in the school (since a similar set-up will often be desired by technicians and other ICT support staff)

◆ personal preference and vision for the direction of ICT resources in the department and in the school

◆ whether the school uses a wireless or fixed cable connection

◆ how much technician support is available

The purchase of the NSG computers was a straightforward process. The first task was to decide on the specification needed. I suggested

1. A set of PCs (because this was what was used in the rest of the school and the technicians felt familiar with the format).

2. Each PC needed to have at least 0.5 GB of RAM, the fastest processor affordable, 40 GB hard disk, and a CD/DVD drive. Each would also need a separate sound card. Many modern computers have sound included on the motherboard and the technicians recommended using this. However, a separate sound card is a superior option because of potential latency problems (this is when there is a time delay between inputting information and hearing it through the speakers). The storage space on the hard disk will be dependent on whether or not programmes are saved on the central server or locally.

3. We also purchased a keyboard as a midi input device for each computer and put the computer keyboard in a tray underneath the desk—so that the music keyboard was always easy to access and use.

The other factor I was keen to build into the system was the ability to play the results of students work back to the whole class. For this reason the computer at the front of the class had an amplifier and speakers connected to the sound card audio output. There were four speakers around the room. Because the computers were part of the school network it meant that the teacher could load a student's work into the sequencer at the front and play it back to the class. Alternatively the teacher could demonstrate a file that s/he had created previously to the whole class, or play sounds as part of a powerpoint presentation to the class. It also meant that there was no need to purchase a separate CD player for this room since audio CDs could be played back in the same manner. This system worked very successfully.

Having planned the basic specification I put the order out to tender and purchased the equipment at a good, value-for-money price. Three quotations are recommended for purchases of this sort in order to meet best value and audit requirements. The purchase was made at a considerably lower price than that offered by specialist music education retailers. The ICT technicians 'built' the computers by adding the sound card and installing the keyboard/mouse etc. The sound card cost about £30 in 2004. It performed perfectly well—although it was possible to purchase a sound card that would cost up to about £500. The advantages of buying a more expensive sound card were not compelling enough until the need was demonstrated.

There were thirty work stations, so that a class of students could access an individual keyboard and computer. I considered this to be very important because I have often witnessed students working in larger groups, sharing one computer, and I have been struck by how inefficient this is for the students. A comparison would be a group of students who are working on a piece of art whilst sharing one drawing canvas, one brush, and a set of paints.

The room size and shape dictated some important aspects of the set-up. The outcome had advantages and a few significant disadvantages as well.

Advantages

1. Students had individual access to a good-quality computer, keyboard, and software that worked very efficiently.

2. They were able to work at a pace that suited them and were not held back by having to share resources.

3. The exposure to these individual resources resulted in fast development of individual capability in using the ICT. Students liked the resources and appreciated the quality of what they were able to produce using them.

Disadvantages

1. The room layout tied up the use of space so that other activities became difficult

2. The room layout had a significant effect on the dynamics of the lesson, the teaching style, and the way that students learn. Because the computers were in a fixed position it was extremely difficult to adjust this layout in order to respond to the ways that students were learning.

The shape of the room was significant—it was very long and narrow. This meant that it was difficult to communicate with students at the back of the room and the teacher needed to make sure that strategies for coping with this were built into lesson planning. Use of network software was very helpful. For example it was possible for the teacher to:

◆ monitor what all students were doing

◆ send an individual message to a student that pops up on their screen

◆ blank off the screen of all computers asking the students to pay attention to a verbal instruction

◆ take control of another computer to demonstrate a point—showing this on an overhead projector if required.

I believe that, ideally, music rooms need to be flexible spaces that can be used for practical sessions with acoustic instruments or seminars. The room shape and use of fixed PCs can tie up the use of the room too much. Overall, however, the advantages significantly outweighed the disadvantages and this room had a very quick and profound effect on learning at NSG because it caused a considerable amount of change in the way that teaching was delivered. More attention needed to be given to discussing these developments so the ICT room did not over-dictate how lessons were planned and delivered. Although the room added excitement and interest for many students and impressed other schools, the debate about lesson content and learning was underdeveloped. This is quite a common issue, even in schools with a high level of ICT infrastructure.

Operating systems

Once a computer has been purchased decisions will need to be taken about a range of factors that affect the software and the interface with the learner. The operating system is the master control program that runs the computer. Software you install 'talks' to the operating system. An operating system performs many important functions. For example:

- The windows, menus, and method of interaction between you and the computer. Prior to the Mac, Windows, and Motif (Unix) interfaces, all interaction was based on commands entered by the user.

- Multi-tasking, which is the ability to simultaneously run multiple programs, is available in all modern operating systems. On a desktop computer multi-tasking is necessary just to keep several applications open at the same time.

- The operating system's file system knows where data is physically stored. Whenever an application needs to read or write data, it asks the operating system.

- It controls devices by sending them commands in their own special language. This is known as a 'driver'. The operating system contains all the drivers for the extra things attached to the computer—keyboard, sound card etc. When a new device is added a driver is installed into the operating system.

- Modern multi-user operating systems provide password protection to keep unauthorized users out of the system. They also provide backup and recovery routines for starting again if there is a system failure.

PC computers usually have a 'windows' operating system installed—94 per cent of computers in the world use windows. Mac computers use something called MAC OS X. A few computers use LINUX—a free, open-source operating system. The operating system will dictate some key features of the computers and how they are used. Software will be written with a particular operating system in mind. Not surprisingly most are for windows. However the MAC operating system is highly rated by users and a considerable amount of music software has been written for it. There is a small but growing list of music software for the LINUX operating system as well. LINUX is a free product and can be adapted according to the needs of the user. Windows and the MAC OS X have to be purchased. A school can save a lot of money by opting for an operating system that is free. It also means that when upgrades are required all the computers in a school can be updated at the same time.

Running music software over a network

An early and crucial decision was whether to run music software on each individual computer or across the school network. Informal advice recommended that teachers run software on a stand-alone computer. I disagree. It is essential that computers should be networked because this enables students to access the internet, all their personal files, and enables the teacher to do the same. All work is stored on the central server, backed up regularly, and more readily available. If students use a stand-alone computer they will be saving work onto that individual computer and will need to use the same one every time they want to work on a project.

However, I was not clear whether or not music software would work successfully across a large network. At NSG we were lucky to have an excellent network manager who was flexible and happy to listen to solutions that supported learning and an ICT technician who was extremely able and creative. The music software was stored on an individual computer. The computer hard drive was partitioned so that a 'ghost' copy was also kept on the drive. If there was a problem with the system it could be restored to the ghost version very easily. The computers were connected to the network and had access to the internet and students could store their files and access information from the central server. However, the network manager had to let go of all the usual controls for these computers. This meant that students could introduce viruses and do other things which make most network managers very nervous! If there was a problem the technician could return the software back to its original 'ghost' format at the click of a button. The infrastructure was also upgraded by checking that the cabling and switches were all of high quality—allowing a lot of data to pass between the server and the music room. This resulted in very stable music software that ran midi and audio files very well, coupled with the students' ability to access the internet and shared resources on the network. It meant they could log on to any computer and access their work. The quality of the learning environment was very high and the provision quickly became popular with a large number of students.

Office-type software

Students will usually need to write down information, edit it, and present it in a format that is appropriate for the audience. They might occasionally need to create spread-sheets and presentations (such as in 'powerpoint') as well. This means that each computer, even though designated for music use, will probably require a word processor, a spread-sheet, and presentation software. Students might be asked to put together a powerpoint presentation on a particular topic or they might need this type of software installed on their computer in order to access a resource that the teacher has developed for them and then placed on the school intranet. Similarly a spread-sheet might be useful where students are asked to model a task that requires specific inputs and outputs—perhaps planning a concert and seeing how income and expenditure match. However, the licences are a considerable financial burden for schools. They represent a cost that has to be planned each year and over time some computers may end up with a later version of a piece of software compared to another computer in the same room—perhaps because the school could not afford to upgrade all the computers at the same time. This lack of consistency and compatibility can become frustrating.

It is possible for students to use something like the freely distributed Microsoft 'notepad' or 'word pad' programs for simple tasks. Word pad will enable students to carry out most writing tasks to a level that will be perfectly suitable for their needs. If this programme is used it should come free with the operating system and mean that a further licence for something like Microsoft Office is not required. Schools spend a lot of money on these office licences—often with no need. Students can use the free programs that come with the operating system or the school can embrace open-source software.

Open-source software

The open-source initiative is a fantastic example of the potentially democratizing power of the world wide web. The principle behind the movement is that the developers make software and the program source code freely available to the community. Other developers can contribute to further refinements and improvements which are then shared with everyone else. The result is a range of extremely powerful software available for free use. Schools, however, are often either unaware of this or too cautious to use it. This means they spend thousands of pounds on unnecessary licences and also maintain out-of-date versions of software because costs are prohibitive.

Schools could:

- use the free 'linux' operating system instead of windows
- use a free and excellent quality programme such as 'Open Office' instead of a commercial product
- use a wide range of free music programs such as 'audacity'.

These strategies will save a lot of money and ensure that each school computer has up-to-date and consistent software that students can download at home. There are further developments which will probably transform the ways that schools can improve access for students. For example, 'Think Free' is an initiative which enables the user to use an office-type program over the internet (through the internet browser) even though the program is not installed on the computer. Once the person has registered on the site and has internet access s/he can use these office programs and save the results into a public or private space. With this and other developments free space is provided for the user to save files. These types of developments mean students will be less disadvantaged if they cannot afford commercial office programs.

Interactive whiteboards and presentation technology

Presentation technologies enable a teacher to communicate with students. For example, when teaching a particular topic to a whole class an interactive whiteboard can be a good way to engage students. The interactive whiteboard is touch-sensitive. A projector, computer, DVD, VCR, or other devices can be connected to it. The teacher can control everything from the front of the room. The whiteboard also comes with virtual pens. These can be configured to any colour or width. The teacher and students can then write notes and pictures which may be saved or printed. The entire lesson can be printed, saved, loaded online, or e-mailed to the students. Students can respond very well to the use of colours and pictures so that lessons can become more motivating and organized. Lessons can be shared with others and saved for future use.

Whiteboards have some potential disadvantages as well. They tend to be expensive and require a certain amount of technical support to set them up. They also dictate that the teacher should spend time at the front of the class rather than moving about the room in a flexible way. This can have a negative effect on the quality of learning. Used without sufficient imagination and thought an electronic whiteboard can have a negative effect on the quality of a student's learning experience. A good teacher will make effective use of an interactive whiteboard but on its own it will not improve learning. Senior managers often, wrongly, assume that purchasing whiteboards is a good thing and makes a good contribution to the use of ICT in their school. I decided not to install one at NSG. Instead I used a gyro mouse. This is a cheap piece of technology. It enables the teacher to move around the classroom whilst still operating any program that is installed on a designated computer. The mouse uses a radio wave and is designed so that it can be moved up, down, or sideways and is able to send these commands to the computer. This computer is attached to an overhead projector which enables the students to see what is on the teacher's computer. There are also several graphics pads available. These can also be very useful. They are relatively cheap and enable the teacher to move around the room whilst interacting with a program. In this way the teacher can engage a whole class, or work with individuals/small groups. It gives access to a wider range of learning styles and activities than just using a whiteboard.

Use of a Virtual Learning environment

A Virtual Learning Environment (VLE) is a piece of software designed to facilitate the management of courses. It helps teachers and learners to access information and resources. The system can track learners' progress. While often thought of as a tool for distance education it can be used very effectively to supplement face-to-face learning. Information is accessed by students on pages that look similar to internet sites. Standard components include templates for content, discussion forums, chat, quizzes, and exercises using multiple-choice, true/false, or one-word-answer formats. Teachers complete the templates which are then released for learners to use. They can also included RSS services (where information is automatically linked and updated from an organization that provides this service).

NSG did not have a VLE and so I introduced one using the excellent open-source, free product called 'Moodle'. This quickly became established by other departments and I developed an AS Music Technology course with a lot of information available to students online—both at school and at home. This included a wide range of text, pictures, sound, and video files. In the second year of the course students' logs showed that there was very good use of resources in lessons and as preparation for coursework and terminal tasks.

There are many VLE systems available and many misconceptions about them. A lot of commercial products are expensive to purchase and maintain. Many schools have VLEs but use them only as places to store electronic files— not really engaging with the variety of learning activities that they can unlock for students. One of the reasons for this is that they are often seen as the responsibility of ICT teachers. VLEs need to be managed and developed by communities of staff who are interested in learning.

Developing specific music ICT skills

Schools might opt to develop and evaluate the level of ICT capability of Key Stage 3 students in order to monitor their skills in a structured way and give positive feedback and reward. For example over the course of a term or year students could be given credit for achieving certain skills, as set out in Table 12.

This kind of structured approach has limitations but, managed well, can provide a sense of direction and opportunities for regular positive feedback as skills are broken down into small, manageable steps.

Making effective use of modern technologies in music education

Modern technology has the ability to transform the way that we teach and learn. This potential is complex and it can be difficult for teachers to get sensible and impartial advice. Students find technology easy to use because it is the norm for them. Using technology effectively will require careful consideration of how we can transform learning so that it is less about

Teacher holds knowledge and releases it to students as required

and more about

Teacher helps the learner to find their way through the knowledge that they need at this stage in their learning

Technology offers us a fantastic opportunity to make music education fit the aspirations and interests of all students. It can enable them to work in contemporary styles and be allowed a more personalized approach. In order to do this effectively we have to evaluate carefully students' learning needs and choose activities and software that will let us achieve these aims. We have to resist the temptation to choose software or styles of learning that just re-enforce our own musical tastes, or to use musical software in a thoughtless way that leads to learning dead ends. Not responding to this agenda can be another example of the hidden curriculum at work.

The advantages of using a computer and music software in lessons are numerous and profound:

- the quality of the sounds used by the students (via a good-quality sound card) can be extremely motivating

Table 12 List of desirable ICT skills for students to achieve

File management	
I can	Example of how I did this (and date completed)
Locate a file on the computer or school network	
Load a programme such as a sequencer	
Load the file I want into the sequencer	
After I have worked on it, resave it in the space I want	
Rename a file if I need to	

Simple sequencer skills	
I can	Example of how I did this (and date completed)
Use the transport control to play, fast forward and rewind a song	
Select a sound and change it to the one I want	
Alter the tempo	
Set the locators	
Cycle between two points using the locators	

More advanced sequencer skills	
I can	Example of how I did this (and date completed)
Use the eraser	
Rename part	
Glue parts together	
Mute parts	
Solo them	
Copy tracks	
Loop tracks	

Drum editor	
I can	Example of how I did this (and date completed)
Open the drum editor	
Enter a part using the pencil tool	

Matrix editor	
I can	Example of how I did this (and date completed)
Open the matrix editor	
Write a part using the pencil tool	

Score editor	
I can	Example of how I did this (and date completed)
Open the score editor	
Change or add notes using the score editor	

Advanced sequencer skills	
I can	Example of how I did this (and date completed)
Export a MIDI file	
Cut and rearrange tracks	
Transpose tracks	
Quantize tracks	
Open the mixer and adjust the volume setting	
Open the mixer and adjust the pan setting	
Use the hyper draw to change volume	
Import an audio file	
Change the colour of the tracks to make information clearer	

- the music that students listen to and respond to out of school is often produced using a high level of music technology
- given the right resources students can make individual progress at a fast rate and not be inhibited by the requirements of a group, lack of instruments, or other resources
- students find the use of technology natural and motivating.

The QCA Key Stage 3 National Curriculum programmes of study included the following information about the use of ICT in music:

ICT helps pupils learn in music by supporting the development of musical skills, knowledge and understanding. ICT acts as a tool and a distinctive medium of musical expression, for example pupils can use ICT for recording or listening to music and for creating electronic sounds. ICT strongly influences the creative process and enables pupils to compose in a variety of different ways.[1]

Whilst this statement is true, it is theoretical and has probably had little effect on developing learning in music education. The two most important factors in allowing technology to provide change for the better are the teacher's pedagogical skills and the support for ICT within school at a senior management level (strong support often leading to an increased level of resources). In a few significant cases music technology has had a major impact on a school and made it more musical. For too many schools music technology has been peripheral, treated with respect (but at some distance), and has made limited impact.

Some potential disadvantages of using modern technologies in music lessons

Along with questions over the reliability of information on the internet raised earlier, ICT does have some potential drawbacks:

- the teacher may feel threatened and lack the necessary skills and experience to use the resource effectively
- resources may be too limited—causing students to lack appropriate levels of access to computers with sufficient hardware and software
- resources may initially seem expensive. However, given the context of a changing children's workforce, less teachers being available to work in schools, and the personal learning that ICT can bring, the investment may actually be very good value for money.

---

[1] QCA, *The National Curriculum Key Stage 3 Music Programme of Study* (London: HMSO, 2007).

◆ students may end up using software in an unimaginative and limited way. This is where the careful input of another student, adult, or teacher with creativity and imagination can be crucial. Using technology does not mean that teaching or learning will necessarily be effective. ICT requires the development of a strong understanding of teaching and how it can support learning. Indiscriminate, over-use of ICT can be negative.

For example, a piece of software may seem initially exciting and motivating for the students and the teacher:

I have found using e-jay an excellent way to motivate pupils. It allows pupils of all abilities to access composing—some just using the given samples, whilst the more able to create their own. I taught this to year 8 for the first time this year as a complete unit with excellent results—after an unsuccessful attempt at a rondo unit with last year's groups. In pupil feedback every pupil said they loved the work and many explained that they felt their confidence had developed. E-jay allowed pupils to develop their understanding of structure and texture, whilst encouraging them to listen to their music and ensuring that it worked as an ensemble. Where many pupils would fail in the performance aspect this allowed them to focus on selecting appropriate sounds and textures to suit their genre. They could then focus on their live performance of the song and think about how to make their vocal part effective.

Pupils were put into groups and their task was to create a pop/dance song. They had to write their own lyrics, make the backing track, record lyrics onto e-jay, add instrumental parts, add a dance routine and then make a video and CD recording.

I would be interested to hear other people's experiences of using e-jay. (posted on a music internet forum 2007)

The music software mentioned has been freely available for several years. It enables students to use a grid system to move prearranged music 'samples' around. Because these are collected and ordered by musical style as part of the supplied software the student can very easily create a piece that sounds like a piece of 'hip-hop' or 'trance' music. The software is easy to use and the results sound initially pleasing and motivating. There are many other programs that do similar things. They are all free or very cheap and have a similar interface (the way the screen looks to the user).

This type of software:

◆ is easy to use

◆ sounds good because the supplied files are of good quality

◆ enables the user to shorten and lengthen files, change tempo and pitch easily (many sound files available are designed to be easily edited or have extra information attached about the tempo that should be used).

It can, however, also lead to a quick sense of boredom because the input from the user can be very marginal—merely a case of moving files around using a painting tool. The user can import files from elsewhere or record bespoke sounds for a particular project, but these extension activities (which can be hugely creative and enjoyable) are rarely explored. Students can be shown how to create a style of dance music they will be very familiar with and enjoy. These DJ skills require a very sophisticated set of musical intelligences in order to select, edit, and merge together different samples and create a new and fresh-sounding musical canvas. The musical landscape is very familiar to students and matches the interests of many. The style is alien to many teachers.

I can remember a lively discussion I had with a group of secondary teachers over this type of software. The teachers were talking at the time about how they liked it and I agreed with them, although I asserted they needed to use it in a musical and imaginative way. To promote further debate I filmed my son (then aged $3\frac{1}{2}$) using the software in a confident way and showed it to the secondary teachers. They were doing similar sorts of activities with years 9, 10, and in one case year 11. My son is not an exceptional child and most reception-age children would enjoy moving sounds onto a grid and listening to the result, especially when it is in a contemporary style. Our conversation turned to what they could do to make activities that continued to engage students once the initial enthusiasm of the software had faded away. My challenge was if a $3\frac{1}{2}$-year-old could use this software confidently how would they ensure that ten years later his learning is supported by the same software (if that is what they choose to use)? I think this provides a good example of how technology can offer possibilities for a teacher to be creative and innovative but can become a cul-de-sac. The transactions often look like this:

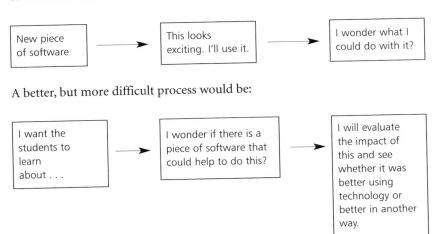

A better, but more difficult process would be:

I accept that it is sometimes difficult not to be seduced into trying all the features that a piece of software seems to offer. However, indiscriminate use will not necessarily support the learning of students.

A follow-up conversation with most of the teachers one year later showed that none of them used this software any more because the students had become bored with it. They had all moved on to using more complex software—but seemed to be repeating the same set of transactions: 'How can I use this piece of technology and what can it do?' Rather than: 'How can I use this piece of technology to help me to get the students to learn in a more effective way that will lead to improved attitudes and achievement?' Buying something more complex and expensive seems to be a waste of time if good use has yet to be made of the simple and cheap program. Some teachers have started to think through the impact that technology can make and started to ask questions about when it is best to use it:

Indiscriminate use of music software can have some drawbacks:

I've noticed a decline in composing standard over the past few years due mainly I think to sequencing software. Do we teach pupils enough about harmony, melody, structure and texture, or do we now tend to sit them in front of a sequencer to experiment? I'm a principal examiner for GCSE composing and all too often I hear compositions that have a plethora of synth sounds creating a confusing wall of sound with little substance. Candidates who have 1000 or more sounds at their disposal can be like kids in a sweetshop and use all of them at once. How can we address this issue without throwing the baby out with the bathwater? (Posted on a music internet forum 2007)

Imaginative planning that leads to effective learning is the answer, rather than just using ICT for the sake of it.

Using music-specific software

A big consideration when setting up ICT music resources is the type of music-specific software to use and where to get it from. A common set of software for a secondary music classroom might include:

- 'sequencing' software
- office-type software such as a word processor
- audio-editing software
- software for learning instruments independently
- software for teaching aspects of musical notation or theory
- software designed to accompany performers or rehearse sections of a piece
- music notation and scoring programmes.

I have dealt with several aspects of software to learn an instrument elsewhere in this book. I am convinced that this, used well, can be of huge benefit to students. It will also become increasingly more sophisticated, with the ability to accompany the students, analyse his/her performance, and monitor their practice sessions. A good instrument-learning programme may be preferable to a bad teacher—although students will always need good teachers. Software to teach music theory notation has its place and some students will find it extremely helpful. This type of software does have the potential to be misused if approached in a thoughtless way, especially with students who do not need to learn music notation to access the music styles that they are interested in. I will consider in a little more detail some of the more common types of music software and their advantages/ disadvantages.

Music-sequencing software

A 'sequencer' is a piece of software that enables the user to:

◆ compose pieces using a midi input device (such as a keyboard, guitar, saxophone, or voice). Most teachers use keyboards. Other input devices such as guitars or drum pads can be of huge benefit to some students but are rarely explored.

◆ download pieces in a midi format for performance or editing.

Most sequencers look similar—so once the user is comfortable with one program others are easy to use and understand.

Sequencers have some other advantages:

1. The data file they use is usually very small—so it does not take up much space and can easily be e-mailed, saved, or stored on a website.

2. The data file uses a standard and universally recognized format such as 'general midi'. This means that a piece created with one set-up can usually be played successfully on a completely different computer. This is very helpful because it means that local, national, and international sharing of resources is extremely easy and not restricted by incompatibility of files. There are hundreds of thousands of midi files freely available on the internet (although some may contravene copyright laws).

3. Midi controllers can also be used to shape the volume, velocity, and dynamics of notes. They can also change the tempo and other expressive factors as well. A midi controller is a piece of hardware (or software) that enables the user to add extra data information to a midi file. This information is stored in the same, universal format and can therefore be read by other software. However, they are rarely explored in a way that utilizes their musical potential.

4. Basic sequencers are very cheap—in fact there are several that are free. Schools frequently spend far more money than they need purchasing software that is expensive and unnecessary. Many seem to assume that the most expensive must be the best without realizing that cheaper software has enormous potential. It is the effective use of the features that matters most, rather than how much it cost in the first place.

These advantages of compatibility and universality have ensured that the sequencer format has remained extremely popular over the last twenty years. Modern sequencers also allow the user to synchronize and play together midi files and audio files (these are much larger recorded sound files).

Disadvantages of sequencers

1. The sound quality produced by a midi file can be poor—sounding artificial and distinctly 'computerized'. This is because the sound is played back by an in-built midi-synthesizer and these artificially created sounds have limited quality. A reasonable quality sound card will make quite a big difference. The inbuilt sounds within many computer motherboards may also give rise to 'latency' problems (where there is a time delay between what is played/recorded and what is heard).

2. Although midi files are small they do not work especially well within a windows environment (the operating system used by PCs) and there can be initial problems in setting up the right drivers in order to make sure that everything works smoothly. Once the system is set up it should be reasonably reliable and cause few problems. A good ICT technician will be able to support with this task.

There are two ways that the sound quality of midi files can be improved quite dramatically. The first involves the use of sound fonts.

Sound fonts

Sound fonts are software 'samples' (short recorded sounds). A sound font will consist of short samples which are triggered by a midi device. A sound font file, or sound font 'bank', will usually contain one or more samples which can be reproduced at different pitches and dynamic levels. Each sample may be associated with one or more ranges of pitches and dynamics. For example, a violin sound font will consist of small recordings of a violin. To make the sound more realistic the pitch that is played on a keyboard or the velocity that is used by a player will trigger a different recording from one that is played lower or quieter. This means that the sounds are much more realistic. It also means that because the sounds are relatively short (they are looped if they need to be sustained) they do not take up too much computer memory. This makes the sounds more realistic and less mechanical. The quality will depend on the sample quality, number of samples used, and how they have been edited. There are hundreds of free sound fonts available because a lot of enthusiasts produce them and make them available via the internet. The software used to create them is also freely available. Sound font banks are integrated with MIDI devices and can be seamlessly used in place of General Midi (GM) in many computer music sequencers. The sound quality of sound font banks is generally superior to standard GM banks, and many sound font banks have been created specifically to replace GM with samples of each corresponding instrument. It is possible to load sound fonts that will turn your computer into a tabla, sitar, or any instrument that someone has created sound fonts for or which you decided to create yourself. The technology is cheap and very readily available. It has the potential to improve dramatically the sound of the pieces that students use. More advanced students can also be encouraged to record and develop their own sound fonts.

VST instruments and effects

Another way to improve sounds is to use a Virtual Studio Technology (VST) instrument or 'plug-in'. Thousands of these exist, making VST the most widespread audio plug-in available. VST plug-ins are pieces of software that often look like particular instruments or effects. They are available for use on all operating systems. A VST instrument (or VSTi) is used to synthesize sound or play back sampled audio. VST instruments include virtual synthesizers and samplers. They can be played with an appropriate software and hardware configuration. Many VST instruments are software copies of well-known hardware devices. Programmers often try to make them look and feel like the original piece of equipment, as well as sounding like them. VST plug-ins can also have effects, such as reverb processors or a 'phaser'. Because VST is a universal standard the plug-in can be used with any modern sequencer software. The user stores the instrument or effect in a specially designated folder and the software will automatically access it when required. Hundreds of free plug-ins are available and they work well with low-latency sound cards. For example a sound card that supports Audio Stream Input Output (ASIO) software can bypass Windows' slower audio system and offers much lower latency times (this is the potential delay between what is played and what is heard). Macintosh computers come with low-latency audio drivers. The result is that the user can create excellent quality sounds and add effects that can be 'recorded' using a standard midi device before being played back using an instrument that sounds far superior. All of this can be done for free. Schools, however, often spend hundreds of pounds on software that they do not need or understand how to use musically.

There are numerous commercial sound banks that can be purchased and installed on a computer to make it sound completely different For example, software manufacturers have recorded all the instruments of the orchestra played by famous players and these can be installed onto the computer. They can then be easily triggered by a cheap or free piece of software, making a piece sound incredibly realistic. These audio collections are usually expensive because they offer very detailed recordings of each instrument. A violin sound will include:

◆ recordings at different pitches (so that it captures the tone of that pitch

◆ a range of dynamics

◆ a range of effects such as pizzicato

◆ crescendo and diminuendo

◆ a range of attacks

These permutations can all be controlled by the user—producing very rich and realistic sounds.

MIDI data can be used to trigger other controls and make pieces sound more effective. A crescendo, accent, or another musical feature can be controlled externally by the person operating a sequencer (even if they are using standard GM sounds). This is very useful for students who are not fluent keyboard players and therefore not able to shape the music in an imaginative way by just recording the piece in one go with all the dynamics and phrasing that they would ideally like to have. Information can be sent to the device via a midi keyboard, drum, guitar, or microphone (to suit the needs of the individual user). It means that an effective teacher does not have to be limited by anything other than his/her imagination.

Audio-editing software

Audio files are different from MIDI files. A midi file saves some data which a computer program can then interpret and use to 'play' a piece of music. For example the MIDI data might include:

◆ which note is to be played

◆ how long it lasts

◆ the level of attack at the start of the note

◆ how quickly the sound decays

◆ which instrumental sound should be used to play this data

All of this information is stored in a file which another program can 'play'. The midi file does not contain any actual sound. Audio files, however, are actual 'recordings' of a sound that can be played back using a piece of software, or on a CD payer. The sound file is usually very good. It depends on the resolution of the file and the quality of the device used to capture the sound. The file will be extremely large. Several can take up a significant amount of space on a server or computer hard disk.

A common format is '.wav'. This is a large, high-quality file and the user is able to edit it in a significant number of ways. To do this an audio-editing program will be required. Sound files can be in other formats as well. Some are specific to particular programs or types of software. Some seek to dramatically reduce file size. An Mp3 file is small because certain frequencies which are inaudible to the human ear have been eliminated and the file is compressed. This results in a file that is of lower quality—but which is usually very acceptable to the listener. Because the file is smaller the user can load a lot of files to an Mp3 player or other device. This format is not suitable for audio-editing without conversion back to a file such as .wav. There are other audio files as well, such as 'aiff', 'wma' or 'ogg vorbis'. They essentially offer the same thing—access to high-quality recorded sound.

Audio-editing software can be free—the excellent open-source program 'Audacity', for example. There are also hugely expensive programs that are used by professional recording studios. Schools often purchase programs that are far more expensive than needed. Some quite cheap midi sequencers contain very good audio-editing programs. This software is included in the price of the sequencer and there is excellent compatibility between the two programs.

Score-writing software

It is relatively common to find secondary schools equipped with score-writing software. This enables the user to input information, usually via a music keyboard, that results in a music score. The interface is based around musical notation and 'notes' are inserted into the score as the player adds information either in real time or note by note.

This software:

◆ produces a good score. This makes it attractive, especially to students with a high level of musical literacy;

◆ is often more useful to the teacher than most students because it requires a high level of understanding of musical notation;

◆ is often extremely expensive and requires frequent costly upgrades. Free, or very cheap software that will do similar things is readily available;

◆ is often used in an extremely limited way that promotes poor teaching and learning skills.

Score-writing software can be useful for AS and A2 students, especially those who are confident about writing music which they can hear in their head. This type of software is far less useful as a creative tool for composition for the majority of students. Purchasing it can therefore result in a school excluding a wide range of students because it gives a strong message that you need to be able to read music fluently in order to be a musician. This is not true. You need to be able to read music fluently if you want to participate in most western classical music activities. The cost of this software can be enormous, especially if several computers are equipped with it. Manufacturers also have a habit of updating the software, at high cost to the user and not ensuring that older files are compatible with new software versions. There is a range of software which has excellent scoring facilities as well as extra features that enable the user to be creative and work in a number of different genres and styles. A good teacher and a musical school will understand how to approach the issue of scoring facilities in a way which has the potential to meet the needs and interest of many students, not just the musically literate ones.

Choosing suitable software

Many schools rely on advice from their local retailer, or in some cases national suppliers who have a reputation for supplying music ICT resources. The problem with this approach is that well-meaning local shops, local peripatetic teachers, or even the respected supplier may not have a deep understanding of learning. This is not surprising—it is not their core business. The result may be that schools purchase equipment and software based on two principles:

- what will make the supplier a good profit
- what has the latest bells and whistles (which may also maximize profits for the supplier)

Some schools rely on extremely informal advice and use this to make major decisions about purchasing equipment and resources that may cost thousands of pounds and have a huge impact on the curriculum for several years. A surprising number of teachers rely on informal advice from someone on the internet. An extract from an internet forum shows the sort of responses that are made to requests for information:

would suggest that you go for stand-alone PCs. You can get a lot of free software, sounds and add-ons from the net. An ordinary PC (around £200 if you shop around) is just fine but you would do well to have a separate graphics card installed (about £20 per machine). Ideally you want a sound-card too. The budget choice is probably between the M-Audio Audiophile 24/96 and the EMU 0404 card. You get a free version of quite a lot of software (including Cubase) with the EMU card. You could also consider the Creative Audigy 4 if you can still get it! (try MISCO for your hardware) The sound-cards are in the region of £40 to £50; if it were me I'd go for the Audiophile. If you can't run to separate soundcards [*sic*] then install ASIO4ALL (off the net or Computer Music magazine disks) this will make the onboard sound chip behave like a low-latency soundcard and it's free! If you can afford it it's worth connecting the ins and outs on the sound card to a little mixer by the computer (about £20) this means that your pupils won't be for ever foraging around the back of the computers and breaking the connections. (posted on internet forum 2007).

The advice is presented in an authoritative way but there is no way of knowing whether or not it is impartial, driven by sound principles, or of good quality. Yet the response from the teacher who posted the query shows s/he intended to act on it. Considerable amounts of money will be committed. Another post gives advice that I believe to be completely wrong and ill-advised. No doubt the person giving the advice is doing it for what s/he believes to be sound reasons:

I stronly [*sic*] suggest that you resist all attempts to get you to connect all the machines to a school network. It's useful to have one machine on the internet, but networking software is usually death for Music applications. You'll spend hours of frustration! I hope this is helpful! Do come back if I can be of further assistance. (posted on internet forum 2007)

This seems to me like a very hit-and-miss approach. One outcome is that schools may purchase software which is far more expensive and complicated than they actually need. There is also a mystique that seems to surround software. Many purchasers feel they must have the most expensive version of something because it is bound to be the best. There is a fantastic range of very cheap and free software available which does everything that these music teachers need. A secondary outcome may be that the software is so complex that functions are not understood/used (despite the fact that it is these that cost the extra investment) or the complexity adds an extra layer of potential pitfall, resulting in technical problems and frustration.

Once the user reaches a point where s/he is not able to do something musical it may signal the need to move onto something more complex and expensive. However, it may take a surprisingly long time to reach the need for further expense and complexity, since most free and cheap music software is powerful enough for what is required. Limitations are most often experienced through the imagination and ambition of the user rather than the limitations of a piece of inexpensive software.

Whilst working with NSG I reviewed the software available and chose a sequencer that cost around £30. I chose it because

1. The software got consistently good reviews from independent magazines.

2. It was relatively cheap.

3. It had a good sequencer, a good facility for creating and editing audio files, and a reasonable level of facility to create standard notation scores as well. In other words it did everything that I thought might be needed for Key Stage 3, 4, and A level courses.

Schools can often benefit from looking at a range of software that is used by enthusiasts who write and arrange music in a contemporary style rather than software promoted for the education market. There are several magazines that cater for this market and they are an extremely useful resource. These magazines often match the interests and tastes of young people. Some of the topics they cover are very contemporary—dealing with the musical styles that will be very familiar to secondary-age students.

There are also hundreds of free plug-ins (extra bits of software that you can use with a sequencer) available that can be used to create all kinds of interesting drum parts, riffs, or 'pop'-type sequences. These are all of great interest to students. However, most schools tend to try to recreate classical-sounding pieces using either a sequencer or score-writing software. This approach may not match the interests of the large majority of students.

Edit screens

A key factor in musical use of software is the approach of the teacher. Many approach the use of a sequencer through the main screen used for recording pieces in real time or the screen that uses notation to insert notes. These can be useful but most sequencers have other features which are excellent for getting a wide range of students to be creative. For example a drum editor can enable students to draw in patterns (including the volume of an instrument) whilst a phrase is looped. This gives them instant feedback on what the piece sounds like and how it might be adjusted. There are also several publications available that represent particular rhythm patterns in this sort of format—so students can use them as a stimulus. The matrix edit window is very useful for students because it enables them to look at a visual representation of a piece of music without being confused or put off by musical notation. The notes can be changed (note length, pitch, and dynamics) very easily and quickly. If a phrase is looped at the same time the student can get feedback on what a phrase sounds like and make further adjustments. This is a very good way to create loops and riffs, especially where the students feels that they have not got any ideas. It is the type of editing that is commonly used in the music industry and by a wide range of amateur enthusiasts but rarely utilized in schools.

The mixer screen is very useful to students in shaping music. Most sequencers enable you to add effects, adjust volume, and carry out a range of other activities, making a piece sound more polished. Most of these can be 'recorded' by the sequencer. This means that adjustments can be made in balancing volume levels as a piece is played (enabling the listener to interact with the music in a very powerful way). This is then 'recorded' into the final piece. A few sequencers also enable the user to change musical parameters. The student will be able to select a track or a section of music and play it half tempo, twice as fast, in inversion, with a crescendo, or in a number of other ways. This can be an excellent way for the student to create very sophisticated musical ideas—which s/he is not able to perform on an instrument.

Many pieces of software have a contemporary look about them—because they are set up to create modern dance-style music or to use specially prepared loops. These can be very effective when working with students who do not have a strong background in western classical music. They are also extremely powerful and effective.

What does a musical school that uses technology look like?

- access to a good level of software and hardware
- decisions about purchases informed by suitability for learning, meeting the interests of the students and a good interface with the learner (rather than the latest thing, what the teacher uses or most expensive piece of kit with bells and whistles)
- creative teaching methods that use a wide range of inputs other than just standard notation
- an open and honest approach that tries to engage the interests of different groups of students
- infrastructure that works well, is reliable, and is constantly evaluated.

This seems like a simple set of guidelines. My experience shows that there are very few schools in England that have started to sort out all of these issues, even amongst those that have a strong reputation for the use of music technology. However, I believe that technology has the potential to transform many aspects of the curriculum and in particular that it can engage a very wide range of students in a positive way. We seem to be a long way yet from this because of a lack of skill, experience, and confidence amongst many teachers. There is a lot of untapped resource available through community musicians and adults other than teachers who have developed a wide range of skills in how to use technology to recreate contemporary popular music. A musical school will have realized this and started to access some of this expertise.

Chapter 9

The community dimension of schools of the future

Music is your own experience, your own thoughts, your wisdom. If you don't live it, it won't come out of your horn. They teach you there's a boundary line to music. But, man, there's no boundary line to art.

Charlie Parker

The purpose of this chapter is to look at the community role of schools, particularly, but not exclusively, in relation to the English Specialist Music College programme. I will consider some of the ways that music can provide a strong feature of this community work. Although I will start by reviewing the brief that was given to these Specialist Colleges I believe that all schools can use music very effectively to work with their local community and to engage people who feel they are not musical and/or at risk of social exclusion. This requires the right vision and understanding of what can be achieved. The Specialist College guidance information is a useful starting point.

These schools were expected to have a clear and important role within their local community. Each had to write a community plan, which included working with at least five schools (including one other secondary school). There was also an expectation that specialist schools would engage other groups in their wider community. Guidance from the Department for Education and Skills (DfES) encouraged links with special schools, a business partner, and a commitment to the principles of inclusion, equal opportunity, and cross-cultural provision. Schools with existing community links were encouraged to build on those as part of their plan. Whilst many were successful, others struggled to be sufficiently imaginative, or to turn ideas into practical activities that worked. An evaluation by OFSTED in 2001 said that:

With few exceptions—notably among the sports colleges—the community dimension was the weakest element of specialist schools' work. Most schools have found their community role challenging to define and pursue. There were good examples of support for other schools, required under the scheme, in about half of the technology, language and arts colleges visited. In the remainder, objectives were vague and support did not focus sharply enough on learning outcomes. Where implementation had resulted in limited benefits, the resourcing and management of the activities were often inadequate.[1]

This matched my own perceptions of many of these schools. Four years later OFSTED carried out a follow-up evaluation:

The community role of specialist schools has improved considerably since the last Ofsted evaluation and is now a strength of the programme. The quality of liaison between specialist schools and their partners is good at four out of five schools. Support for primary schools is good, but links with other secondary partners are more varied in quality.

Many community groups benefit from additional support, but specialist schools often find it difficult to establish links with local businesses. Only half of specialist schools have strategies to help partners become independent of support over time. About half of specialist schools have good systems for evaluating the impact of the support they provide.[2]

Revised guidance from the Specialist Schools Trust in 2006/07 signalled a move from a separate 'community development plan' to a more holistic approach. A community element was an expected feature within the school development plan. This was significant because it placed the community element at the centre of the school's work. It was also expected that all specialist schools would need to review both their school and community performance within their self-evaluation form (SEF). The SEF in UK schools was a document, and a process, used to regularly self-analyse performance and inform external agencies such as OFSTED of progress being made.

Guidance on the community role of Specialist Music Colleges

It was suggested that Music Colleges might work with partner schools in a number of ways. These included:

- providing access for pupils from other schools to its specialist facilities
- providing master classes for year 6 gifted and talented pupils in music
- using communication technologies—web-based or broadcast radio—to reach and hear from school partners
- developing ICT skills in music for pupils from partner schools

---

[1] OFSTED, *Specialist Schools: An Evaluation of Progress* (London: HMSO, 2001).

[2] OFSTED, *Specialist Schools: A Second Evaluation* (London: HMSO, 2005).

- providing technical expertise to support teachers using music-specific technology and equipment in partner schools
- making opportunities available for pupils from primary schools to learn a musical instrument
- enabling pupils from partner schools to access live performances in music
- enabling professional musicians to work with pupils in partner schools
- working with disaffected pupils from partner schools using music to raise self-esteem or motivation
- providing professional development for non-specialist teachers in partner schools in delivery of music.

It was also suggested that when working with the wider community a Music College might:

- provide access to specialist music facilities and technology for groups in the community
- use the school as a venue for local groups with an interest in music
- coordinate activity amongst local music groups for joint projects and festivals
- promote skills such as DJ and mixing, and sound recording for youth and community groups
- provide courses for adult learners in music, instrumental tuition, and music technology, and learning opportunities for local business/employers (including public sector employers) to help meet the identified learning needs of their employees.

These helpful and wide-ranging ideas had the potential to help a secondary school work very effectively and musically with its local community.

Schools within their local community

Although the community role of specialist schools was a key priority for the English government there were competing priorities championed by different departments within government, so although there were some common themes the detail was seldom well coordinated. A good example was the concept of extended schools providing a central point of contact for communities accessing a wide range of universal and specialist children's services. Having Extended Services within schools forms a natural synergy with the development of a community role for Specialist Colleges. Schools needed to make sense of these complementary activities and their different agendas and timescales. Schools provide a good community resource because there are lots of them, they are geographically spread, and often form a natural community focal point—particularly in rural areas. The idea of a school at the heart of its local community is not new, not restricted to UK schools, and not necessarily the exclusive territory of state-funded schools. Privately funded public schools can also have a well-defined and important community element to their work, particularly the larger and more established schools.

The Governors and Management of Stowe School respect the value of their position in the local community and the contribution it makes. We endeavour to instil in all our staff and pupils a strong sense of social responsibility and respect for the local community. A strong ethos of the school is to encourage all 'to think deeply, think for themselves and to think about others.' In the features below we aim to give a broad overview of the wide range of activities which Stowe undertakes as part of this commitment.

Luffield Group:
Stowe works in partnership with local schools as a member of the Luffield Group. This group was formed in July 1997 to promote co-operation between the secondary and preparatory schools of the small towns and villages lying between Bicester, Northampton and Milton Keynes on cross-curricular matters and events where mixing students from different schools is valuable. The co-operation and bonding between pupils from all the different schools results in some outstanding achievements and seeing so many children with diverse educational experience working and playing together is an extremely rewarding experience. (Stowe School website 2006)

This type of provision can be found in many of the large and well-known public schools. The model is one of a strong school reaching outwards, for the benefit of its local community. The partnership tends to be one way. An alternative and more radical approach involves developing buildings and resources that are actually 'co-owned' by the community. Examples of this approach can be found all over the country. A well-known project was developed in the Cambridgeshire Village Colleges during the 1930s. The Village Colleges were, and still are, extremely successful schools with a very strong community element. I taught in one for many years and had the privilege of being involved in a wide range of community activities. Henry Morris, who developed the concept, took great pride in the architecture and design of the Village Colleges because he saw the buildings, landscape, and public works of art as powerful educators and cultural influences. He believed that the practice and enjoyment of the arts was as necessary to people as food and air. He therefore placed a special emphasis on the way the Village Colleges supported cultural activities, encouraged local artists and the display of artistic work. Public schools often seem to place a high premium on the quality of their buildings and their favourable funding resources means they use high-quality, aesthetically pleasing buildings which seem to make strong statements about the educational values they promote. It is a strong marketing feature and makes a statement about the school to its local community and in some cases to a regional or national audience.

A school such as Eton College probably suggests 'traditional' values, high quality, and Oxbridge Colleges. It may therefore complement parents' views of the school as a musical school, but in a narrowly defined sense. This will probably be appealing and reassuring to the parents who can afford to send their child to the school. It doesn't suggest modernity, popular cultural values, or more informal links with the community it serves. Compare this to the modernistic architecture of the English government's Academies programme and Building Schools for the Future project (both developed to transform schools and buildings). What effect do they have on the local community and will they want to participate in activities at the school and feel ownership of it? These are questions that are difficult to answer. However, the design of the building and the way that the school interacts with its stakeholders will be crucial to its success and the engagement of particular groups, especially with those for whom education is a relatively low priority.

Caroline Chisholm School in Northamptonshire was completed in 2005 as part of a Private Finance Initiative (PFI) project. Here the vision of integrated education provision has moved on from the Village Colleges. The PFI company owns the buildings and facilities, which they rent to the school for a period of twenty-five years. At the end of this time the building is handed over to the school. The school rents the facilities from 8 a.m. to 6 p.m. Outside these times the PFI company (or its sub-contractor) sells the facilities to other providers and might choose to set up adult classes—if they make a reasonable profit. The musical activities on offer to the community are therefore likely to be shaped by a private provider and one of their aims will be commercial. This may have a profound effect on the shape of community music provision:

Local Community Groups and Organisations

We can offer you a regular meeting place, stage functions and special events with or without catering. Open after 5.00pm during school term, from 9.00am on weekends and throughout the school holidays.

Kajima Community provides a complete range of activities at the school including: adult education, athletics, football, rugby, cricket, badminton, volleyball, basketball, tennis, keep fit, aerobics, martial arts, dance, drama, theatre, music events, concerts, gymnastics, youth activities, birthday parties, dances, shows, banquets, promotional launches, wedding parties, meetings, conferences, corporate hospitality and almost any other activity you would like to attend or organise.' (Caroline Chisholm School website 2006).

The Village College vision of education from the cradle to the grave has been tempered by the benefits and restrictions of the marketplace.

What was the local community for a school such as NSG?

Like other Specialist Colleges NSG included partner schools (one secondary, one special, and three primaries) in its initial bid for Music College status. Unlike many Specialist Colleges they did not form a discrete and tight geographical area around NSG. This is partly because NSG takes students from across the whole of Northampton—over fifty primary schools. Being a girls' school also had an impact on the shape of community provision. Should the school be working just with girls? How does this fit with the fact that it is the only Specialist Music College in Northamptonshire? Many Specialist Colleges create a natural link with feeder schools—relatively easy in a rural area with a tightly defined catchment area. It provides them with a good marketing opportunity to engage with these schools and their parents. The fact that NSG admitted students from across a wide area, coupled with the determination of senior leaders to be a resource for the local community, meant that I tried hard to ensure that community provision responded to the needs of:

♦ Northampton (not just schools that had a link with NSG and not just girls)

♦ Northamptonshire (as the only Specialist Music College)

♦ The national scene (as a school that by being the first was helping to lead the way).

An outcome was that I think the NSG community dimension felt different to many Specialist Colleges. This was a real strength because the community work was relatively new and there were no preconceptions that needed to be broken down. There was also a sense in which the inclusive philosophy of the school could flourish. This meant that NSG worked with a very wide range of groups:

♦ Partner schools within the bid

♦ Local residents

♦ Primary and special schools across Northampton

♦ Early years

♦ Local venues

♦ Students at risk of exclusion

♦ Local festivals

♦ The elderly

♦ Adults within the community

♦ All schools across the UK

◆ Community music groups

◆ Other Northants schools

NSG had an extremely useful 750-seat theatre (Spinney Hill Theatre). This had been used as a regular venue for concerts and productions in the past but use had declined since the Borough Council had built a 1,700-seat concert hall in the late 1980s. An early task for the school was to adjust the acoustic in the theatre to make it less dry and more acceptable for live performances. The theatre provided a key focal point for many of the community activities.

The 2004 initial Specialist College bid included a community position statement:

There is already significant community involvement in the school. Site open until 9pm every weekday and at various times over the weekend, is staffed and the Theatre is stewarded for any public performances. Wide range of usage in the Theatre, Drama studio, Dance studio, Swimming Pool, Sports Hall, and classrooms and activities range from the Jesus Army to Arts Theatre to badminton. The 750 seat Theatre is well used and could further develop to provide a wider range of musical attractions/recitals for the local community, possible link with Community Arts Theatre, Northamptonshire Touring Arts.

Many of our Asian students have a strong musical tradition within their community, which we celebrate eg at the Diwali and Eid Festivals through assemblies, when students play their music and dance for the school. (extracts from 2004 community section of NSG bid)

The bid also included some priorities for development:

◆ to support teachers in the primary schools in Northampton to raise achievement in music at KS2

◆ to organize music workshops for gifted and talented primary pupils not currently learning a musical instrument

◆ increase uptake of music tuition in schools in disadvantaged areas with a low uptake of music tuition and offer a term's free taster sessions to targeted students in Year 6

◆ to organize ten sessions over two years for year 5, 6, 7 students with behavioural difficulties, sessions to include use of music and drama

◆ to support collaborative teaching in AS and A level Music in cluster schools

◆ to host more singing days for primary pupils

Once the school started as a Specialist Music College in September 2004 a number of factors affected the community provision:

1. There was scope to be far more ambitious, daring, and forward-thinking.

2. My secondment meant that I could use part of my time to focus on this area whilst other staff coped with the demands of bringing together a school that now included three extra year groups and a considerable focus on the new PFI building project.

3. The appointment of an administrative assistant who had the community dimension as a clear and discrete responsibility enabled many activities to move forwards unhindered by the distractions of school activities.

4. As the first Music College NSG had a particular status that helped engagement with others.

5. These drivers for change were tempered by the reality of finding sufficient partners who had capacity and the inevitable internal resistance to change during a period of turbulence.

Community activities at NSG during 2004–2005

The first year was characterized by plans to deliver the aims set out in the successful bid to become a Specialist Music College. It became clear fairly early on that there was scope for more extensive and ground-breaking work. A key factor in moving forwards was making links with the right people and organizations locally, regionally, and nationally. It was also important to find enthusiasm for change and development rather than resistance and blocking tactics. I will describe some of the activities that took place during the first year. Far more happened than space allows me to describe.

An early project involved a partnership with Yamaha UK. Yamaha promoted a tour with a group of musicians who gave a free concert—the 'Visions' tour. This was then followed up by members of the audience (mainly primary-age children) having the opportunity to try out an instrument. Around 800 local children came to the concerts where instruments were played in an ensemble and demonstrated individually. These students then tried an instrument of their choice, many for the first time. The project got the community provision off to a flying start and created a lot of enthusiasm. The feedback from teachers and pupils involved was very positive.

The Yamaha Day was simply amazing for staff and students alike! Just looking at all those eager faces, the band must have realised they had them in the palm of their hands—a most rewarding experience. The presentation was very slick and, for me, hit just the right note (no pun intended)—it was visually sensational. The members of the band were not only extremely accomplished musicians but could enthuse the students at just the right level. Compliments too to the supporting crew—a vital link in any production! (Julie Shaw, Director of Music, Northampton School for Girls)

There were also more mixed views about the day:

I recently had the privilege to be involved with Yamaha's Vision Tour to Northampton School for Girls (a music specialist school) and I commend Yamaha for its own vision. No expense seemed to have been spared in the production; live music delivered in a totally professional way and in such an electrifying format can't help but raise the profile of instrumental and vocal work in our schools.

It was clear from the feedback after the performance that all the students went away inspired, having had a brief hands-on experience with a variety of instruments. You had to admire the way Yamaha's instruments survived the onslaught of one child after another and still continued to function even when slightly buckled.

The problem for those of us running music services is how we meet the demands for support raised by such an event. Is it even fair to raise expectations in this way?' (Peter Dunkley, Head of Northamptonshire Music Service)

Is it fair to raise expectations? A key theme of this book is that we absolutely should and that we should challenge any message that suggests otherwise. Peter was of course being cautious and reflecting a very pragmatic approach. I say, let us celebrate raised expectations and then try to cope with them. The alternative hidden curriculum approach takes the view that if it is inconvenient it is best not to encourage the young people to participate. Traditional approaches can result in the exclusion of key groups of students. Exclusion is a strong word, but many students wanted to learn an instrument and were not able to, for a variety of reasons. In this sense they had been excluded. NSG gave their own students an opportunity to follow up their initial trial with a lesson given by post-16 students. Fifty year 7 students, who expressed an interest in learning a new instrument, were given a free 'taster' lesson in December 2004 and a few girls went on to start lessons as a result of the project. Many more would have liked to but space on the instrumental timetable did not 'allow' this, so the instrumental teachers 'selected' girls for the spaces that were available. A number of students wanted to learn an instrument but were not able to and this raised some particular issues for me about access and fairness over instrumental tuition. The way this issue was addressed is covered in Chapter 7. The provision for the primary students who attended the event was also patchy. Expectations had indeed been raised but the opportunities were not available.

Researching the views of partner schools

During the autumn term I carried out research with local schools (not just those named in the bid) about the support that they would like to receive from NSG. Some key themes emerged. Singing was a particular feature. NSG therefore sent the local schools a questionnaire asking what type of support they would like and Julie Shaw from NSG was given one day a week for a year to work with local schools. NSG also ran a CPD session for primary teachers on singing. I organized a very successful singing day for 450 local primary-aged children led by Carol Pemberton from Black Voices. This workshop electrified the teachers and children. It was a good example of how singing, which can be a mundane activity, can enthuse a hall full of students. A key to this was the inspiring repertoire. This was followed up by a very successful singing Easter School which hosted 200 singers for two days and led to the setting up of a community choir for pupils in years 5, 6, and 7 called 'Voices—the Northampton Children's Choir'. This then became a regular weekly event.

Other priorities were identified as well:

- support for general class teachers in primary schools
- support with artists working in schools
- support for post-16 music education
- specific support for Special Schools

The programme of community activities therefore addressed these issues over the next eighteen months.

Launch event and celebration day

Because NSG had so many competing priorities in September 2004 I decided to delay holding a 'launch event' to celebrate becoming a Music College until March 2005. Regular meetings were held with staff representatives from across the school in order to try to ensure that there was widespread support and acceptance for an event that involved the whole school community. The planned format had some key features:

- involvement of a well-known musician—a female to emphasize to the girls that music was a possible career option for those who had the skill and deter-mination. The intention was also to focus the professional community's attention in on the school as well. Evelyn Glennie accepted the invitation to join the school for this important event.
- ensuring that every student in the school—all 1,700—were involved in the day in some way.
- promoting diversity in musical styles and cultures in order to offer a positive and wide-ranging experience for the students.
- commissioning new work in order to contribute to the professional community of composers, stretch the horizons of the students, and invest in the music of the future.
- reaching out to the local community—not just the school community.

During the day a wide range of NSG student groups gave concerts and these were attended by every student in the school. Members of the local community, including local residential homes for the elderly, were invited. Every single lesson taught during the day, no matter what subject, included music as a key element.

NSG commissioned a new piece called 'Blood Moon' for orchestra from local composer Tom Williams. The contemporary language stretched the musical horizons of the students considerably and took them out of their comfort zone. Workshops were held for pre-school children and students in years 7 and 8 attended samba workshops. The concert was featured on local television and certainly made a big impact on the local community. Evelyn Glennie's positive reaction, and feedback from others who attended the concert suggested that the event put NSG on the map at a local, regional, and national level.

It was truly an honour for me to participate and share with you in such an incredible evening of music making. You all gave a remarkable evening displaying immense proficiency in all your musical endeavours which was highly infectious, greatly admired and frankly I shall not forget the evening. You are setting a standard of participation that is high and this alone will be an inspiring benchmark for future pupils and staff to surpass. Your hard work and dedication is such a success story for me to broadcast nationally and internationally. (Evelyn Glennie, 2005)

I had wanted to make an impact on all the students at NSG—even those who were not directly involved in the evening concert. Every student was given a commemorative programme and they all experienced music in lessons and attended a concert during the day. However, my research into the views of students showed that despite this a significant number still felt that music in school was something that they viewed as being outside of their lives.

The programme cover was designed so that it had an inclusive feel to it—avoiding too many overt references to white, western art music. The artist Quentin Blake demonstrated fantastic generosity by supplying a drawing free of charge. The concert included music from a wide range of styles and cultures.

Other activities

NSG hosted a very successful music conference in November 2004 organized by the Local Authority Advisory Service. This involved 120 primary and secondary teachers in an exhilarating and interesting programme of events and workshops. The partnership between NSG and the Local Authority was very strong and provided a lot of mutual benefits. It reflected the inclusive approach taken by the school and the head teacher in particular, to working with the local community. NSG was seen by managers as a resource, rather than being primarily concerned about what could be gained from a relationship. I believe that this was a brave and enlightened approach.

During the autumn of 2004 NSG I applied for a grant from Youth Music and worked in partnership with 'Weapons of Sound' to produce a school-based junk orchestra. The project also enabled four partner schools to do the same. The aim was to increase access to music-making for those who had no previous experience. A key part of the project was the recruitment of workshop leaders from the sixth form who were soon confidently running sessions for pupils from years 7 and 8. The workshop leaders had to provide a CV and attend an interview in order to give them a vocational experience. I deliberately chose leaders who had little musical experience, much to the consternation of some of the music staff. A few could not see how the sixth-form workshop leaders would be able to run a group that was of sufficiently high quality. The girls who participated may not have reached the highest levels of performance skills but loved being in the group and the vast majority would not have had the opportunity to participate in music-making if the group had not existed. They may also not have been encouraged to keep coming to the group if it had been run by an 'expert'. This group did a lot to increase the cross-section of students who were participating in extra-curricular music-making at NSG. They also contributed to some excellent music workshops as part of the NSG music Easter and Summer Schools.

This project was facilitated by Weapons of Sound, part of an exciting and extremely influential community music initiative based at Estover Community College in Plymouth. Their outstanding work demonstrates how vision and energy can make a strong contribution to the local community. The approach at Estover is firmly rooted in the notion of a high level of participation.

The Estover Percussion Project has expertise in developing, managing and funding music and dance within the community. Since 1991 people throughout the region have enjoyed the sounds of Real Steel, Weapons of Sound, and Jam Samba—the original and still successful founders of the Project. As a pioneering community music project, it's our job to open up new opportunities and re-engage disaffected young people. But we think it's just as important to have fun with music as to win prizes. Our aim is to help you enjoy music from access to excellence. The Soundhouse is a unique collaboration between Estover Community College and Estover Percussion Project. It brings together cutting-edge technologies, leading youth bands, musicians, teachers and a truly unique learning environment. (Extracts taken from Estover Community College's and the Soundhouse's websites 2006)

The partnership between NSG and organizations such as Weapons of Sound provides a good example of how schools can use community music organizations with an inclusive policy to increase participation and access to music-making for a wide range of students in the school and the local community. To be successful the sixth-form workshop leaders did need someone in school who was able to challenge the notion that extra-curricular groups are always for particular students, rather than potentially participative and enjoyable. The first year had been characterized by the exploration of new relationships, establishing structures within NSG to manage projects and the realization that the potential for future development was enormous.

Community activities 2005–2006

Everyone at NSG was moved by the plight of the thousands of people who died during the tsunami of 26 December 2004.

Deep under the Indian Ocean, at the epicentre of the quake, the 20m (65ft) upward thrust of the seafloor set in motion a series of geological events that were to devastate the lives of millions. Billions of tonnes of seawater, forced upward by the movement of the seabed now flowed away from the fault in a series of giant waves. Thirty minutes after the shaking had subsided, the first wave, travelling eastwards, crashed into Sumatra. On the shores directly facing the epicentre, the waves reached heights of 20m (65ft), stripping vegetation from mountain sides 800m (0.5 mile) inland, capsizing freighters and throwing boats into the trees. The city of Banda Aceh, just a few kilometres further round the coast was almost completely destroyed, killing tens of thousands of people in just 15 minutes. (BBC news website 2004)

NSG hosted a concert to raise money for children in the tsunami-hit Tamil Nadu state of India. The concert, which took place on Tuesday 11 October 2005, featured a group of four very talented percussionists who mesmerized the audience with some truly amazing percussion playing. During the day the group took part in percussion workshops at Eastfield Primary School and Preston Hedges Primary School, as well as entertaining year 7 and 8 students in Spinney Hill Theatre. The proceeds from this concert were split between the victims of the tsunami and the more recent earthquake in Pakistan.

I also commissioned various artists to work with partner schools. This meant I was able to use my awareness of a wide range of musicians and offer local schools the chance to participate in a workshop at a reduced rate. I was able to ensure that the artists were of high quality and that they represented a culturally and musically diverse range of styles. For example Lucky Moyo has been a professional singer, dancer, choreographer, and arts lobbyist for more than twenty years and has performed all over the world. An accomplished workshop leader, Lucky believes that the experience of sharing is at the core of each activity. His hugely popular workshops are conducted with a communal and 'feel free to experiment' approach. The schools gained a huge amount from participating in a range of similar workshops.

Activities to support singing with the local community continued and we hosted further singing days in the Spinney Hill Theatre for primary-school children in the local area. These were led by Juliet Russell, a member of the singing group 'Sense of Sound'. The participants had a fantastic day and were able to give an impressive performance incorporating multi-part harmonies. Sense of Sound are an innovative group of musicians who develop community projects based around contemporary vocal styles. They have used a wide range of techniques to develop successful and enjoyable projects in schools and informal settings. Their work illustrates again the wealth of expertise that exists within the informal sector and which schools can learn from and utilize. Sense of Sound take singing to a new dimension. For example:

- The Water Music Project—creating an original a cappella vocal piece with four schools and 100 school children between the ages of 9 and 13, taking Handel's *Water Music* as inspiration
- Girls Can—A recording and composition project for teenage girls
- Young Artist Development programme for talented young people who want to develop their musical, vocal, song-writing, technical, and performance skills
- International Exchange: In 2005 Sense of Sound took a group of young people from the UK to La Reunion in the Indian Ocean to work on a collaborative music and dance project
- Cyril Jackson Sings (as part of Isle of Dogs Music/Trinity College of Music)—to stimulate singing activities in Cyril Jackson junior school in East London.
- 4 Corners Project—Working with residents from the '4 Corners' of Liverpool, this reminiscence project was designed to document the history and subsequent changes that many of Liverpool's residents were facing
- Voices—working with nearly 500 residents from Liverpool, Sense of Sound ran satellite workshops throughout the city for adults and young people
- Fireworks—this project involved Lewisham's young string players, young dancers from Laban, and GCSE students from a Lewisham school. (Sense of Sound, 2006)

NSG made good links with several similar organizations that provided high quality activities that were also inclusive and innovative.

Celebration day 2006

Building on the success of the previous launch event in March 2005 I persuaded the school to make this an annual project. The format replicated the previous year with music in all lessons taught during the day, concerts for all students, projects with the community, commissioning of new work, and cultural and stylistic diversity as a key theme in the cross-section of activities. The programme cover was designed to promote the idea that girls can play a brass instrument—contradicting the stereotype that was evident in the choice of instruments by NSG girls. The trumpet player Alison Balsom was an outstanding ambassador for music. She engaged fully with the school during the day, performed in all the daytime events, and in the evening activity as well. Her down-to-earth approach and interest in what was happening were exceptional. Needless to say her playing was also an inspiration.

I commissioned a new piece from Lin Marsh for the concert. It exceeded everyone's expectations and was performed by 350 children with incredible enthusiasm and enjoyment. The song was typical of Lin's work. The words captured contemporary issues brilliantly and the music was written in a style that was extremely accessible, but with outstanding integrity. Lin visited all the schools involved and led some inspiring sessions for the pupils. She also provided an exceptional role model in being able to work with young people from a wide range of backgrounds and experience. The song was made available free to every school in Northamptonshire and beyond via the NSG website.

A key element in the activities and workshops was the involvement of a group of students with special educational needs. The group, made up of children from Fairfields, Greenfields Special School, and Rowan Gate Special School, worked during the day to produce a piece that was performed as part of the evening concert in Spinney Hill Theatre. Some of the pupils had profound learning difficulties or physical needs. Their involvement in the concert stunned the audience and sent out a very strong message that music can be for all students, regardless of ability or disability. The day involved a wide range of artists from around the world. For example, Mamadou Cissahko is an outstanding musician from Senegal. He has travelled and performed in many countries using the Kora, a twenty-stringed African harp, drums, and voice. He worked with children at Eastfield Primary School, teaching drumming with African Djembes. There were many other artists and workshops as well. The outcome was summed up by year 3:

Thank you for showing us how to play the Djembes. We learnt about the base, tone and the slap, and the energy song. We appreciated it. (Year 3, Eastfield Primary School)

Other community activities

NSG made a strong contribution to the Northampton Music Festival. This was a professional festival involving a mixture of artists from around the world as well as community-based activities. NSG supported local choirs and singers joining together in a performance of the Mozart Requiem—this was rehearsed during the day and then performed during the evening. The majority of the orchestral musicians were aged between 16 and 18. The support of the school enabled many adults and young people to join together in a high standard and memorable community music event. The school worked with the Harmonie Band to give local schools the opportunity to compose music to accompany 'One week' by Buster Keaton. The students developed their music over a two-day period and then performed it live to a large audience as they accompanied and enhanced the silent movie. The band entertained us with their magnificent accompaniment to *The General*, a classic Keaton film.

I worked with the Northamptonshire Complementary Education Centres. Four Complementary Education Centres provide full-time programmes of education for permanently excluded pupils and two provide an alternative to mainstream school for pregnant young women and those with babies. NSG worked with all the centres in 2006, providing an exciting contemporary music project. Every student in each centre had the opportunity to attend a series of workshops which involved playing instruments, recording, composing, and associated activities such as DJ skills. The students involved often had difficult backgrounds and negative perceptions about education. They responded very well to the opportunity to work with music in a relaxed and contemporary style.

'Gigajam' is an online course for learning the guitar, bass guitar, drums, and keyboard. I wanted to develop access to this sort of resource for students so that more could be engaged in learning an instrument and a more contemporary ethos could be created. I had planned to develop these resources myself but discovered that someone had got there first! Gigajam provided a set of resources that included:

- lessons with embedded video clips
- a piece of software called xtractor which allowed the player to perform to an accompaniment
- analyser software which enabled the player to perform a piece and have it 'marked' for accuracy.

The concept behind the lessons is good. Each student is able to follow an individual course on their chosen instrument. The range of instruments matches the interests of a large majority and enables them to have lessons in an informal way. I have picked up some of these issues and themes in Chapter 7. Courses were set up so that students were encouraged to purchase equipment they could use at home. We also put the courses onto the internet so the students could access them from anywhere. This facility was extremely popular and resulted in about 100 students a week attending after-school sessions and developing their performing skills. They paid a small fee for this. This resource was popular with students from local schools. A useful feature of the lessons was that separate instrument lessons integrate so all students at the end of the first lesson can put their part together into a group performance. The project was integrated into a wider community pop and rock project that involved DJ skills, dance music, or song-writing. These were extremely popular. The Pop and Rock school at NSG expanded in September 2005 and gave local students the chance to learn how to play an instrument and get involved in song-writing, music technology, recording, and live performance.

I ran Easter and summer schools during 2005 and 2006. These were extremely popular—attracting over 100 students on each day. The activities offered were designed to appeal to students who wanted to try out a musical activity but might lack specific experience. They included singing, samba, DJ skills, or world percussion. No previous expererince or skills were expected. NSG supported the Camrose Centre by providing a worker to develop early-years provision. The Camrose Centre is a community centre in Northampton. It is located in an area identified as facing particular challenges and provides a very wide range of services such as:

◆ Respite day care

◆ Support for men as carers, recently developing initiatives to support young fathers

◆ Health advice drop-in sessions

◆ Maternal Mental Health Pathway, for identification, early intervention, and treatment of post-natal depression

◆ Financial support for day care

◆ Childminding hub

◆ Speech and Language support, through individual and group therapy

◆ Support for community groups—Bangladeshi Mums and Tots, Somali Women's group, Bangladeshi Girls group, Time for Toys and other Playgroups

The NSG early-years worker provided sessions for two classes of 3/4-year-olds. We provided home packs for each child participating in the classes containing a picture songbook, CD, home activity cards (they describe the class activities for the parents' benefit), small music box (for storing materials at home), and stickers. The Home Packs encouraged parental involvement in their child's daily activities and ensured that the music continued within the home.

Virtual and community resources

I developed a set of resources for specific community groups which were made available online. The first project involved activities for AS and A2 students studying music and music technology. Resources were developed covering set works and other information that students could access and use to enhance their learning and revision. The resources covered all examination boards, so were not just restricted to students at NSG. A training day was held for teachers from around the country, several of whom agreed to help with further development. A project was set up in conjunction with the Local Authority Advisory Service. This aimed to develop a set of resources for general class teachers in primary schools. A working group was created to write materials made available to all schools in Northamptonshire. The project was led by the LA Music Adviser and included a CD with resources for every school as well as access to free CPD events. The materials were evaluated very highly by the teachers who took part in the project.

The primary project was set up to support class teachers teaching their own music lessons at KS2. Each writer was asked to work with their pupils to help devise and trial the materials, give feedback, and think about what the pupils would like to see on the website. We asked children what they did and didn't enjoy about music at school and what they would like to help them learn. The majority of pupils in year 6 enjoyed singing and playing instruments. Many of them commented that they wanted to learn keyboards and do some more 'modern' music. The year 6 resources included:

- 'This Life of Mine' by Lin Marsh, commissioned by NSG and copyright free to all schools participating in the project
- original compositions and an interview with the internationally renowned composer Trevor Wishart
- a new song written as the basis of a year 6–7 transition project.

There were seven diverse projects covering a range of topics that were all trialled in local schools, with input and feedback from pupils. The projects contained

- lesson plans with clear learning objectives and assessment strategies
- 'powerpoint' presentations
- listening activities, performance, and composition tasks
- video clips of the materials being used with pupils

- very clear guides for teachers and pupils on how to use ICT (from how to plug in a microphone to editing and manipulating sound files)
- links to free downloadable software and commercial programmes
- weblinks—links to resources sites for music teachers.

The site also contained pupil pages and discussion forums and an online festival (a site where pupils could upload their performances and compositions for other schools to hear). The first set of projects included those listed in Table 13.

Table 13 Seven projects trialled in local schools in 2006

Name of project	Description
Film school	Through a range of exciting multi-media resources pupils will learn about film music and create a soundtrack to a film that reflects either the mood, character or the action.
This Life of Mine	This project is based on the original composition by Lin Marsh. There are tips on how to teach the song and a composition project linked to it
Vox	Exploring the voice and graphic notation. This project focuses on the work of contemporary composers such as John Cage, Cathy Berberian, Sheila Chandra. There is original work by the composer Trevor Wishart.
Sound Mutate	This project includes a very clear guide to audio-recording using free software such as 'Sound Recorder' and 'Audacity'. Pupils will create, manipulate, and share compositions within class, school, or even inter-school groups.
African rhythms	This is a very user-friendly guide to exploring African rhythms. It contains very clear sound clips and tips for teachers including how to create effective sounds with junk instruments.
Dance riff and loops	This project has been written in response to the pupils' request to do some pop music. Pupils will listen to and analyse how riffs and loops are used in music from a range of styles and cultures. They will learn about house, garage, jungle, drum 'n' bass and create a loop-based dance composition.
Transition project	This project is based on a new song written for year 6 pupils going into year 7. It is intended for clusters of primary schools to work on with their secondary colleagues. Resources are excellent and presented in a user-friendly way to support both music coordinators and non-specialists

Pupils said that they would like to do some work on pop music in their lessons. One project explored riffs and loops and how they are used in music from a range of styles and cultures and more specifically in drum 'n' bass, jungle, and garage dance music. Each project outlined learning objectives and then a brief description of the lesson content. For example:

All students will be able to:

1. Know about riffs and ostinati in music from a range of styles and cultures

2. Know some key features and structure of dance music, for example, use of samples, loops, drum machines, mix in groove, mix out

3. Be able to choose samples from a selection and begin sort them into a simple dance structure using software such as Dance Ejay with help

Most will be able to:

1. Understand how riffs/ostinati are used and be able to compose their own pieces based on layers of riffs

2. Know some vocabulary and use it appropriately to compare and contrast dance music styles, for example, mix in, mix out, groove, sample, loop, bpm

3. Understand the basic structures of dance music styles and begin to create a piece in five sections using loop-based software exploring rhythm, texture, and timbre

Some will have made more progress and will also be able to:

1. Use some appropriate vocabulary to describe the music e.g. off-beat, riff, syncopated, time-stretched, bpm, loop, texture, timbre

2. Analyse pieces of music with understanding and compare and contrast pieces of music, justify answers, explore the characteristics of the vocabulary

3. Compose pieces with an understanding of key features of style and structure. They will begin to create and select their own loops and samples to drop into a dance mix.

There were also detailed lesson plans linked to resources such as worksheets, powerpoints, websites, video examples of pupils doing activities, and teachers demonstrating good practice. They included a range of teaching resources such as the following card sort activity from the riffs and loops project

Renegade Master by Fatboy Slim
Card sort

- Copy the following onto six pieces of different coloured card
- Select six envelopes

- Cut up and put one set of cards into each envelope
- Ask pupils to work in pairs or groups
- Each pair or group has a set of cards
- They need to listen to the piece of music and sort the cards into the order in which they appear

Mix in	Rhythmic section where DJ mixes previous track into the new one
Groove	Made up of vocals, drums, bass, guitar samples, scratches, vocal sample ('jump') Instruments drop in and out are looped, cut, and repeated
Break down	Vocals only and then joined by other samples. Texture thickens, rhythms speed up
Groove repeat	Much shorter version of groove section. Main loop reappears
Mix out	Rhythms and vocals samples only giving DJ time to mix in the next track

I believe that the community provision at NSG between 2004 and 2006 was very good. The approach was very inclusive and embraced a wide range of musical styles. NSG used its community provision in a very effective way because the head teacher and other senior managers saw themselves as an out-ward-looking community resource. NSG managed to have a big impact on local schools, community groups, and set up very good links with a wide range of organizations. In doing so it also raised its own profile to a very high level. Was this then the provision of a musical school? I think that in many ways it was. In particular the engagement with special schools, students who had less previous experience of music, and the use of a wide range of musical styles was exemplary.

Conclusion

This section brings together the various strands covered in this book. I will start by setting out the key themes that emerge before suggesting some next steps. I have noted that what I have set out is a personal view, based on a mixture of experience in a large number of settings, research findings, and, I hope, common sense. What I say is challenging and consequently will not be universally popular. I hope that at the very least I might promote debate. In my transactions with schools and other settings I have encountered many people who agree with these views and many other people who acknowledge them but find it hard to change their practice. I believe that music education needs to address some, or all, of these issues and I believe it can do this. Music education in England is, quite rightly, highly regarded by many other countries. In particular the attention given to class music-making has been much studied and admired. I am under no illusions about everything being better in other countries.

Music is very important to nearly all young people. There may be just a tiny few who for some reason do not respond to it. I am not able to say whether this is based on their experience (and therefore capable of modification) or whether it is based on some physiological characteristics that mean they were destined to be like this. We are talking about small numbers and every case will probably be slightly different. Almost all babies and young children respond naturally to music in a variety of forms. They love to sing and play instruments. Noise is an important early stimulus. Much music-making in nurseries and other settings is spontaneous, integrated with other activities, and assumes that everyone will participate. At this stage there are, thankfully, no tests of musical ability and most of the adults involved in music-making seem to understand that babies and toddlers will respond to sounds with enthusiasm. Very few seem to be on the lookout for musical 'talent'. Given the right environment most young people will continue with this approach to music until at least the end of year 6 (when they move into secondary education). However, cultural influences at home, in schools, and other settings mean that many become disengaged with music as an active participatory activity in schools, even though they continue to love music and listen to it avidly. In many cases this is before year 6. Boys are much less likely to be active participators as they move into year 4, 5, and 6. There is no good reason why this should be the case. Maturity makes them more aware of their emotions and understand that music gives access to these feelings in a very direct and slightly unpredictable way. Their enthusiasm for these expressions of emotion will need to be controlled in front of their peers. At this stage adults will often start to introduce terms such as 'can't sing a note', 'tone deaf', and 'no musical talent' when describing themselves to students. This is presumably because at some stage they have come to the conclusion that this is true, probably because someone else helped them to reach this view. They prepare young people to take on the same sort of role in the future. Why? The reasons are complex but I believe they relate to the labels they were given by adults, sometimes on purpose but often more indirectly. I do not believe that these 'unmusical' labels are accurate and I feel that anyone can participate enjoyably in musical activity as a performer (which is where the focus of these comments seem to be directed) if s/he is given the right encouragement and opportunity. Some people will make more progress than others, through a combination of social factors, amount of effective practice, or other reasons. I don't think that anyone should ever feel that they have no musical talent. On hearing the suggestion it would be better if they 'don't sing' or are 'not suited to an instrument' they will give up or never start. I knew a very well-respected violin teacher who confessed to me once that he looked upon the fact that several students would give up during a year as a measure of success. He did not believe they should be playing in the first place. What utter nonsense. How can we move forward with teachers like these? How many students have similar negative experiences?

The stage at which students disengage and start to think of themselves as having little musical talent depends on the adults they encounter. In a good primary school, with an inclusive approach, they will maintain their enthusiasm and love of participation until the end of year 6. However, primary schools increasingly offer tuition on musical instruments, often from year 4 onwards and at this stage there is often a separation between those who learn an instrument and those who do not. Learning an instrument conveys a different status and these students are regarded by teachers, parents, and students as being 'musical'. In some cases tests or other criteria will have been used to select these 'musical' students. The subsequent behaviour of adults towards the musically selected group and the rest (the 'non-musical' students) is crucial in shaping perceptions. A lot of this is hidden and may also be unconscious. It can be observed in the types of interactions, expectations, and transactions that take place. Sometimes you have to observe things closely to notice. I can recall a queue of year 6 students at the desk of the Head of

Music in a well-known secondary school with a very strong reputation for music. They were there to sign up for music lessons at the secondary school. I detected the teacher's particularly enthusiastic approach to students who played an instrument already, were white, female, presentable, and had a middle-class demeanour. The rest were treated rather more frostily, although still within the bounds of professional courtesy. The message, however, was clear enough and I know the students picked it up because they told me later. I feel uncomfortable recording this example but it provides evidence of the very powerful 'hidden curriculum' that shapes the experiences of almost all students. It happens across the country on a regular basis, even in this age of equal-opportunity legislation and awareness.

By the time students reach secondary school these sorts of musical and 'non-musical' distinctions are often confirmed in the minds of senior managers, teachers, staff, and students. A good secondary school may offer an inclusive approach in year 7 that helps to address the issue and offers an opportunity for all students to learn an instrument and feel musical. In reality most do not, often through not wishing to tackle the real practical difficulties such an approach would demand. It is easier for schools and teachers to deal with the needs of a small group of selected students. Somehow or other this approach in music is condoned and accepted as the norm because many people seem to assume that there are musical students (and therefore unmusical students). The special group are known as the 'musicians'. We have specialist schools, funded by central government, to cater for the needs of the most 'talented' because we feel that they need to be treated differently. An approach that separated out the artists, thespians, mathematicians, or pole jumpers would probably not be deemed acceptable. Music gets away with it and the key difference seems to be that we teach some students in schools to play an instrument. In order to make things manageable we select the ones that we regard as being 'musical' using a variety of improbable techniques that do not stand close scrutiny and which fly in the face of equal-opportunities legislation. In doing so we shape the perceptions students have about music. A student with special needs may not even get a look in because s/he might be thought of as unsuitable by default. Few students in Special Schools probably get the chance to learn an instrument. This is strong and unpalatable stuff, but it is out there and happening every single day.

Despite all this, students respond to enthusiastic teachers. It doesn't really matter what the enthusiasm is for. It could be a brass band, ocarina, or a choir. It is the sense of belonging, the sense of achievement, and an alignment with the positive adult role model that matters most. Some students also like the social cohesion that comes from being associated with a group. Being in the band means that you belong. When I first started teaching I worked at a school near Twickenham and recall going to a rugby match where a school brass band started the proceedings. The standard of the playing was incredible. Years later I happened to visit the school where the brass band came from. The band consisted of twenty-two pupils who were all selected by the teacher and rehearsed four times a week. When I visited they were still playing the same piece I had heard at Twickenham years before (although it was a different group of students). They had five pieces in their repertoire, which they could play to a very high standard. None of the band members played with another group, because the teacher would not allow them to. Each could play little more than their individual band part. Everywhere they went they received prizes and accolades for their performances. The rest of the school had a keyboard lesson once a week (if they remembered to bring their own headphones into school) and little ambition was shown for their progress. When the teacher retired the band stopped and the members felt devastated because of the strong loyalty they had felt towards it. None of them was equipped to transfer to another band until they had gone through a process of re-education and training. They could only function within that very narrow and enclosed environment. Was this a musical school? Many in the community felt it was. The school had a national reputation but by my definition it was anything but.

Despite these factors almost all secondary-age students love music. They listen to it a lot and will spend a lot of money on this interest because it is so important to them. They recognize music's importance as a mood-enhancer, marker of important occasions, and in promoting social bonds. They understand the powerful link that music has with their emotions. They like music that is contemporary in style, although this style is constantly shifting and hard to pin down. The style issue covers a variety of different genres and is further complicated by commercialism, social trends, and pressures. This group of students represents about 90 per cent of the school population. They probably did not have the opportunity to play an instrument and may regard themselves as being unmusical. They certainly do not engage strongly with music in school and do not relate school music to their love of music. I find this disappointing. These students responded to music as toddlers and young children (because this is what human beings do) but somehow missed out along the way. Having taken this 'wrong' turning there seems to be no way back, unless they happen to bump into an enlightened and determined adult who refuses to assume that they are unmusical. The hidden curriculum means that many adults probably rarely openly describe these students as being unmusical. However the behaviour of the adults may give the clear impression that they are. This approach makes the adults' life more manageable even though they might not realize that this is one of their motives. This is surely a key barrier to creating a musical school.

By the time they reach secondary school the 90 per cent who do not learn an instrument want activities that are energetic, kinaesthetic, and involve active participation. These ideally involve the contemporary musical styles they are interested in. School music is often a million miles away from this. Modern technology provides an opportunity to involve students in contemporary styles in an exciting and engaging way. It gives them access to sounds and genres that they find familiar. Music technology is becoming increasingly important in schools and other settings. The classically trained teacher may purchase score-writing software that s/he finds useful for writing band arrangements and which the musically literate students use at A level. The use of non-notation-based software and musical styles appears threatening, alien, and may even be classed as unmusical (when it is clearly not). Many young people can use music technology very effectively to create pieces that are imaginative, interesting, and highly complex. This contemporary style of music does not require musical literacy but is rarely pursued within formal settings. This can make the curriculum seem at odds with the interests and experiences of the large majority of young people.

The way that students learn is changing rapidly because society is changing in response to technological advances. Teaching needs to adapt to this and the best music teachers have grasped these issues. These teachers are few and far between. Knowledge is increasingly less important, since it can be accessed very easily in a variety of formats. Organizational skills, participation, self-discipline, and teamwork are valued in the world of employment and are extremely relevant to many aspects of the world of music education. Or can be. In too many cases the teacher's role is still one of the expert deciding the knowledge that will be given to students at a particular time. The National Curriculum has gone through a series of adaptations and moved from its very prescriptive function fifteen years ago to become increasingly general. It probably makes little or no impact on the lives of music teachers or the students that they teach. Many 14+ examination courses are still more suitable for students who learn an instrument and have a reasonable degree of musical literacy. Sometimes this is hidden due to the way that teachers and examiners interpret well-meaning specifications. It may be stated that a student does not have to be able to play an instrument to access a course but teachers make it clear through their language and assumptions that it will be better if students who do not play an instrument consider an alternative option. The Key Stage 3 curriculum can be a key barrier to progress since it may provide many students with a series of activities that occupies them for three years but does not leave them feeling music is a viable option aged 14 onwards. Drama and art could suffer from similar problems of elitism and cultural narrowness but seem to have successfully addressed these issues and are more popular as examination choices.

Schools are seen as having an increasingly important role to play within the community. They are seen as a potential focus for universal services and have the ability also to link with a range of voluntary and community organizations. They are well placed for these roles. The potential for music education to reach out to a wide range of adults and young people is enormous. However this requires a vision for music that is inclusive and socially less divisive.

The music education sector is extremely diverse. Diversity can create great richness. It can also support lack of consistency and expectation. We have numerous societies for every aspect of music education and music-making. We have a Music Education Council which is an umbrella organization designed to glue these things together. Despite this the funding that central government puts into music education is not regulated and although new initiatives are inclusive and culturally diverse, schools remain powerful transmitters of an exclusivity that assumes musical talent. We have Specialist Music Schools where students are chosen, at a young age, to devote their lives to an intensive study of playing a musical instrument. Parents of these students support this approach enthusiastically. Newly created Specialist Music Colleges were set up to improve the quality of experience within the state-funded mainstream schools. The philosophy behind them was very sound but the reality is far more diverse and may actually contribute to traditional and divisive values. We seem to need a National Music Association with a core set of values that all other organizations that access any funding will be required to be part of.

Music education is not unique. Football has a development programme for children which includes the training of a wide range of volunteers, a charter standard for affiliated clubs, and central and regional officers who support the development of excellence programmes and grassroots participation. The FA promotes strongly disability participation and the idea that football is an activity for all to be involved in as well as something that young people with exceptional abilities can excel in. The FA also promotes the idea that football is not just about skills development. The training programmes for young people are structured to include psychological, social, and physical development. Of course within this framework the parents and volunteers involved can be a barrier as they unknowingly impose their own values on the transactions that take place.

Having outlined the issues I want to turn to some possible ways forward. There are no easy solutions. I recognize that many recent projects and initiatives promoted by central government have helped to address these issues in a positive and transformational way. With this in mind I am going to suggest a few short- and medium-term priorities that I believe might make a difference.

1. Ensure that every organization that receives any central government, local government, or lottery funding signs up to an agreed statement of equal opportunities. This statement would need to be drafted to cover aspects of disability, culture, and contradict the idea that participation in musical activities should be related in any way to 'musical ability testing' or the notion of musicians and non-musicians. Work would be required to put together such a statement and ensure that it was a condition of funding that each organization signed a declaration and agreed to be monitored on the application of the policy.

2. Music Services, or private organizations in receipt of central or local government funding should be required to sign up to this statement and have performance targets which related to the ethnicity, social profile, and other features of their local community. In particular they should be encouraged, through funding mechanisms, to increase the proportion of local students learning instruments with funding incentives and penalties for high or low participation rates.

3. Schools should be required to sign up to this equal-opportunities statement because they receive public money that is spent on music education—either through class music or the provision of instrumental tuition. They should receive similar incentives for high participation rates.

4. Specialist schools (which receive additional funding) should be expected to lead the way on the participation and access element of their provision.

5. Some form of high-quality CPD should be organized that covers specific key issues that will make a difference in transforming music education. For example:

- effective use of ICT (including the use of contemporary styles)
- encouraging the use of contemporary musical styles in all areas of music teaching
- understanding and meeting different learning styles
- curriculum development and transformation to meet the needs of all students
- working with the community in an inclusive way
- developing curriculum pathways that meet the needs of all students

- ◆ group instrumental teaching and innovative approaches that enable more students to be able to participate and continue with learning an instrument or taking part in some form of group music-making

All of this will require regulation and monitoring and therefore sounds a bit heavy-handed. The aim would be to develop a more inclusive approach and make this become embedded and evident in the work of schools/colleges, Music Services, individual teachers, and other funded organizations. There are many good things going on in music education, sometimes against the odds. There are some fantastic teachers and much of what we have is world class. I also feel that the tide is turning towards a more inclusive approach. We need to hang onto this and grapple with some fundamental principles. We need to ensure that music education moves from selective nineteenth-century Conservatoire principles to a more egalitarian and inclusive approach. We also need to promote excellence. It is a tricky balancing act. I hope that we have the vision and the courage to try.

Index